D0553992

The Thirteen Pragmatisms

Until his death in December, 1962, Arthur O. Lovejoy was Professor Emeritus of Philosophy at the Johns Hopkins University. Among his books are *Reflections on Human Nature; The Reason, the Understanding, and Time;* and *Essays in the History of Ideas.*

The Thirteen Pragmatisms

and Other Essays

ARTHUR O. LOVEJOY

The Johns Hopkins Press: Baltimore

Distributed in Great Britain by Oxford University Press, London
Printed in the United States of America by Vail-Ballou Press
Library of Congress Catalog Card Number 63-11890

This book has been brought to publication with the assistance of a grant from The Ford Foundation.

PREFACE

Since the publication in 1936 of *The Great Chain of Being,* Professor Lovejoy has been thought of as primarily a historian of ideas. His contributions to epistemology have been obscured by his activity in opening up a new territory of research into which his juniors have rushed with all the enthusiasm of pioneers. The founding of a journal devoted to that study, Lovejoy's acceptance of the editorship of that journal, his unfailing kindness in reading and criticizing papers sent him by aspiring historians made it impossible for him to continue that long series of philosophical papers which had culminated in *The Revolt Against Dualism* and had given him a distinguished reputation in technical philosophy. As a matter of fact he had always combined the two interests. As early as 1904 he had published his monograph on *The Dialectic of Bruno and Spinoza,* which was an analysis of a metaphysical technique, and at the same time he had published *Some Eighteenth Century Evolutionists,* which was a contribution to the history of a science. This was not after all surprising in a man who had called himself a temporalistic realist, for such a man would be likely to see in every idea traces of the historical moment in which it was expressed. As he says in his article on "William James as Philosopher," reprinted in the present volume,

"All philosophies . . . are the result of the interaction of a temperament (itself partly molded by a historical situation) with impersonal logical considerations arising out of the nature of the problems with which man's reason is confronted." To discover in a philosophy this interaction has always been his purpose, and in these essays on the various pragmatisms one sees the discovery in process.

Every logical system has to be based on premises, and what will seem self-evident to one man will seem dubious or problematical to another. Moreover the personal vision of no man is all-inclusive and the wider his angle of vision, the less likely is he to see the details of his intellectual landscape. It has always been part of Lovejoy's critical technique to ask himself just what an author is saying and then to put it down in straightforward literal sentences. He thus untangles the premises from their implications, sorts out ambiguities, and above all indicates clearly where a switch from one meaning to another has occurred. This technique he has used upon himself as well as on others. In his statement of his own position, "A Temporalistic Realism," which appeared in *Contemporary American Philosophy* (1930), he laid down his own premises as if he were writing a legal brief, just as he did in *The Revolt Against Dualism.*

The essays in this volume are then critical and are, with one exception, directed against pragmatism. "The Thirteen Pragmatisms" is an exercise in logical analysis and is, so to speak, a challenge to a group of philosophers who have taken on a collective name to show how their apparent diversities are to be reconciled. The distinctions which he made in that article and which led to logical confusions are expounded in such papers as "Pragmatism and Realism," "Pragmatism vs. the Pragmatist," and "Pragmatism as Interactionism." There can be few living philosophers who would call themselves orthodox followers of this train of thought, and hence these papers can be studied without that sense of personal injury which deadens the critical faculty and obscures one's insight. Here it is the logical technique which counts; the author's keenness in spotting double meanings and his ability to rephrase them in univalent form. In spite of his admiration for William James himself as a teacher and writer, Lovejoy turned a cold shoulder to the seductions of a brilliant literary style and asked James just what he was driving at. Yet this was done with rare courtesy and with appreciation of a great thinker's generosity and imaginative power.

In admitting the contributions of temperament to philosophy, Lovejoy also ran the risk of what he has called mind-reading. Though he has always insisted upon the part which temperament must play in thinking, he has also insisted that no critic can assume the position of a psychoanalyst. One simply does not know why James, for instance, was so open-minded, so in love with the unfinished, the multiple, and the changing. We know that such attitudes were characteristic of him, but the philosophical critic who is interested in reasoning alone must accept them as fundamental and leave it at that. They orient a man's thoughts, explain his acceptance of certain ideas and his reluctance to accept their contraries, but they are prelogical and hence prephilosophical in the sense that they need not be clear to the man who is possessed of them. They are part of what might be called his protophilosophy, though the neologism is not Lovejoy's. By bringing them into the light of day, Lovejoy translates them into sentences which can be submitted to validation or simply to the test of clarity. To cite but one example out of scores, when someone argues that a given practice is bad because it is unnatural or another good because it is natural, one confers a benefaction upon him by asking him which of the sixty-odd meanings of "natural" he is thinking of.

This is to be sure an unpopular way of writing. We philosophers do not seem to be any fonder of exposure than other people are. Though most of us take pride in our rationalism, we hesitate to accept its consequences. One of them is obviously the impossibility of believing in both the affirmative and negative of a proposition. Either all knowledge can be formulated in a consistent set of sentences or it can not. If it can, then the act of knowing is robbed of its temporal, historical, personal character. But if it can not, then the world is in a state of change and what is true today may be false tomorrow. But this would seem to involve one in accepting the reality of time and of logical gaps. In "The Anomaly of Knowledge" (p. 236 below), Lovejoy argues that knowledge itself contains one of these gaps, in that knowing as a psychological fact is here and now whereas its object may be in the future, the remote past, or almost anywhere. The problem of the epistemologist is to explain, if possible, how this can happen or, if he cannot explain it, to accept it as one of his fundamental data, just as a botanist would have to accept the fact that some plants have flowers and some do not. The desire to find out just what facts are imposed upon a philosopher has always been illustrated in Lovejoy's critical method, whether he was writing about emergent evolution, psychophysical dualism, or the reality of time. If one wishes to attack him, this is the place to do so. But one must be prepared to prove that the supposed data are really fictions or illusions. In his case this would involve one in proving, for instance, that the idea which I am now entertaining of the character of Julius Caesar is identical with that character itself in date and location; that my idea, if true, is *existentially* one with that of a friend which is also true; that the image of which I am aware of a picture hanging in the next room is also in the next room at this moment; and that two physical objects can be in the same place at the same time.

Now there seems to be clearly present to Lovejoy the realization that no two minds are existentially the same however much they may agree, and it may be this conviction which has led him both to emphasize the temperamental element in philosophies and the necessity for co-operation if productive work in philosophy is to be done, as well as above all, the tentative or hypothetical nature of philosophizing. None of this implies to his way of thinking that agreement is impossible or that truth is nothing more than opinion. Quite the contrary, he gives one the impression that once the temperamental factor is clarified, it might be discounted or perhaps eliminated by the man who is its victim. If several philosophers can be brought to agree on the definition of key terms and on what data they will accept, they may also be brought to agree on their conclusions. Finally he believes that probability is better than fantasy.

His motto has been *De deux choses l'une.* But he is only too happy to consider the *deux* before choosing one of them. His investigations into the history of certain ideas have been, as it were, a study of cases of men drawing certain conclusions which were not implicit in their premises. In these essays on pragmatism the situation is similar. But he is above all showing that certain conclusions were drawn which were illicit and this largely because of an initial confusion. To take but one example from the present volume, in the essay on "Pragmatism and the New Materialism," he tries to show that if the pragmatist believes that ideas are plans of action, then he cannot also believe that only material things exist. Why? Because if he is a materialist, he must believe that "it is possible to describe the phenomenon called 'planning' wholly in physical terms, i.e., in terms of masses actually existing, of positions actually occupied, of molar or molecular movements actually occurring, *at the time when the planning is taking place.*" The clash in opinion then turns out to be whether "a past or possible future state of the material world" can be also "at the moment at which it is represented in the experience of the planner, a part of the real material world." The issue is reduced thus to one question alone, that of dates. The legal analogy is, I think, fairly clear.

If the question should be raised of why a collection of essays critical of views taken a generation ago should be reprinted now, one answer—and only one of several—is that they afford the student of philosophy a set of cases in which he need not take sides but which give him an analytical method which he can practice for himself on contemporary issues. The very fact that these essays are on the whole critical gives them a heuristic value which dogmatic or expository essays would not have. This is the sort of value of some of the Platonic dialogues in that though they come out with the Scotch verdict, the process of reaching it is both illuminating and chastening. At a time of mounting anti-intellectualism, this should prove a welcome antidote.

George Boas

Baltimore
September 1962

Acknowledgment

The Johns Hopkins Press acknowledges with gratitude the assistance of Mr. Bernard Mathews, Jr., in reading proof and in helping to bring this book to publication after Professor Lovejoy's death in December 1962.

CONTENTS

I

THE THIRTEEN PRAGMATISMS *

Part I

In the present year of grace 1908 the term "pragmatism"—if not the doctrine—celebrates its tenth birthday. Before the controversy over the mode of philosophy designated by it enters upon a second decade, it is perhaps not too much to ask that contemporary philosophers should agree to attach some single and stable meaning to the term. There appears to be as yet no sufficiently clear and general recognition, among contributors to that controversy, of the fact that the pragmatist is not merely three but many gentlemen at once. Some recent papers by Perry set, as it seems to me, the right example in discriminating a number of separate pragmatistic propositions and discussing each of them by itself. But perhaps even these papers do not insist so emphatically, as it is worth-while to do, upon the utter disconnection and even incongruity that subsists between a number of these propositions; and there are one or two important ambiguities of meaning in certain of the pragmatists' formulas which do not seem to find a place in Perry's careful

* First published in *The Journal of Philosophy,* V (1908), pp. 5–12, 29–39.

enumeration. A complete enumeration of the metamorphoses of so protean an entity is, indeed, perhaps too much to expect; but even after we leave out of the count certain casual expressions of pragmatist writers which they probably would not wish taken too seriously, and also certain mere commonplaces from which scarcely any contemporary philosopher would dissent, there remain at least thirteen pragmatisms: a baker's dozen of contentions which are separate not merely in the sense of being discriminable, but in the sense of being logically independent, so that you may without inconsistency accept any one and reject all the others, or refute one and leave the philosophical standing of the others unimpugned. All of these have generally or frequently been labeled with the one name and defended or attacked as if they constituted a single system of thought—sometimes even as if they were severally interchangeable.

I shall try to put down all the logical doctrines of importance that seem to have been improperly reduced to unity in current discussions; and I shall try to exhibit the fact of their reciprocal independence in as clear a light as possible. To contribute to the determination of the truth or falsity of any one of these doctrines is no part of the business of the present discussion; for I venture to think that the question of truth has sometimes been not very profitably dealt with during the past ten years, in the absence of a sufficiently considerate prior clearing up of the question of meaning. The pragmatist school itself seems, thus far, more distinguished for originality, inventiveness, and a keen vision for the motes in the eye of the intellectualist, than for patience in making distinctions or the habit of self-analysis.

And its critics, on the other hand, have occasionally made haste to take the utmost advantage of this unassorted commingling of doctrinal sheep and doctrinal goats in the ample fold of pragmatic theory and have made the apparently caprine character of some members of the flock a warrant for the wholesale condemnation of the entire multitude. In view of this situation, nothing seems more indicated than an attempt at clear differentiation of the separate pragmatist assertions and tendencies.

Certainly it is probable that the following list could be extended. I hope that it will be found to include all the genuinely independent contentions that are most frequently illicitly identified, and all the ambiguities of meaning that are so central and important as to call for serious consideration from both the defenders and the critics of the several opinions to which the one name has been applied.

1. Primarily, it is obvious, pragmatism—the pragmatism of Peirce, and of James's Berkeley address—was merely a doctrine concerning the meaning of propositions, concerning the way in which the really significant issue in any controversy could be determined. It maintained that one meaning of any proposition whatever is reducible to the future consequences in experience to which that proposition points, consequences which those who accept the proposition *ipso facto* anticipate as experiences that somebody is subsequently to have. Now, a theory about the meaning of propositions is not the same thing as a theory about the criterion of truth in propositions; a formula which professes to tell you how to ascertain precisely what a given assertion really signifies does not thereby profess to tell you whether or not that as-

sertion is true. James, at least, in his recent book and elsewhere, has clearly noted this distinction between pragmatism as a theory of meaning and pragmatism as a theory of truth; Schiller does not appear to do so, since he identifies the "principle of Peirce" with a view concerning the mark that "establishes the *real* truth and validity" of a proposition.[1] But I do not think that even James has sufficiently insisted upon the logical disconnectedness of the two theories. Indeed, the whole topic of the relation of meaning and truth might advantageously receive more extended discussion than it has yet had. It may at first sight seem that a close logical relation can be made out between the two, in at least one direction. To know what a proposition exactly means may appear to involve a knowledge of just where to look for the evidence of its truth and for the test by which its claim to truth can be brought to proof. If a judgment *means* merely certain future experiences, it might appear that its truth could be known only through—and, therefore, only at the time of—the occurrence of the predicted experiences. But I can not see that this really follows. The assertion "God exists and mere materialism is false" may possibly mean only the anticipation of a cosmic future different in specific ways from that which the acceptance of the contrary proposition would lead one to expect; but the criterion of the truth of the assertion need not be correspondingly future. Its truth may conceivably be known *now,* through a mystical intuition or by a "necessity of thought"; or (and this is apparently good pragmatist doctrine about knowledge) it may be a

[1] "The Definition of Pragmatism and Humanism" in F. C. S. Schiller, *Studies in Humanism* (1907), p. 5.

proposition that we are obliged and entitled proleptically to accept as a true acceptance of the postulate, because it satisfies a present (not a future) need. The experiences whose occurrence constitute the meaning of the judgment may have one date; the apprehension of the judgment's validity, or legitimacy as a belief, may have quite another. According to one of the pragmatist theories of truth, a proposition is known as true (in the only sense of "true" which that theory regards as intelligible) at the moment at which it effectually operates to put an end to a felt inner discord or to open a way through a practical *impasse;* but the matter to which the proposition refers not only may be, but normally will be, subsequent to that moment of acceptance and mental relief. A "plan of action" presumably relates to the future; but the determination of its "truth," or whatever kind of acceptability is pragmatically to pass for such, can not be postponed until the future to which it relates has been "verified" by becoming past; else all our "true" plans of action would, paradoxically, be retrospective, and we should have to say that the pragmatic man never is, but always is about to have been, blest with knowledge. If, then, the legitimacy of a belief is, upon pragmatist principles, to be known at one moment, while the experiences which it "means" may run on into later moments, it appears to follow that the fullest knowledge of the belief's meaning may throw no light whatever upon the question of its legitimacy. That—until the belief has (presumably) *lost* all meaning by coming to refer purely to past experiences—still remains, from the standpoint of pragmatism as a theory of meaning, a separate and unsettled question; it is impossible to infer that the pragmatist theory of validity is any more correct than another. The acceptance of either one of these theories, equally known as "pragmatism," leaves you an entirely open option with respect to the acceptance of the other.

2. This pragmatic theory of meaning, as used by James, who has been its principal expounder and defender, seems designed to function chiefly as a quieter of controversy, a means for banishing from the philosophic lists those contestants between whose theories there appears, when this criterion is applied, to be no meaningful opposition, in whose differences there lies no issue that "makes a difference." In this application, however, the criterion clearly exhibits a radical ambiguity. The "effects of a practical kind" which our conception of an object must (we are told) involve, the "future consequences in concrete experience, whether active or passive," to which all significant propositions must point, may consist in either: (a) future experiences which the proposition (expressly or implicitly) predicts as about to occur, *no matter whether it be believed true or not;* or (b) future experiences which will occur *only upon condition that the proposition be believed.* The consequences of the *truth* of a proposition (in the sense of its correct prerepresentation of a subsequent experience to which its terms logically refer) and the consequences of *belief* in a proposition have been habitually confused in the discussion of the pragmatic theory of meaning. Taken in the one sense, the theory is equivalent to the assertion that only definitely predictive propositions—those which by their proper import foretell the appearance of specific sensations or situations in the "concrete" experience of some temporal consciousness—have

real meaning. Taken in the other sense, the theory does not require that propositions *refer* to the future at all; it is enough that, by being carried along into the future as beliefs in somebody's mind, they be capable of giving to that mind emotional or other experiences in some degree different from those which it would have in the absence of the beliefs. No two doctrines could be "pragmatically" more dissimilar than the pragmatic theory of meaning when construed in the first sense, and the same theory when construed in the second sense. If the formula includes only "future experiences" of the class (a), it has the effect of very narrowly limiting the range of meaningful judgments, and of excluding from the field of legitimate consideration a large number of issues in which a great part of mankind seems to have taken a lively interest; and it must assuredly be regarded as a highly paradoxical contention. But if it includes also future consequences of class (b), it is no paradox at all, but the mildest of truisms; for it then is so blandly catholic, tolerant, and inclusive a doctrine that it can deny real meaning to no proposition whatever which any human being has ever cared enough about to believe. In James's *Pragmatism* his criterion is applied to specific questions sometimes in one sense and sometimes in the other; and the results are correspondingly divergent. Using his formula in the first sense, he argues, for example, that the only "real" difference between a theistic and a materialistic view of the universe is that the former entitles us to predict a future in human experience that contains certain desirable elements for the expectation of which materialism gives no warrant. In other words, the whole "meaning" of theism is declared to be reducible to the anticipation of a specific cosmic or personal future; and the only genuine issue between it and the opposing doctrine lies in the question of the legitimacy of this anticipation. "If no future detail of experience or conduct is to be deduced from our hypothesis, the debate between materialism and theism becomes quite idle and insignificant." Supposing matter capable of giving us just the same world of experience as a God would give us, "wherein should we suffer loss if we dropped God as an hypothesis and made the matter alone responsible? Where would any special deadness, or crassness, come in? And how, experience being what is once for all, would God's presence in it make it any more living or richer?" [2] "Treated as it often is" (i.e., treated nonpragmatically), "this question becomes little more than a conflict between esthetic preferences," between different ways of talking about, imagining, or explaining the ancestry of precisely the one, identical, actual world of past, present, and future experiences; and such differences in esthetic preferences are treated by James as "abstract" things that really make no difference. In the spirit of this chapter of James's book—which is the spirit of the Enlightenment at its narrowest, most utilitarian, least imaginative—one might go on to eliminate from consideration, as pragmatically meaningless, a large part of the issues over which metaphysicians and theologians have divided; one might show that (apart from the having of the beliefs themselves, which from the present point of view does not count) it makes no difference whether you believe or reject most of the dogmas of theology or the hypotheses of speculative philosophy. For

[2] William James, *Pragmatism* (1907), Lecture III, *passim.*

these largely refer to alleged permanent, unvarying factors of reality from which no specific contents of experience (beyond, once more, the experiences directly arising from the presence of those factors) can be clearly deduced. The trinitarian presumably does not necessarily anticipate "concrete future experiences" different from those anticipated by the unitarian; nor need the pantheist expect the cosmos to behave in a manner other than that expected by the pluralistic theist. Later in James's book, however, we find his criterion taken in the opposite sense; for example, while the author observes of the monistic doctrine of the absolute that "you can not redescend into the world of particulars by the Absolute's aid or deduce any necessary consequences of detail important for your life from your idea of his nature," just this nonpredictive doctrine is credited with genuine pragmatic meaning, because "emotional and spiritual" consequences flow from the belief in it (*Pragmatism*, pp. 273–74). And in *this* spirit, all beliefs with which human emotions have in any degree become entangled would have to be regarded by the pragmatist as *ipso facto* meaningful and serious. It would not even be necessary that the beliefs should, in the ordinary logical sense, have any intelligible import at all. There are some who feel pretty sure that those who adhere, for instance, to the nihilistic monism of the Vedanta, or to the Athanasian doctrine of the Trinity, never really *conceive together* the elements of the propositions that they affirm; but no one can deny that, out of the maintenance of the posture of belief toward these propositions, believers derive highly distinctive and vivid experiences which they could scarcely have in any other way. And for all such beliefs our pragmatist—who, but a moment ago, seemed so narrow and ferocious an Aufklärer—would now be compelled to find a place among the significant issues.

This pragmatic theory of meaning thus breaks up into two possible doctrines that are not merely different, but incongruous. We seem to be justified in calling upon the pragmatist to make an election between them. If I may, for a moment, go beyond the province chosen for this paper, I venture to predict that neither choice will be found welcome; for I suspect that all the charm and impressiveness of the theory arises out of the confusion of its alternative interpretations. It gets its appearance of novelty and of practical serviceableness in the settlement of controversies from its one meaning; and it gets its plausibility entirely from the other. But (when the distinction is made) in the sense in which the theory might be logically functional, it seems hardly likely to appear plausible; and in the sense in which it is plausible, it appears destitute of any applicability or function in the distinguishing of "real" from meaningless issues.

3. But the pragmatic theory of meaning in its first sense —with its characteristic emphasis upon the ultimately predictive import of all judgments—leads to a theory concerning the way in which judgments are verified; in other words, to a theory about the meaning of truth. If all judgments must refer to specific future experiences, their verification consists in the getting of the experiences which they foretold. They are true, in short, if their prediction is realized; and they can, strictly speaking, be known to be true only through that realization, and concurrently with the occurrence of the series of experiences predicted. James presents this doctrine

with an apparent exception in favor of "necessary truths"; which, since they coerce the mind as soon as they are clearly presented to it, are (he seems to admit) verified "on the spot," without waiting for the presentation in experience of all empirical phenomena that may be referred to by them. But even this exception is not recognized entirely unequivocally; and in any case, for the great mass of our judgments, their truth consists in the correspondence of the anticipations properly evoked by them with subsequent items of experience; and the verification of their truth comes only when the whole series of such items which they foreshadowed has been completely experienced. "All true processes must lead to the face of directly verifying experiences *somewhere,* which somebody's ideas have copied." "Truth *happens* to an idea. It becomes true, is made true by events. Its verity *is,* in fact, an event, a process: the process, namely, of its verifying itself, its veri-*fication.*" [3]

Now, I have already tried to show that such a theory of truth is neither identical with, nor properly deducible from, the original pragmatic theory of meaning—in either of its senses. I wish now to make more fully clear the precise import of this theory of truth, and to show its contrast with another type of theory of truth which also and, I think, more properly figures as pragmatism. Observe that the words quoted give us a theory of truth which is obviously not at the same time functionally serviceable as a theory of knowledge—which seems a strange trait in a pragmatist theory. According to this phase of pragmatism, judgments are not known to be true until they become true, and until they be-

[3] James, *op. cit.*, pp. 215, 201.

come true they have no use or importance (and, as I have suggested, they even ought to be said, on some "pragmatist principles," to have no meaning), for their reference is to the dead past. Our intellect is condemned, according to this doctrine, to subsist wholly by a system of deferred payments; it gets no cash down; and it is also a rule of this kind of finance that when the payments are finally made, they are always made in outlawed currency. Now, of course, what we practically want and, indeed, must have from a theory of knowledge is some means of telling what predictions are to be accepted as sound *while they are still predictions.* Hindsight is doubtless a good deal more accurate than foresight, but it is less useful. No one is likely to deny that a valid proposition (in so far, at least, as it is predictive at all) must "lead us finally to the face of some directly verifying experience"; but I can conceive no observation which it can be more unprofitable to dwell upon than this one. If this were all that a pragmatic epistemology had to tell us, it would assuredly be giving us a stone where we had asked for bread.

But, of course, there is a form—or more than one form—of pragmatic epistemology that offers to meet the real needs of the situation in which the problem of knowledge arises, that seeks to tell us what predictive judgments ought, and what ought not, to be believed, before the "veri-*fication*" of those judgments in actually possessed experience makes the question concerning their truth as irrelevant and redundant a thing as a coroner's inquest on a corpse is—to the corpse. And these pragmatist theories about the criterion of truth—i.e., about the marks of the relative validity of propositions—which attempt to be really functional ought to be completely distinguished from this sterile doctrine which insists that the only true proposition is a dead proposition.

Part II

The purpose of this paper, as indicated at the beginning of the former installment, is to discriminate all the more important doctrines going under the name of pragmatism which can be shown to be not only distinct, but also logically independent *inter se*. Three such divergent pragmatist contentions have thus far been noted. "Pragmatism" was primarily a theory concerning the "meaning" of propositions; but this theory, because of a latent ambiguity in its terms, breaks up into two: (1) The meaning of a proposition consists in the future consequences in experience which it (directly or indirectly) predicts as about to occur no matter whether it be believed or not; (2) The meaning of a proposition consists in the future consequences of believing it. The first of these was seen to suggest (though it by no means necessarily implies) the third variant of pragmatism, namely, a doctrine concerning the nature of truth; viz., that the truth of a proposition is identical with the occurrence of the series of experiences which it predicts and can be said to be known only after such series is completed. "Its truth *is* its verification." This contention, that judgments acquire truth only in the degree in which they lose predictive character and practical bearings, has been shown to be wholly barren and useless, since its affords no answer to the real epistemological question concerning the criterion of the truth of propositions whose specific predictive implications have not yet been experienced.

4. It is, however, not difficult to see through what associations of ideas some pragmatists have been led to emphasize this notion of the *ex post facto* character of all truth. Largely, it would appear, it derives its plausibility from its resemblance to the ordinary empirical doctrine that those general propositions are to be regarded as true which, so far as they have been applied, have been found to be realized in past experience. This latter doctrine, from which the former is often not clearly distinguished, may be set down as another of the things that pragmatism is frequently supposed to be. It is the doctrine sometimes sententiously expressed by the observation that those propositions are true which "will work" or "which you can live by." What the evolutionary empiricists who are fond of this observation almost always really mean by it is that those judgments are true which hitherto *have* worked; in other and more precise words, that I am, in advance of the actual realization or verification of the future experiences which may be predicted by a given judgment, entitled to regard it as true if it is *similar* to, or is a special application of, a general *class* of judgments which historical records or my own memory tell me have thus far had their implied predictions realized. But this is by no means identical with the principle previously mentioned and vigorously insisted upon by some pragmatists, that each *individual* judgment can *become* true only through,

and contemporaneously with, the presentation in consciousness of those specific subsequent experiences which it points to and prognosticates.

5. If, now, we are to set down this evolutionary empiricist criterion of truth as one expression of pragmatism—at least as that is popularly understood—it is necessary to add that this formula, too, suffers from ambiguity, and therefore breaks up into two quite distinct criteria. The ambiguity is analogous to that already pointed out in the pragmatist's theory of meaning. A belief may "work" in two very different senses, either by having its actual predictions fulfilled, or by contributing to increase the energies or efficiency or chance of survival of those who believe it. The Jews, for example, believed persistently for many centuries that a national Messiah would come in the next generation to restore the independence and establish the supremacy of Israel. In one sense, this belief did not work; for the events which it predicted did not occur. But biologically considered it worked wonderfully well; for it assuredly did much to produce the extraordinary persistency of the Jewish racial character, and the exceptional energy, self-confidence, and tenacity of purpose of the individual Jew. Many beliefs involving false predictions are biologically unfavorable, namely, if they lead to physical conduct ill-adapted to the conditions of the believer's physical environment. You can not "live by" the belief that fire will not burn. But, also, some false or never-realized predictions, and many beliefs having apparently no predictive character—and no capacity for empirical verification—have shown themselves to be excellent things to live by. And if we are to take the doctrine that

the true is the "livable" in its second and more unquestionably pragmatistic sense—if we are to identify the validity of beliefs with their biological serviceableness—we should apparently have to classify as "true" many judgments which predict nothing, and many which confessedly predict what is not going to occur.

6. Partly, however, what I have called the theory of the *ex post facto* nature of truth is a somewhat blurred reflection of a certain metaphysical doctrine which, although not always very explicitly put forward, appears to me to have a rather fundamental place in the characteristic mode of thought of most representatives of pragmatism. This is the doctrine of the "open-ness" of the future, and of the determinative or "creative" efficacy of each "present" moment in the ever-transient process of conscious judgment, choice, and action. The two parts of the doctrine obviously enough go together: if the process truly brings into being at each new moment a genuinely new and unique increment of reality, then, so long as any moment's increment has not yet been brought forth, it can not yet be called in any intelligible sense real; and if, similarly, the thing that is to be is a sheer nonentity until it enters into actual, temporal experience, the moment in which it becomes an experience must be credited with the creation *ex nihilo* of a new item of being. This doctrine of what M. Bergson calls a *devenir réel,* and of the creative function of consciousness, which is the pregnant ontological preconception from which a great variety of confused pragmatistic ideas have proceeded, unquestionably has certain epistemological implications. Such a metaphysics ap-

pears to imply the partial contingency and (from the standpoint of any "present" knowledge) indeterminateness of the future content of reality. But these implications are not synonymous with the *ex post facto* theory of truth in the generality with which that has usually been expressed. The future may be—and by the same pragmatists, when they adumbrate this sort of metaphysics, apparently is—regarded as presenting to our understanding only a narrow margin of the unpredictable; its general character and the greater mass of its content may be supposed, without departing from the conception in question, to be predetermined by the accumulated and crystallized results of reality up to date, of which any possible future and novel increment of being must be the child, and to which it must be capable of accommodation. And at all events, there is nothing in this sort of thoroughgoing metaphysical temporalism which justifies the denial of the possibility of the making of "true" judgments about contemporaneous or past (but not yet consciously verified) realities.

7. It is a frequently repeated observation of pragmatists, in moments when they are more mindful of the psychological than of the metaphysical antecedents of their diversely descended conceptions, that the true, in its more generalized character, is "the satisfactory"; it is, says James, that which "gives the maximal combination of satisfactions." Or, in Perry's careful formulation—with an amendment which we have recently been told, upon good authority, would make it entirely acceptable to a pragmatist—"the criterion of the truth of knowledge is the satisfying character of the practical

transition from cognitive expectation to fulfillment, or the resolution of doubt into practical immediacy."[4] Now this doctrine which identifies the truth with the satisfactoriness of a given judgment may mean any one of three things. It may, in the first place, be a simple psychological observation—from which, I fancy, few would dissent—indicating the genus of feelings of which the "emotion of conviction" is a species. To doubt, to inquire, or to have before the mind certain potential material of judgment that is not yet accepted as true is, of course, to experience dissatisfaction; a specific sense of discomfort and of nonfulfillment is the emotional concomitant of the doubting or the deliberative moment, and is doubtless the principal spring which prompts men's search for truth. And to believe, to hold true, whatever more it may be, is always at least to be satisfied in some degree with one's mental content of the moment, to find it good, or at all events not so bad as some contrary judgment which, for its sin of insufficient satisfyingness, has been shut away into the outer darkness of nonacceptance.

8. But this psychological truism, that to pass from doubt to belief is to pass from dissatisfaction to a relative satisfaction, is quite a different thing from the first of the pragmatist epistemological contentions that appear to be based upon it. This asserts that the way to determine whether a proposition is true is to apply the test of "satisfyingness"; and to apply it directly and *simpliciter*. There is, according to this version of the nature of truth, to be no attempt to determine the differentia which distinguishes the species "conviction" from the genus "satisfaction," or the subspecies "highest dis-

[4] A. W. Moore, in *Journal of Philosophy*, V (1908), p. 576.

coverable type of certitude" from "conviction" in general; and there is to be no arranging of satisfactions in a hierarchy and no pretension to define the conditions under which a maker of rational judgments *ought* to be satisfied. From many expressions of pragmatist writers it would appear that while the term "satisfaction" is "many dimensional" one dimension is as good as another; and that the final and decisive warrant for belief—the mark of the valid judgment—is the capacity of the judgment to yield the maximum bulk of satisfaction, measured indifferently in any of its dimensions. But since the dimensions *are* many, it may manifestly turn out that the greatest total volume may not give the potential maximum of any given dimension taken singly. The liking for luminosity of meaning, or for conceptual consistency, or for completeness of empirical verification may fail to get full satisfaction in a judgment; but the judgment may, it would seem, still be "true," if it compensates for these limitations by a preponderant satisfactoriness with reference to other desires or interests: by its congruency with our habitual ways of belief, or its charm for the imagination, or its tendency to beget a cheerful frame of mind in those who accept it.

I think it possible that some pragmatists may at this point protest that they know of no one who seriously holds this view; certainly, it appears to me to be a curious view to hold. But I think one is justified in calling upon all of the name who reject this doctrine to take (and faithfully observe) an oath to abstain from a fashion of language which they have much affected; to refrain from identifying the true with the satisfactory *simpliciter*, to cease speaking of satisfaction as a "*criterion*" of validity, and to confine their assimilation of the two concepts to the much more qualified and commonplace thesis which follows.

9. This is pragmatism number seven *plus* a more or less explicit admission that our "theoretic" satisfactions have a special character and special epistemological pretensions; that our "intellectual" demands—for clear meanings, for consistency, for evidence—are *not,* and can not be, satisfied, unless their peculiar claim to precedence in the determination of belief is recognized; and that this claim is a legitimate one to which men should (though they often do not) subordinate their impulse to accept any conclusions that have any other kind of satisfactoriness. According to this view, "satisfaction" is still insisted upon as an essential mark of the apprehension of "truth"; but it is precisely a satisfaction which is not to be had except upon condition that other possible satisfactions be ignored or, in many cases, flatly rejected. Between this and the preceding (eighth) doctrine some pragmatist writers seem to waver. James, for example, often uses expressions (some of which have been quoted in the two foregoing paragraphs) implying the doctrine of the commensurability and equivalence of all satisfactions. But he elsewhere (e.g., in a controversy with Joseph in *Mind,* 1905) expressly distinguishes the "theoretic" from the "collateral" satisfactions connected with the processes of judging thought; and he does not appear to deny that the former may conflict with the latter, or that, in the event of such conflict, they ought to be preferred. To the objection offered by his critic, that if such admissions be made the pragmatist's criterion of validity is not practically distinguishable from the

intellectualist's, James opposes nothing more relevant than a sketch of the genesis and evolution of the demand of the human mind for consistency.[5] This sketch purports to show —if I understand it—that the desire (more characteristic of some minds than of others) to avoid self-contradiction is historically engendered through the crystallization of repeated experiences of uniformity in "things" into fixed subjective habits of expecting specific uniformities—habits so fixed that when such an expectation is disappointed "our mental machinery refuses to run smoothly." How the transition from the idea of uniformity to that of consistency is accomplished here remains obscure to me; but even supposing the evolution of the one into the other to be completely and convincingly traced, these interesting historical speculations do not show, they do not even tend to suggest, that the demand for consistency in our judgments as we now find it—playing its captious and domineering role among our mental cravings—is not quite distinct from all its fellows and their rightful, though their often flouted, overlord. In the present sense, then, the pragmatist's criterion of truth, whether right or wrong, seems entirely destitute of any distinctive character; it is simply the old, intellectualist criterion supplemented by the psychologically undisputable, but the logically functionless, remark that, after all, a "theoretic" satisfaction is a kind of satisfaction.

10. Another pragmatism, and one that undoubtedly has real epistemological bearings, is the doctrine of radical empiricism conjoined with the doctrine of the necessity and legitimacy of postulation; the doctrine, in other words, that

[5] *Mind,* N.S., XIV., p. 196.

"axioms are postulates" and that postulates are as valid as any human judgment ever can be, provided they be the expression of a genuine "practical" need. This may look like our eighth kind of pragmatism over again, expressed in other terms; but in certain important particulars it is really a distinct theory. It contains, in the first place, a special negative contention: namely, that there are no strictly compulsive or "necessary" general truths, no universal propositions that can force themselves upon the mind's acceptance apart from an uncoerced act of voluntary choice. And on its positive side, it identifies the true, not with those judgments which slip so easily into the mind that they afford a present emotional state of satisfaction, but with those that man's active nature requires as working presuppositions to be followed in its reaction upon present experience and its instinctive endeavor to shape future experience. This doctrine seems to me to be quite unequivocally expressed by Schiller in a well-known essay in *Personal Idealism.* "The 'necessity' of a postulate," we are told, "is simply an indication of our need. We want it, and so must have it, as a means to our ends. Thus its necessity is that of intelligent, purposive volition, not of psychical, and still less of physical, mechanism." "Behind the 'can't' there always lurks a 'won't'; the mind can not stultify itself, because it will not renounce conceptions it needs to order its experiences. The feeling of necessity, therefore, is at bottom an emotional accompaniment of the purposive search for means to realize our ends." [6]

11. A kindred but a much less thoroughgoing doctrine

[6] F. C. S. Schiller, "Axioms as Postulates," para. 11, in *Personal Idealism.*

seems to constitute one of the pragmatisms of James. The author of *The Will to Believe* would, I suppose, still vigorously deny the possibility of reaching "necessary" conclusions with respect to many issues, including some of the greatest importance in relation both to the purely utilitarian requirements of our living and to our higher interests; and he would, clearly, still maintain the propriety and the practical inevitableness of voluntary postulation in such cases. But that there are *some* truly coercive and indubitable truths, some items of a priori knowledge inhering in the native constitution of a rational mind, James pretty fully and frankly declares in his recently published volume of lectures. "Our ready-made ideal framework for all sorts of possible objects follows from the very structure of our thinking. We can no more play fast and loose with these abstract relations than we can with our sense experiences. They coerce us; we must treat them consistently, whether or not we like the results." [7] This, obviously, is no doctrine that axioms are postulates or that behind every "can't" there lies a "won't"; it is the doctrine that axioms are necessities and that the action of voluntary choice in belief is always limited by a permanent system of a priori principles of possibility and impossibility inhering in the nature of intellect, at least as intellect is now evolved. It is compatible, at most, with the opinion that there are not so numerous, nor so useful, axioms as some dogmatic philosophers have supposed, and that, when axioms fail us, postulates must in many cases be resorted to.

12. A point of pragmatist doctrine separable from (though not inconsistent with) either of the two last mentioned is the

[7] James, *op. cit.*, p. 211.

assertion of the *equal* legitimacy of those postulates (such as the uniformity of causal connection, the general "reliability" of nature, and the like) which appear indispensable as presuppositions for effective dealing with the world of our physical experience, and of those which, though lacking this sort of "physical" necessity as completely as they do the logical sort, yet seem demanded in order to give meaning to, or encouragement in, men's moral strivings, or to satisfy the emotional or esthetic cravings of our complex nature. It is conceivable enough that some pragmatists should refuse to recognize the equal standing of these two classes of postulates and should accept the first while rejecting the second; and it is a fact that not all who find a place for both agree as to the number and range of the second sort. The more extremely liberal forms of the doctrine of the right to postulate freely and to treat postulates as truths tend to lapse into identity with the eighth variety of pragmatism which identifies the true with the "maximally satisfying"; but in its more cautious and critical forms, the argument from the practical inevitableness of certain scientific to the legitimacy of certain ethicoreligious postulates must be regarded as a distinct type of pragmatist epistemology, and perhaps the one which—if pragmatism ought to have practical bearings—best deserves the name.

13. Lastly, there remains a second pragmatist theory of the *meaning* of concepts or judgments—which brings us back to the topic, though by no means to precisely the doctrine, with which our enumeration began. It may be expressed thus: an essential part of our idea of any object or fact con-

sists in an apprehension of its relation to some purpose or subjective interest on our part; so that no object of *thought* whatever could be just what, for our thought, it *is*, except through the mediation of some idea of purpose or some plan of action. The language of some pragmatist writers might lead one to suppose that they consider the *whole* meaning to be reducible to this teleological reference; but such a view does not seem to me intelligible, and it does not appear certain that any one really intends to maintain it. But it is evident that there are several logicians who think it both true and important to declare that a relation to a purpose constitutes an intrinsic and a determinative element in the connotation of any notion. It is, I suppose, such a principle that Moore intended to illustrate in recently pointing out that, however objective the virtues of a given candidate for office may be, he could neither be "clean" nor a candidate were there not present in the mind of every one so representing him the idea of possible voting to be done. And I suppose the same view is, in part at least, what Schiller has sought to enforce in insisting that nobody can be "lost" except with the aid of the existence in the universe of some purpose in some mind, requiring the presence of the "lost" person (or of the persons from whom he is lost) in some place or relation from which he is (or they are) excluded by virtue of his "lostness." [8] Schiller appears to me to have entangled this theory of meaning in a confusing and illegitimate manner with questions about "truth" and "reality"; but to pursue this distinction would involve a somewhat long

[8] *Journal of Philosophy*, IV (1907), p. 42, and pp. 483, 488.

and complicated analysis which may not here be undertaken.

These thirteen pragmatisms have been set down, not in a topical order, but according to the leading of those associations of ideas through which the ambiguities of the several doctrines, and the transitions from one to another, become relatively intelligible. But it may be useful to arrange them here in a more logical manner, while still retaining the original numbering. Those forms of theory, the separate enumeration of which results from distinctions made by this paper, but overlooked by pragmatist writers themselves—in other words, the doctrines formulated by pragmatists in more or less equivocal terms—are indicated by the sign (a); each group of doctrines hitherto improperly treated as single and univocal has a common superior number:

I. *Pragmatist Theories of Meaning.*

1. The "meaning" of any judgment consists wholly in the future experiences, active or passive, predicted by it.

2. The meaning of any judgment consists in the future consequences of believing it (a^1).

13. The meaning of any idea or judgment always consists in part in the apprehension of the relation of some object to a conscious purpose (a^1).

II. *Pragmatism as an Epistemologically Functionless Theory concerning the "Nature" of Truth.*

3. The truth of a judgment "consists in" the complete realization of the experience (or series of experiences) to which the judgment had antecedently pointed; propositions *are* not, but only *become,* true (a^2).

III. *Pragmatist Theories of Knowledge, i.e., of the Criterion of the Validity of a Judgment.*

4. Those general propositions are true which so far, in past experience, have had their implied predictions realized; and there is no other criterion of the truth of a judgment (a^2).

5. Those general propositions are true which have in past experience proved biologically serviceable to those who have lived by them; and this "livableness" is the ultimate criterion of the truth of a judgment (a^2).

7. All apprehension of truth is a species of "satisfaction"; the true judgment meets some need, and all transition from doubt to conviction is a passage from a state of at least partial dissatisfaction to a state of relative satisfaction and harmony (a^3). This is strictly only a psychological observation, not an epistemological one; it becomes the latter by illicit interpretation into one of the two following.

8. The criterion of the truth of a judgment is its satisfactoriness, as such; satisfaction is "many dimensional," but all the dimensions are of commensurable epistemological value, and the maximum bulk of satisfaction in a judgment is the mark of its validity (a^3).

9. The criterion of the truth of a judgment is the degree in which it meets the "theoretic" demands of our nature; these demands are special and distinctive, but their realization is none the less a kind of "satisfaction" (a^3).

10. The sole criterion of the truth of a judgment is its practical serviceableness as a postulate; there is no

general truth except postulated truth, resulting from some motivated determination of the will; "necessary" truths do not exist.

11. There are some necessary truths, but these are neither many nor practically adequate; and beyond them the resort to postulates is needful and legitimate.

12. Among the postulates which it is legitimate to take as the equivalent of truth, those which subserve the activities and enrich the content of the moral, esthetic, and religious life have a co-ordinate place with those which are presupposed by common sense and physical science as the basis of the activities of the physical life.

IV. *Pragmatism as an Ontological Theory.*

6. Temporal becoming is a fundamental character of reality; in this becoming the processes of consciousness have their essential and creative part. The future is strictly nonreal and its character is partly indeterminate, dependent upon movements of consciousness the nature and direction of which can be wholly known only at the moments in which they become real in experience. (Sometimes more or less confused with 3.) [9]

Each pragmatism of the thirteen should manifestly be given a name of its own if confusion in future discussions is to be avoided. The present writer has neither the necessary

[9] It is impossible to bring out the nature, motives, and reciprocal relations of dependence or incompatibility of these theories in any such condensed formulas. I hope no reader will attempt to take the above recapitulation as a substitute for the analytical discussion contained in the preceding paragraphs.

ingenuity nor the ambition to devise a nomenclature so extensive. But however the several theories be designated, the fact of their difference, and of the incompatibility of some of them with some others, can hardly, just now, be too much insisted upon—in the interest of pragmatism itself. What the movement commonly so named most needs is a clarification of its formulas and a discrimination of certain sound and important ideas lying behind it from certain other ideas that are sound but not important, and certain that would be important if only they were not unsound. The present attempt to list the chief varieties and to clear up the hidden ambiguities of a doctrine nominally one and indivisible is accordingly offered as a species of *Prolegomena zu einem jeden künftigen Pragmatismus.*

II

PRAGMATISM AND REALISM *

Professor Montague's interesting and characteristically lucid series of papers on this topic is, I hope, to be continued. In those which have thus far appeared certain considerations pertinent to the subdivisions of the topic already dealt with have, as it seems to me, been overlooked. These considerations I think it worth-while to point out, in the hope that Professor Montague may take occasion to revert to them in some subsequent installment of the series. The determination of the historic affinities and logical implications of a doctrine so influential and so characteristic of our time as pragmatism has, at the least of it, great historical interest to those who desire to understand, logically and psychologically, the complex and curious interplay of intellectual motives from which the ruling tendencies of the time result. There is, to be sure, in a sense, no such thing as pragmatism; that doctrine is not a well-defined substantive entity, a logical brick that can be passed from hand to hand, microscopically analyzed, and broken into pieces, all without essential alteration or loss of identity. Few of the historic schemes of doctrine for which we happen to have names are

* First published in *The Journal of Philosophy*, VI (1909), pp. 575–80.

things of that sort; and for that reason, most of the innumerable controversies of the past over the question whether one -ism or -ity is compatible with another have been unedifying examples of circular reasoning. Whether, for example, Christianity is compatible with pantheism—a subject that has been much debated—depends, obviously, entirely upon your definition of Christianity; but the term "Christianity" as the name of a collection of historic phenomena—the opinions or tendencies of persons called Christians—has at all times embraced a great number and diversity of elements. It is possible to take any one of these that you please, declare it to be "essential" or "fundamental," and then proceed to prove anything you please upon the question at issue. But there is no objective reason for considering one more essential as a characteristic of the historic complex termed Christianity than any other, unless it can be historically shown to be either (a) the sole, or (b) the most emphasized, teaching of the actual originator of the movement, or, at least, (c) a teaching never previously expressed or emphasized, a novel contribution to the world's stock of ideas. So, too, pragmatism is a historic complex of mixed philosophical motives and tendencies. There is danger, on the one hand, that in discussing its affinities with other doctrines one pick out arbitrarily some one element of the complex, or a few elements, and by analyzing the implications of these prove the pragmatist to be a realist, or a solipsist, or a positivist, or an anarchist, or an ontological Mormon, or what you will. On the other hand, it would be equally an error to assume at the outset that there is no one pragmatism *par excellence*, no trait of the group of doctrines going under the name and usually combined in the same minds, which is so peculiar and exceptional historically as to deserve better than any other to be regarded as distinctive and essential. Only, it remains to find, in the specific instance, the criterion of such essentiality and to discover the feature of the doctrine in which it is realized. To these ends it is requisite, first, to make a complete enumeration of all the more important ideas or logical motives emphasized in the actual utterances of persons willing to call themselves pragmatists; second, to see whether any one of these motives separately, *or the fact of their combination,* is, historically speaking, a relatively novel and distinctive contribution of this particular movement to our collection of more or less coherent and intelligible types of doctrine upon philosophical issues. Unless these precautions are taken, discussion upon the affinity of pragmatism for some other -ism will not really deal with any "objective" or historical thing called pragmatism, but only with the compatibility *inter se* of certain propositions arbitrarily drawn up by the person who starts the discussion.[1]

Now, Professor Montague's argument may, I think, be objected to on the grounds (1) that it hardly sufficiently recognizes one decidedly important and much-emphasized motive

[1] Pragmatism as a term bandied about in philosophical discussion ought *not* to mean merely the total complex of doctrines that chance to be joined together in the minds of persons—or in the mind of the first person—denominated pragmatists. If we are to use this type of term and are to avoid muddle, we must, I should insist on the one hand, give it some historical reference to some real stream of tendency; yet we should, on the other hand, subject that tendency to both logical analysis and historical comparison, in order to pick out what is original and distinctive in it, if, indeed, there be any such distinctive factor.

in the teaching of the pragmatists; (2) that it overlooks the fact that there is something novel and unique in pragmatism and that this unique characteristic consists chiefly in the *transformation* of the instrumentalism, of which he speaks in his second article, through its conjunction with the neglected factor—so that the instrumentalism of the pragmatist is not mere instrumentalism, but an instrumentalism of a special coloring.

1. One of the things that the pragmatism of James is, certainly, is a modern expression of the motive which in certain other expressions is known as nominalism or positivism. In his original volume of lectures on the subject, James showed very plainly that he was in the line of the great nominalistic tradition of English thought, a successor of William Ockham, of Hobbes, of Locke and Hume and Berkeley. The problems of philosophy, even the aspirations of religion, were to be simplified by confining thought to its proper objects of reference, by explaining to the mind the real limits of the meaning of every proposition it could frame. And the secret of this simplification was to lie in reducing all meaning and all verifiable truth to a "pointing" to "particulars in concrete experience." Enumerate those particulars and you have the whole meaning of any proposition; discover the smoothness and satisfactoriness of the transition from the particular concrete experience to which it pointed, and you have verified truth. The doctrine was, indeed, in a sense the last and completing word of the whole secular movement of nominalistic empiricism; where the medieval nominalists had applied the demand for the reduction of the meaning of abstractions to concrete and em-

pirically verifiable particulars, chiefly to the miscellaneous hypostases of Platonic realism; where Hume had applied the same demand to the notion of cause, and Berkeley to that of material substance; James applied it, in a still more fundamental manner, to the notion of truth itself. The truth was to be reduced to truths; and each truth must be statable in its "cash value." "Truth" was to be the name not of a mysterious essence, nor of an abstract quality, nor of a bare relation; it was precisely a kind of experience, having in each case a time and place and individual *quale* in the flux of experience. The typical nominalistic motive—the simplifying, clarifying, *denkökonomisch* motive; the typical nominalistic method—the definition of universals as collective names for particular items in experience; the typical nominalistic result—the rejection as negligible, if not demonstrably unreal, of all entities incapable of being brought within the compass of concrete experience—these are all conspicuously present in the most authoritative exposition of the pragmatic doctrine. Professor Montague seems to me to have scarcely noted sufficiently the role of this familiar and ancient motive in the new movement.

Now, nominalistic empiricism in epistemology has always made for idealism in metaphysics. Idealism, though it is a good deal more, is primarily the application of the law of parsimony to ontology. It refuses to multiply entities beyond necessity; and it finds no necessity for adding anything to their immediate, empirical face-value. That a tendency of thought in which the nominalistic temper is so marked should be thought naturally to incline to realism is surprising; that any part of it should be held necessarily to imply realism indicates a paradox on the part either of the holder of the doctrine or of the critic who finds such an implication latent in it.

2. It is true, however, that pragmatism also means instrumentalism. But its instrumentalism, it seems to me clear, should be construed in the light of its nominalism, of its demand for the reduction of all meanings to concrete particulars of experience stated in their most "economical" terms. Professor Montague has taken pragmatism too atomistically. What has been called pragmatism is, as I have maintained, a medley of diverse logical motives. Some of these I believe to be actually incompatible with one another. Most of them have on occasion been put forward separately and disconnectedly by pragmatist writers. Yet it can not be denied that several of them are capable of being harmonized. And when we are interpreting pragmatism we ought to take as many of its elements together as logic permits, and let the elements thus synthetized modify and interpret each other. We may thus be able to see in at least some phases of pragmatism a more or less novel doctrine, even though its constituent parts be not novel. It would be a new compound in intellectual chemistry.

Instrumentalism certainly—as "the courageous application of Darwinism to the life of reason"—is, in its most general definition, by no means a novel doctrine. The substance of it is to be found in the evolutionary empiricism of Spencer: thought is an incident of organic adjustment to environment, and its categories are the result of successful and biologically advantageous adjustments. In Spencer this doctrine appears in a realistic form and with an intellectualistic temper, very much after the fashion sketched out by Professor Montague on pages 486–87, 489–90; * such a form and temper are thus not uncongenial to instrumentalism, in the extremely broad sense there given it. But pragmatism is not simply a re-editing of the evolutionary empiricism of Spencer and Fiske and of a host of Darwinizing epistemologists. Its distinctiveness consists precisely in the fact that it combines instrumentalism and the method of nominalism. It does not take the doctrine that knowledge is an instrument as meaning that it is a copying or duplicating instrument, designed to receive an impress or decalc of an "environment" there independently. Pragmatism appears to propose a simpler, more economical, more rigorously empirical, and concretely verifiable, way of construing the instrumental relation.

It remains, indeed, to ask whether these two motives, instrumentalism and nominalism, are truly harmonious. Professor Montague thinks not (pp. 486–87). But in this I think one must say that he merely exhibits that double vision characteristic of the realist by temperament and connatural predestination without really presenting to those of a more nominalistic turn of mind convincing reasons for thus beholding the entire universe as twins. Certainly he begs a good deal of the question, marching to his realistic conclusions very calmly without casting a glance by the way at the most characteristic arguments and cherished distinctions of

* In the *Journal of Philosophy,* VI (1909) ; Professor Montague's series of articles is entitled "May a Realist Be a Pragmatist?" and appear on pp. 460–63, 485–90, 543–48, 561–71. The references in this essay are to pp. 460–63 and 485–90.

the pragmatist. For the pragmatist—whether he eventually professes realism or not—quite explicitly defines his more *denkökonomisch* way of interpreting the instrumental function of knowledge. He recognizes, indeed, that a serviceable instrument must somehow fit into something other than itself; instrumentalism always implies *some* sort of correspondence. But this correspondence, the pragmatist points out—if I have ever at all understood him—need not be a correspondence of something in conscious experience with something independent of conscious experience; it need only consist of a system of cross-references within the unbroken context of experience itself, between temporally sundered moments of the flux of existence. If one thing more than another is the *bête noire* of nearly all of those called pragmatists, I had always supposed it to be the copy-theory of the judgment. It is, in fact, as much on instrumentalist as on nominalist grounds, as I understand it, that the pragmatist has objected to that theory. It does not serve any useful purpose whatever for an idea to match either a simultaneously-existent, or an eternal, objective; what is pragmatically important is that this moment's thought should forecast, or advantageously lead into, some future moment's experience. In short, pragmatism substitutes intertemporal for transsubjective reference in its interpretation of the criteria alike of "serviceableness" and of "objective validity." This does not seem to me an altogether true or adequate view; but it seems to me a definite and intelligible one; and in so far as instrumentalism is a part of the group of doctrines that have been designated at various times as pragmatism, it seems to me to be this particular, this nominalistic, variety that is so far novel, distinctive, and important as to deserve to have the designation applied to it. This kind of instrumentalism I personally believe to be idealistic in its logical tendency; but, since the defense of that view would require further argument, I will in the present discussion not go so far; I will say only that it does not either necessarily or naturally make for realism. It leads *either* to idealism or to a *tertium quid,* a view in which the traditional subject-object dualism which constitutes the starting point of the ordinary controversy between realist and idealist is abrogated and transcended. Into an examination of the relational theory of consciousness I do not want here to enter. I am content, therefore, to leave it as a pragmatic alternative to idealism, maintaining only that, at any rate, if it is in any degree a new or distinctive theory, it must be distinct from dualistic realism of the ordinary sort; while if it is not distinct therefrom, it is incompatible with the nominalistic instrumentalism of the pragmatist. In any case, Professor Montague's realism (e.g., p. 487) seems as frankly dualistic as any ever was and as fully committed to the copy or duplication theory of knowledge. This, I should agree, is the one perfectly intelligible and clearly definable realism, the only one rightly to be so called. And it is such realism that I understand to be here in question. In view, then, of what has been said above of the characteristic *nuance* of pragmatic instrumentalism, and in view of Professor Montague's failure even to essay to show that that *nuance* results from an inconceivable combination of ideas, I can not see that he has proved that "an instrumentalist *must* be a realist." I even apprehend that it would be difficult for any one to prove (though I know the task has been attempted) that the pragmatist *may* be a realist. He ought to be either an idealist or what for the present I can only call an antidualistic *x*.

III

PRAGMATISM AND THEOLOGY *

That branch of philosophy known as the theory of knowledge is not generally conceived to be either the most humanly interesting or the most practical part. Yet to religious belief, and to the general ethical temper of individuals and of generations, it is shown by historical experience to have, after all, very close and pregnant relations. Theoretically, epistemology, since it professes to determine the criteria of truth and the scope of real knowledge and legitimate affirmation, should affect natural science as vitally as theology. But in practice it has usually not done so. Natural science has gone on its way, using the working hypotheses that were found empirically serviceable, without greatly caring about their ultimate foundations or their precise logical status and implications; and it has perhaps more often shaped the epistemological tendencies of a period than been shaped by them. But theology has been less able to be indifferent to what the epistemologists were saying. The reasons for this are various and for the most part obvious. Religion, dealing largely with supersensible realities and involving affirmations usually not susceptible of empirical testing and

* First published in *The American Journal of Theology*, XII (1908), pp. 116–43.

verification, has occupied intellectual territory requiring a title-deed of a different sort from those provisional ones that served the purposes of science adequately enough. The success of the procedure of science has itself often suggested a question as to the possibility of the acquisition of real truth in fields so remote and by methods of mental action so different from those which characterized the scientific investigation of nature; and such doubts, once raised, made inevitable for the serious religious consciousness some attempt to find, by a more profound examination of the nature and limits of knowledge than was indispensable for science alone, a proper and defensible place for itself in the mental world. Constituting, also, a more ultimate and decisive human reaction upon life than does scientific curiosity and inquiry, religion has naturally been brought into contact with more ultimate issues respecting the intrinsic character and the degree of actual accessibility of truth; and the craving for certitude and for a mental quietude and confidence that no imaginable doubt could shake may be considered a peculiarly religious need. This assurance has often been sought in the way of the mystic; but mysticism itself is only a form of rather impatient epistemology.

Such being the relations of the theory of knowledge to theology, the appearance and rapid spread of a comparatively new and ostensibly revolutionary epistemological doctrine is necessarily an occurrence of moment to the theologian. Few such doctrines, certainly, have spread so rapidly or got themselves talked about so universally in so brief a time as that known as pragmatism; and none appear to have more direct bearings upon religious issues. Unfortunately, it is more the diffusion of a name than of a theory that has to be recognized in a good deal of the current talk about the pragmatists' opinions. The term pragmatism, like "transcendentalism" before it, has far outrun any precise ideas which might be supposed to be its proper traveling companions. Even those who profess themselves pragmatists do not invariably appear to have an altogether clear apprehension of the exact meaning of their theory, or to agree with one another as to its bearing upon specific metaphysical and theological problems. In view of this prevalent confusion and uncertainty as to the import and ulterior implications of the doctrine, perhaps the most serviceable thing that can just now be done is to attempt to discriminate the several fairly distinguishable contentions—of which the most important is much more than an epistemological theory—which appear to be concealed under the one name; to set aside those that appear to be lacking in consistency with themselves or with demonstrable facts, or destitute of any important application; and only after the completion of this analysis, to seek to determine the significance and value for theology of the residuum that remains. Fortunately, the distinguished American philosopher to whom we owe both the name and the origination of the whole movement has just published a volume[1] in which he attempts, more systematically than ever before, both to clarify and to justify the pragmatistic doctrine. Any consideration of pragmatism at the present juncture is likely to touch the point most nearly and to serve the reader best, if it takes Professor James's book for its text.

[1] William James, *Pragmatism,* (1907).

One broad distinction, and a consequent limitation of the scope of this paper, must be made at the outset. The word pragmatism has been applied not only to quite dissimilar theories, but to theories bearing upon two entirely separate questions in epistemology. As first employed by Professor James and as still often used by him, the term designates a doctrine about the *meaning of propositions*—about the conditions under which a proposition can be said to have real meaning, and the way in which the genuine and vital issue in the case of any controverted question, theological or other, can be made clear. As used by many others, and frequently by James, the word indicates a certain theory as to the nature of truth or the *criterion of validity* in propositions—the theory, namely, that what, in general, entitles a proposition to be regarded as true is its functional value as an instrument to the satisfaction of a vital need or to the accomplishment of indispensable activities; in other words, the theory that (I quote these phrases with their ambiguities all upon them) a proposition is true "in so far as it will work," and that "ideas become true just in so far as they help to get into satisfactory relations with other parts of our experience." Now these two doctrines—the doctrine about meaning and the doctrine about truth—are not only distinct but independent. A proposition which is found to have definite meaning, according to the first sort of pragmatism, is not therefore held to be true by the second sort of pragmatism. And it is perfectly possible to accept the first sort without being logically compelled thereby to accept the second. To all who care anything for clear thinking it must appear a misfortune that two conceptions which—though they, of course, have elements in common—are essentially different in meaning, and possibly in value, should have come to be called by the same name.

It is impossible within the limits of a single paper to discuss adequately both sorts of pragmatism in their relation to theology. Here, therefore, I shall undertake to deal only with the first sort. It is the one more strictly entitled to the name. It is in some respects more fundamental—for a theory telling us whether any given proposition has any real meaning and what its meaning is, begins, so to say, farther back than does a theory telling us which, among the propositions that possess meaning, are true. The first kind of pragmatism, moreover—James's theory of the import of propositions—is relatively more novel and has been a good deal less discussed. The pragmatic theory of truth—pragmatism in the second sense—so far as it relates to theology, is a variant or a more generalized statement of a type of doctrine tolerably familiar in the religious thought of the past century, the type which makes a thoroughgoing theoretical skepticism the preliminary to—and the justification of—the postulation of whatever propositions are held to be called for by one or another sort of "practical" consideration. For these reasons, and because, in philosophy as in other serious business, it is well to clear up one thing at a time, and to take time to try to do so thoroughly, I shall here ask the reader to consider primarily—and as exclusively as the logic of the matter itself permits—the pragmatic theory in the first of the two senses which have been indicated.

I

Pragmatism, first of all, then, is a doctrine which undertakes to provide us with a criterion by which we can judge not what beliefs are true, but what differences between beliefs contain enough of significant meaning to be legitimate and intelligible subjects of discussion. As a theory concerning the meaning of propositions, it has no power either to sanction or to condemn any particular meaningful proposition; the function which it professes is simply to put out of court, as unfit for consideration, a large class of propositions which it declares to be really destitute of meaning. It asserts, essentially, that the import of any proposition framed by our minds consists in some reference to the future—as it is usually added—to "concrete future experience, whether active or passive." We are characteristically temporal, active, purposing, willing creatures, with our faces toward the future; the whole significance and interest of that ever-vanishing pin point of time which we call the present lies in its transitive character. If that present is engendered of the past, it is fed out of the future; it is in the vital sense of such transition and of purposeful control and direction of it that we really feel our life. And our intellectual faculty of judgment, like all the rest of our organic functions, is adapted to this forward-looking process of conscious life and instrumental to it. To judge is not to mirror things as they are, but to forecast things as they are to be and to make adjustments for dealing with them. A judgment, accordingly—says the pragmatist—

which contains or implies no such reference to the future has no meaning at all; and the meaning of propositions which have this reference is precisely and fully stated when you have made clear what that specific and concrete future experience is to which they point.

It was, as has been said, in this sense that the term was originally used by Professor James when he first gave it to the world as a name for a short and easy method in philosophy, in a now celebrated address delivered at Berkeley in 1898; and although he has also contributed notably to the development of the other sort of pragmatism, hereafter to be discussed, this theory about the meaning of propositions, which others of the school have a good deal neglected, may be regarded as peculiarly James's form of the doctrine. It is copiously illustrated in his newly published volume.

> To obtain perfect clearness [he says, *Pragmatism,* p. 46] in our thoughts of an object, we need only consider what conceivable effects of a practical kind the object may involve—what sensations we are to expect from it, and what reactions we must prepare. Our conception of these effects, whether immediate or remote, is then for us the whole of our conception of the objects, so far as that conception has any positive significance at all.

And the application of this criterion of meaning to a special case is exemplified by the controversy between the materialistic and the theistic conceptions of the nature and source of the world. That controversy has meaning, says Professor James, only because, and in so far as, theism implies the expectation of future possibilities in the world different from those implied by materialism. Suppose the world to have no future; and then (*Pragmatism*, p. 96),

> let a theist and a materialist apply their rival explanations to its history. The theist shows how a God made it; the materialist shows, and we will suppose with equal success, how it resulted from blind physical forces. Then let the pragmatist be asked to choose between their theories. How can he apply his test if a world is already completed? Concepts for him are things to come back into experience with, things to make us look for differences. But by hypothesis there is to be no experience and no possible differences can now be looked for. . . . The pragmatist must consequently say that the two theories, in spite of their different-sounding names, mean exactly the same thing, and that the dispute is purely verbal. . . . If no future detail of experience or conduct is to be deduced from our hypothesis, the debate between materialism and theism becomes quite idle and insignificant. *Matter and God in that event mean exactly the same thing*—the power, namely, neither more nor less, that could make just this completed world—and the wise man is he who in such a case would turn his back upon a supererogatory discussion.[2]

[2] For the sake of accuracy of citation, it is necessary to mention that James adds in brackets at this point the following proviso: "I am supposing, of course, that the theories *have* been equally successful in their explanations of what is." The proviso is a rather peculiar one. It seems to mean that if the theories had *not* been equally successful in their purely retrospective explanation of the sources of the supposed moribund world, there *would* be a difference of meaning between them. And this is equivalent to admitting that the pragmatic doctrine asserted in the same paragraph is untrue. But one must, doubtless, regard this, not as a retraction, but as a momentary and unintentional lapse.

With the spirit that engendered this doctrine—and, in particular, with the temper and purpose of Professor James's latest book—it is impossible for any save the most crabbed of scholastic metaphysicians not to feel a great deal of sympathy. The book is a sharp and emphatic demand—enforced with wonderful humor, with an unequalled insight into human nature, and with a sense for concrete realities rare among philosophers—for a philosophy and theology that shall be in touch with the life of human beings who live in a temporal world, who hope and fear and strive and achieve. And one of the primary aims of it, though not the only one, seems to be to put an end to the waste of energy and the needless discord that results in a world so full of real business to be done, from the jangling and (as the author considers them) the purely verbal and sterile controversies of many of the philosophical and theological schools. One could not, indeed, convincingly call the book an eirenicon. Professor James's usual method of peacemaking is to try to annihilate both combatants in the quarrels of which he disapproves, using his pragmatic formula as a bludgeon to that end. But this betokens at least so much of the spirit of the peacemaker as is implied by a strong dislike for the spectacle of avoidable quarrels. And it is perhaps this militant part of that spirit which, as human nature goes, is assured of the most general sympathy. But it neither befits the philosophic temper, nor is it pragmatically safe, to permit one's sympathy with the general spirit of a doctrine, or one's respect for the practical purposes of its author, to absolve one from a patient and analytical examination of its precise meaning, and of the validity of it in the specific form in which its author has expressed it. The pragmatic theory of the meaning of propositions is put forward primarily as a contribution to logic or epistemology; it implies that a correct view upon the logical question which it raises is worth having; and it purports to give a coherent and true account of a certain matter that is not intrinsically unverifiable. The coherency and truth, therefore, of that account we ought now to examine more closely. For the success of Professor James's somewhat aggressive peacemaking depends entirely upon the solidity of his weapon.

Now, in examining into the truth of the pragmatist theory in this first of its two senses, we must first of all ask how the validity of a theory concerning the meaning of propositions is to be tested. There appears to be no imaginable way of testing it, except by ascertaining what we do in point of fact mean by our propositions—in other words, by introspection. If a certain philosopher contends that no judgment made by a human mind ever contains any meaning beyond—let us put it algebraically—x, y, z, we do well to look into our judgments; and if we find in some of them certain elements of meaning which do not seem to be quite satisfactorily described as either x or y or z, we are justified in concluding that the philosopher's contention, as a generalization, is simply not true. Now applying this kind of test to Professor James's pragmatism, it is easy to find at least two classes of propositions, either of which constitutes a negative instance fatal to the theory as it is formulated. It is, indeed, so easy, that I find it scarcely conceivable that a great master of psychological analysis can ever have set up a general rule to which the exceptions are so obvious; and I go back and read again and again all the ways in which James states his theory with a feeling that they must mean something other than that which they, nonetheless, appear explicitly and unambiguously to affirm.

In order that, in presenting our negative instances, we may avoid all difficulty over the question of idealism, let us confine ourselves, first, to one class of judgments: those, namely, concerning the real existence, *für sich,* not of things, but of persons. My belief that Professor James now consciously exists and is probably at this moment engaged in writing about pragmatism, certainly (whether true or false) means, for me and for anyone who is unwilling to call himself a "solipsist," a good deal more than the mere expectation that I shall in the future have evidence of Professor James's existence and shall continue to be instructed and stimulated by further profoundly interesting contributions to philosophy and psychology. The belief, for one thing, refers primarily not to the future at all, but to something conceived as strictly contemporaneous with the moment at which the belief itself arises. And something similar is, in fact, true of all beliefs which have either a contemporaneous or a retrospective reference. The pragmatist seems to forget so commonplace a circumstance as that most of our beliefs refer to matters that have a date, and that the date is not always future. When I try to imagine what Galileo's state of mind was while he was recanting, at least the temporal part of my meaning, the "pastness" of the incident with which it is concerned, cannot be identified with any "future practical consequences in my experience" or anybody's else. Yet one cannot suppose that the pragmatists intend to deny the validity of the temporal distinction—they are the last philosophers in the world who could be expected to do so. As little do they seem actually to reject that other nonpredictive element in my meaning, in the instances cited—namely, the "externality" of the mental state referred to, the fact that what my mind is trying in some degree to reproduce is the conscious state of another, numerically distinct mind. *Some* objective practical consequences are usually (by no means invariably) implied by propositions of this sort; but they are implied only mediately or inferentially. These implied future aspects of the judgment's meaning constitute not its essence, but only the means to its verification. The complete *verification* of most judgments about concrete matters of fact is, indeed, usually subsequent to the making of them; and beliefs about past facts which contain no incidental implications as to possible future experience are (except in one important class of cases, to be noted) not in the strictest sense verifiable at all. If somebody has a theory that Queen Elizabeth was married to Leicester, but makes it a part of the same hypothesis that all possible evidence bearing upon the point has been completely destroyed, he says what is foolish and unimportant, because by his own admission no one can ever find out whether it is true or not. But he is not saying a thing that has no distinct and intelligible meaning. To maintain, then, that a belief which is empirically unverifiable is *ipso facto* meaningless appears not only unwarranted but absurd.

II

Our pragmatist seems, in fact, to have confused these two quite different things: the meaning or import of a judgment and the means to its verification. Recognizing this confusion, it seems advisable—in order that we may not take advantage of a mere infelicity in the formulation of the doctrine—that we restate the theory in a corrected and more promising form. What it, so far, appears to reduce to is the contention that propositions are *verifiable* only in so far as they imply anticipated future practical experiences. The pragmatist might offer this corrected principle as a criterion of the limits—not, indeed, of the meaningful, but of the verifiable; and, by implication, therefore, as a means of distinguishing the properly debatable from the undebatable. And in so doing the pragmatist would, if his criterion were sound, be at length doing something practically useful. He would, in effect, be setting up a sort of practical syllogism, which should have the function of regulating controversy, theological or other, and quieting the strife of tongues. The syllogism would run:

1. It is foolish and immoral to dispute about matters the truth of which cannot be verified.

2. All dispute about propositions that do not contain the implication of specific future practical experiences resulting from their truth is dispute about matters which cannot be verified.

3. Therefore, all dispute about such propositions is foolish and immoral.

No one is likely to quarrel with the major premise. The point now at issue is whether the minor premise (2)—the revised version of the first sort of pragmatism—is admissible. In one of the later chapters (*Pragmatism*, Chap. vi) of Professor James's book his theory—though confused, more or less, with another quite different doctrine—seems substantially to have assumed the form of this minor premise. All verification, we are there told, in the last analysis consists in the comparison of a concrete experience with a judgment of anticipation which had preceded it and had pointed or led to it. There are, indeed, certain indirect verification-processes that appear to lack this character; but they are merely provisional substitutes for the real thing. ". . . All roads lead to Rome, and in the end and eventually all true processes must lead to the face of directly verifying sensible experiences *somewhere*, which somebody's ideas have copied."[3]

Now a full discussion of this point would involve us at once in a consideration of pragmatism in its second sense as a theory of the criterion of truth. For you cannot tell what propositions are verifiable and what are not, until you know in what the verification of a proposition consists; and you cannot know this without knowing the generic nature of the mark or quality which distinguishes all "true" judgments from all false ones. Upon that larger discussion I do not now wish to enter. But one or two observations may be introduced here which will not necessarily bring up the broader epistemological problem. In the first place it should be evident that—whatever others may say—no one who admits that there are such things as "necessities of thought"—or "ex-

[3] James, *op. cit.*, p. 215.

ternal truths," or "self-evident propositions," or "a priori knowledge"—can consistently hold the view under consideration that only empirically predictive judgments are verifiable, and that all verification consists in the comparison of an anticipation with a subsequent concrete experience. For a "necessary" truth, an axiom, is, by hypothesis, precisely the kind of thing that is automatically self-verifying. It may imply a prediction; all general propositions do so, since they profess to apply to all future, as well as past and present, cases of the kind of thing you may be talking about. But if they are really self-evident propositions their verification does not depend nor wait upon the realization of the future facts which happen to come within their scope; their truth is known, as the jargon of the logicians implies, "from beforehand." And, further, there appears no reason why there should not be truths of this character which do not point to any subsequent, concrete, sensible verification. "Eternal" truths seem likely sometimes to deal with eternal matters; or they may deal with past matters, the necessity for the reality of which is involved in the necessity of some general truth which covers them. The elaborate systems of metaphysics and rational theology built up by the whole series of post-Kantian idealists constitute affirmations which do not imply the possibility of their own verification, for our minds, by any future sensible experience. But the pragmatist (though he may dissent from their actual arguments) cannot rule these systems out of court at the outset as by their very nature unverifiable, unless he refuses to admit the existence of necessities of thought. For what each of these systems professes and (however unsuccessfully) strives to be is a sequence of necessary and interconnected truths which leads from some common and admitted fact of experience to the discovery of the ulterior and unescapable implications of that fact. Here again, then, the pragmatic contention can only be maintained at the cost of a further and very questionable doctrine—that of the nonexistence of any a priori and necessary truth. Some may be prepared to pay this cost, and with them we must deal hereafter. But many—and Professor James, in particular—are not of their number. The author of *Pragmatism* gives very full and liberal recognition to the reality of eternal truths, which constrain the mind to assent in advance of experience and independently of any comparison of an anticipation with a subsequent sensible verification.

> Our ready-made ideal framework for all sorts of possible objects follows from the very structure of our thinking. We can no more play fast and loose with these abstract relations than we can do so with our sense-experiences. They coerce us; we must treat them consistently, whether or not we like the results.

These observations appear to be true, but they do not appear to be consistent with the doctrine about the nature and limits of the verifiable which constitutes the restated form of the pragmatic theory.

It could be shown, if space permitted, that even apart from the restricted field of necessary truths, we have ways of reaching conclusions which, though not absolutely coercive, we regard as convincing, about matters concerning which, at the moment when we make the judgment, we have no anticipation whatever of any subsequent experience, on our own part or on that of any other person. But it is needless to multiply negative instances. A single class of exceptions to a generalization is as effective as a multitude in showing the generalization to be untrue. The second formulation, then, of James's sort of pragmatism seems also to break down. We can as little maintain that verifiability is limited to the reference in judgments to future sensible experience, as we can that the meaning of propositions is so limited.

III

There still, however, is left something of the original pragmatist contention; there is a residuum to which the pragmatist would cling—and to which, so far, he is entitled to cling—even after his first two more imposing affirmations have successively been abandoned. This is the assertion that even if propositions lacking a reference to "concrete future experience" may have both meaning and verifiability, they can at all events have no importance or practical interest or religious value. It is to this and no more than this, I think, that a great part of the argument of James's book reduces. The substance of his pragmatic doctrine is to be found in this view which defines what constitutes not the intellectual meaning nor the logical validity, but the moral worth and human significance of propositions. It is impossible to suppose that the author of this first form of pragmatism really thinks that, if the world had no future, there would be no difference of meaning (in the popular and the logical sense of that word) between the materialistic and the theistic accounts of the world's origin and past operation—when the very sentence in which he enunciates this paradox betrays that the author himself, irrespective of any future reference, very clearly contrasts the meaning of the one account with that of the other. It is equally impossible to suppose that he fundamentally and consistently thinks that all verification depends upon the *ex post facto* comparison of a prediction with an experience predicted, when in the same discussion he sets forth, with characteristic felicity in exposition, certain modes of verification of a wholly different character. But there can be no doubt that he thinks that propositions which have no bearing either upon future experience or future conduct have no useful function in human life.[4] What, he constantly asks, shall it profit us—creatures whose connatural

[4] This doctrine is, of course, not particularly new. I find, for example, in a forgotten German logician of the eighteenth century, whom, by coincidence, I chance to be reading just after writing this paragraph, the following distinction between "dead" and "living" knowledge: "Whenever a piece of philosophical knowledge (*eine gelehrte Erkenntnis*) is capable of putting in motion man's appetitive or volitional faculty, and actually does so, it contains grounds of action (*Bewegungsgründe*) and is *living*. Any knowledge which can, or does, have no influence upon the will, is a *dead* knowledge. . . . There are three things requisite in order that any piece of knowledge may be called living: (1) it must be perceptual [by this he means, not abstract or symbolical]; (2) it must arouse some rational feeling of satisfaction or dissatisfaction (*Vergnügen oder Missvergnügen*); (3) it must at the same time rationally represent this satisfaction as not only future, but also as capable of being furthered or hindered by our own powers" (Meier, *Vernunftlehre*, 1752, paras. 263, 266). Meier goes on to reason that only "living" knowledge is truly important. This comes near to making a pragmatist of the logician whose book (from which the quotation comes) was used by Kant as the textbook for his university classes.

business is to act and whose treasure is in that concrete future that our desires or our ideals foreshadow and our choices may help to form—what shall it profit such as we to hold beliefs which define no expectation and prescribe no action? Unless a proposition puts before man's volitional nature the promise of some hope realized, the possibility of some risk to be faced, the means that may be seized upon for some desirable consummation, what does it humanly signify whether the proposition be affirmed or rejected?

It is really upon such considerations as these, I think, that James chiefly relies when he tries to justify even his technically logical theory; it is, in the last analysis, by means of this practical test that he seeks to distinguish the legitimate from the illegitimate subject of controversy in theology or elsewhere. Thus the issue between a spiritualistic or theistic, and a materialistic, conception of the world *may* be of great importance, a question upon which we have every reason for employing the best energies of our minds. But it is so only if you mean by theism a belief which justifies you in hopes and expectancies to which the other view gives no sanction.

> Give us a matter that promises *success,* that is bound by its laws to lead our world ever nearer to perfection, and any rational man will worship that matter as readily as Mr. Spencer worships his own unknowable power. . . . Doing all that a God can do, it is equivalent to God, its function is a God's function, and in a world in which a God would be superfluous; from such a world a God could never be lawfully missed.

This, it will be noted, is very far from saying that the idea of self-evolving matter and the idea of divine personal agency are—even in their past relations—ideas of identical logical import; it implies, in fact, quite the contrary. It says merely that if the materialistic and theistic hypotheses pointed to identical and equally valuable cosmic futures we should have no serious motive for caring to know which is the true hypothesis. But since, in reality, "materialism means the denial that the moral order is eternal, and the cutting off of ultimate hopes," while "spiritualism means the affirmation of an eternal moral order and the letting loose of hope," our moral interests and the sanction of our forward-looking emotions are at stake in the matter; and it is for that reason that "we have here a genuine issue, which as long as men are men will yield matter for serious philosophic debate."

In its "pragmatic" residuum, then, the first sort of pragmatistic doctrine must be regarded as essentially a practical and ethical attitude; James's attempt to convert it into an epistemological theory is an untenable and a superfluous exaggeration. He has apparently been led by enthusiasm, and by an instinct for the effective and emphatic way of putting things, to translate a strong conviction concerning the relative importance of propositions into a logical doctrine concerning the import of propositions. The value of this third transformation of pragmatism we have now to consider. We shall find it open to a very different sort of objection from those which it was necessary to urge against the preceding two.

It must be borne in mind that we are not now concerned with the analysis of the meaning of a proposition nor with the verification of the assertion contained in it; we are now interested in its functional value, *its relation to the future in any way*. In order, therefore, to come up to the requirements of our present pragmatist formula, a proposition need not be expressly predictive; its reference to the future need not be a verbal or even a logical part of its own content. So long as it actually bears upon, affects, or predetermines the future, and can be apprehended by us in advance as capable of doing so, it must escape the pragmatist's condemnation. In his original statement,[5] even of his doctrine about meaning, James explicitly made his pragmatic criterion take in every kind of future consequences of a proposition's being true—"active or passive, direct or indirect, express or implied;" and certainly, when the criterion drops its masquerade as a logical theory and presents itself now purely as

[5] There is, however, in James's recent book a radical ambiguity in the statement of the pragmatic criterion. The "future consequences in experience of the proposition's being true," in which the meaning or the importance of any proposition is declared to consist, may either (a) include only the future experiences which the proposition predicts as about to occur, no matter whether it is believed or not; or (b) it may also include the future experiences which will follow if the proposition is believed. James applies the formula sometimes in one sense, sometimes in the other, and his results vary accordingly. When he takes the formula in sense (a), it tends to exclude a variety of beliefs—or all except certainly restricted elements in those beliefs—from consideration, as meaningless or unimportant. It is, for example, applied in this sense in the passage cited, referring to the issue between materialism and spiritualism. More usually, the criterion is applied in sense (b); and then it appears able to exclude no belief that anyone really cares about. It does not, for example, permit the relegation of either the Vedantist, or the modern idealistic monism to the limbo of nonsignificant issues. Neither doctrine is in any concrete way predictive; but, as James recognizes, the holding of either makes a difference in the life of the believer; and both, therefore, are acknowledged to have pragmatic value.

a means of discriminating practically significant from practically trivial differences of opinion, it must necessarily be taken with this latitude of meaning. Any judgment, then, which by being true, and known as true, entails future consequences in any way different from those which would follow upon its falsity, is as "pragmatic" as need be and fully meets all the demands that our pragmatist can ever make of any judgment.

This being recognized, I do not see how anyone can question the entire truth of the formula. A belief which turned an absolutely blind eye, a dead face, to the future in which alone value still remains possible for us would be a thing itself utterly and inexpressibly valueless and unimportant. But just the obviousness of this fact suggests to us the question which may still be asked about the present pragmatic principle—one concerning, not at all its truth, but its applicability. Doubtless, no beliefs that neither enable us to prognosticate any future experience nor prescribe any future behavior can be useful or interesting or morally or religiously serviceable. But *are there any such beliefs?* Do judgments of this sort exist in nature? Assuredly, we must answer, they must be few in number and of a wholly peculiar character. For *any belief which I am supposed to be capable of carrying with me into the future,* ipso facto *constitutes an item of my future experience; it will in that future engender its own concomitant states of thought and feeling and call for its appropriate reactions, and it will therefore have importance and efficacy corresponding to the degree of interest and of influence which there attaches to it*—no belief, while held, being wholly destitute of such interest and influence. This is the consideration which compels me unwillingly to conclude that the pragmatic enterprise of ruling out a whole class of propositions in advance, on the ground of their nonfunctional character, is a completely hopeless, or rather a completely redundant, undertaking.

That this is no verbal and sterile quibble may be seen by reverting to Professor James's own chosen illustration and using that once more as a test case. Suppose that a theistic and a materialistic account of the source and essential nature of the world both implied in all other respects exactly the same futures; suppose, for example, that we *could* put a thoroughly optimistic construction upon materialism and infer from it the "success" of all our highest ideals of social good or of individual perfection. There would still inevitably remain one difference between the two views, arising precisely from the fact that they are two views and not one. If the theistic view be true, and accepted as true, then our future will contain an additional item of fact; our sensible experiences, even though no other than those which the materialistic theory might have led us to expect, will be construed by us as the expression of a personal consciousness behind them; and this will give to them a reinterpretation and will awaken in us a sense of communion, which may very well come to seem the most significant element in our whole universe of discourse. A future world with a God in it will, both for our intellectual modes of representation and for our feeling, be incommensurably different from a world with no God in it, even though all the choir of heaven and furniture of earth be the same in the latter as in the former world. From no standpoint save that of a shop-keeping sort of utilitarianism—which is the last attitude that anyone could regard as characteristic of the originator of the pragmatist movement—can it be maintained that my experience, when I have a set of physical sensations which I ascribe to the working of unconscious automata, is "equivalent" to my experience when, having the same sensations, I ascribe them to the agency and purpose of conscious, feeling, loving, or hating minds analogous to my own. And between a theistic and a nontheistic way of construing the facts of experience —even the facts up to date—there is, at least for a large class of minds, a far more pregnant difference. There is an eloquent and familiar passage in Romanes's early writing, *A Candid Examination of Theism,* in which he gives expression to his sense of all that he had lost out of the universe through that abandonment of theistic faith to which he found himself constrained; and it was as much in the vanishing of a spiritual presence from Nature, as in the quenching of hopes of personal immortality or cosmic "success," that the tragedy of his intellectual illumination seemed to him to consist. Throughout the reflective poetry of the nineteenth century there sounds an often recurrent cry of protest or of lamentation before the seemingly irresistible march of a purely mechanistic conception of the world; and the expected consequence of that threatened triumph which these poets have bemoaned has been not usually the darkening of the hopes of the future, but the disenchantment of the present, through the baffling of man's imaginative craving for meaning, purpose, fellowship, and kinship in the outer world of physical phenomena. Better—the modern poet has sometimes cried, reversing the argument of Lucretius—the somewhat disorderly and capricious, but responsive and essentially personal, Nature of paganism than a cosmos never so neat and regular in its behavior, but empty of any consciousness either of our existence or of its own.

> We yearn for fellowship with lake and mountain;
> Our conscious souls seek conscious sympathy—
> Nymphs in the forest, naiads in the fountain,
> Gods on the craggy height and roaring sea.
>
> We find but soulless sequences of matter,
> Fact linked to fact by adamantine rods;
> Eternal bonds of former sense and latter;
> Dead laws for living gods.[6]

It is from entirely the same point of view that the melancholy preacher in James Thomson's *City of Dreadful Night* brings to his pessimistic and despairing congregation, as the first and deepest consolation remaining to them, an assurance that the evil universe in which they suffer has at least no purpose nor personality behind it. "The facts of experience"—this is the burden of his message—"are as bad as you think them; but it is not necessary to make that evil intolerable by conceiving it as the expression of a conscious will."

> There is no God: no fiend with names divine
> Made us and tortures us; if we must pine,
> It is to satiate no Being's gall.

In neither of these cases does the idea of a divine presence imply any change in the facts external to itself; yet both to

[6] Grant Allen, "Magdalen Chapel," in *The Lower Slopes* (1894).

the poet who finds those facts in themselves beautiful and to the poet who finds them monstrous, that idea is what, by his personal rejection of it, chiefly gives the coloring to his total experience and determines his emotional reaction upon life. The belief in God thus, even where it predicts no future experiences that might not have equally been predicted by the negative of that belief, still predetermines a difference in experience. It is the difference in the belief that *makes* the experience different.

The question of theism, considered apart from its prophetic implications, is doubtless the most important example of the existence of real issues which turn upon propositions that have of themselves neither a predictive nor a prescriptive reference to the future. But it is not a unique example. Any nonpredictive proposition whatever will possess, in greater or less degree, the same kind of *pregnancy* of future differences in experience, if any strong feeling or any lively need of the human imagination chance to be implicated in it. Logically speaking, the difference between a proposition's truth or falsity is always, in this sense, a pregnant one, since, once more, the experience even of the vaguest and mildest affirmation of the proposition is bound to be different from the experience of its negation. The presence of the associated emotions or special interests determines only the degree of the difference, not its existence. When we look about us or turn the pages of history, we find scarcely any limit to the number and variety of the affirmations which different minds have been desirous of carrying along into the future with them, though none of the other elements entering into that future were thereby deducible. Occasionally we find men caring in this way about purely past matters of fact—for example, the aristocratic origin of their own family, or the saintliness of the character of Jeanne D'Arc, the historicity of Moses, or the reality of the miraculous conception. In some of these cases such purely historical beliefs appear significant merely because they are supposed to be inextricably involved in some complex body of truths that has a predictive side to it. But examples are not wanting of retrospective judgments that have of their own force taken a singular hold upon the imaginations of great masses of men. More usually, however, the pregnant sort of nonpredictive belief relates to some permanent or nontemporal element or aspect of the world that does not manifest itself in any specific, efficacious relation to the other phenomena of experience. Of these purely descriptive or interpretative beliefs, the provinces of metaphysics and religion afford an inexhaustible supply of illustrations. Many persons, for example —as Professor James has himself remarked, in a passage that is an admirable example of sympathetic humor—find great inward satisfaction, and even a very practical sort of relief from unhealthy mental perturbation and restlessness, in simply being able to apply the numerical adjective "one" to the world with considerable frequency. It is not any particular or working kind of oneness that they care about; the vaguer it be, the better it is able to arouse those subtle reactions that seem to be especially associated with the idea of unity. Others, again, are analogously affected by the number three—for there is a trinitarianism that is much wider than orthodox Christianity—and are strongly sensible of the need of representing the general nature of things under the form of a triad. Perhaps the great majority of mankind finds some sense of an ultimate mystery and ineffableness in things almost indispensable and therefore resents any doctrine which conceives the universe as nothing more than a neat system of regularly moving atoms, completely calculable by a sufficiently good mathematician. It is for this reason that Mr. Spencer and those of like mind cling to their "unknowable power" and are not content with even the most serviceable and "successful" matter.

Now, we are, of course, accustomed to recognize that not all of these "needs" are equally legitimate and serious; and it is generally agreed that the question of truth or falsity is more urgent and more important in the case of some of these nonpredictive but pregnant beliefs than in the case of others. It is, indeed, questionable whether any belief that a considerable part of mankind have cared about is unimportant, if true. We should be somewhat shy of any doctrine which proposes to deny to even the most outlaw sort of belief its day in court—its opportunity to be tested by the two ultimate questions: First, does the proposition expressing it have any definite, intelligible and consistent *logical* meaning? Second, is it in any way verifiably true? Still, it would doubtless be an advantage to have some canon whereby we could arrange these purely descriptive and interpretative judgments according to their relative seriousness and significance, in advance of any consideration of the evidence for their truth. It should, however, by this time be entirely clear that pragmatism, even in its amended form, is incapable of providing us with such a canon. It has no facilities for either excluding from consideration, or even for subordinating, any proposition. Every affirmation that is not pure nonsense is either true or false. If true, and if its truth be verifiable, the acceptance of it will be a fact which alters the future of somebody. Thus every belief that actually waits at the gates of anyone's mind wears at least some shreds of the pragmatic wedding garment. A doctrine which confines itself to the distinction between propositions that have, and those that have not, future consequences can furnish no criterion for distinguishing, *within the limits of the former class,* the important from the unimportant. And virtually all propositions, we have seen, fall within those limits. The pragmatic principle itself, indeed, comes very near to being an exception. But it is not really one. It cannot, it is true, perform its chosen role of extinguisher of controversy. But (in the diminished sense to which we have now seen it reduce itself) it is undoubtedly true; and it expresses a certain descriptive generalization about a common characteristic of our judgments that may conceivably awaken some obscure emotional reverberations in some minds.

IV

Our results thus far appear to be chiefly negative. But after this clearing of the much-incumbered ground, it is possible to discover the more clearly in the philosophy of James an insight more profound and much less questionable than any of these variations of pragmatism. It is not properly an epistemological insight at all, but a directly metaphysical one; and it is not reducible to any of the pragmatist formulas. But it springs, nonetheless, I think, from the same root as they and is the substance of an idea of which they are vague adumbrations. Those who have followed Professor James's writings from the beginning must have long since seen what aspect of human experience, what sort of moment in life, has presented itself to him always as the central and illuminating fact, the fixed datum to which any philosophy that could be considered sound must be required to do justice, the point at which we have most reason to suppose that the inner and ineffable nature of reality is directly revealed to us. This is the moment of voluntary choice—the moment in which, in the presence of alternative real possibilities, and with the consciousness that some actual content of the future now truly hangs trembling in the balances of volition, the mind somehow reaches its fiat and, by the "dumb turning of the will," performs the daily miracle of excluding one of those real possibilities thereafter and eternally *from* reality. And it is to this sort of experience as a touchstone that James comes back in his latest book, when he attempts finally to settle what he himself declares to be the gravest and most momentous of philosophical issues—the issue, in general, between monism and pluralism. He is, confessedly, not in the least helped to his own settlement of this issue by his pragmatic criterion in the first sense; for both of the opposing views are recognized as having pragmatic meaning and potential value in experience. Nor is it upon any merely general application of pragmatism in the second sense—of the conception of the true as simply the morally or practically serviceable—that he bases the main outcome of his reflection. It is rather upon a more original and an entirely specific principle (which has this in common with the first sort of pragmatism, that it, too, is the expression of a sense of the necessity of maintaining the vital significance of the relation of present action to future experience) that James rests his characteristic metaphysical doctrine. This principle may be expressed thus: no proposition is to be accepted as legitimate which, directly or by implication, *denies to the future the genuine character of futurity and contradicts the reality of open possibilities* at any present moment of conscious choice between alternatives. It appears to be a reasonable, a natural, and even a necessary, presupposition of all action and of all reflection that future time is future; that in the act of choice something is chosen; that in the process of deliberation there *is* a process and there is something determined thereby; that possibilities, before decision, have just that kind of reality which it is, *at the moment of decision, impossible to think of them as not having;* and that at the moment after decision one bit of this kind of reality is extinguished forever. This is for James, at the least of it, a hypothesis which has the right of way in philosophy, and one which no conflicting doctrine can show to be illogical or untrue. "Our acts, our turning-places, where we seem to ourselves to make ourselves and to grow, are parts of the world to which we are closest, the parts of which our knowledge is most intimate and complete. Why may they not be the actual turning-places and growing-places which they seem to be, of the world—why not the workshop of being, where we catch fact in the making, so that nowhere may the world grow in any other kind of way than this?" [7]

[7] James, *op. cit.*, p. 287.

This presupposition is, indeed, so natural to every man that it may seem to many a mere commonplace. But the implications of it for philosophy and theology are, on the contrary, revolutionary. In particular, it leads to the rejection of a mode of religious thought that has influenced many minds—and minds of a high order—in our time. This is the doctrine—which has received its most systematic and persuasive presentation at the hands of Professor Royce, but is to be found also in many other and less coherent forms—that all which enters, or has entered, or shall enter, into the experience of any conscious life is eternally embraced in one Absolute Experience. This all-including Divine Life, we are told for our comfort, is itself, in its timeless existence, eternally triumphant; the world that is, is the world that the Absolute wills and finds very good; even our suffering and sin and shame are, every single jot of them, indispensable elements in the bliss and glory of the Universal Self who alone sees and understands the whole. This doctrine is, by its philosophical defenders, declared to express only what is necessarily implied by the very conception of the existence of such a thing as truth; its technical basis, in other words, is epistemological,[8] and the rejection of it involves the denial of the soundness of its epistemological premises. But apart from all purely dialectical considerations, it has seemed to many to possess profound religious value. Thus an anonymous correspondent, whom James quotes, finds that the

[8] One form of a kindred epistemological argument for a supratemporal and eternally perfect Self, manifesting itself in the temporal experiences of humanity, is familiar in the writings of Thomas Hill Green.

thought of the limitations, failures, and sufferings of himself and others becomes endurable "only on one condition; namely, that through the construction, in imagination and by reasoning, of a rational unity of all things, I can conceive of my acts and my thoughts and my troubles as supplemented [not merely to be supplemented] by all the other phenomena of the world, and as forming—when thus supplemented—a scheme which I can adopt and approve as my own." Such a conception of all evil as completely taken up into, and required by, the total plan of things—and of this total plan as eternally willed and approved by a timeless Consciousness that knows and possesses all the content of it from the beginning—may be said, indeed, to be necessarily involved in any thoroughly optimistic view of the world. Whoever says that the universe of our experience is through and through, and in all its items, rational, the expression of a single Reason and a single Will—whoever intends to maintain literally that because God's in his Heaven, *all's* well with the world—implies some such doctrine as this to which the philosophers of idealistic monism have given systematic and logical expression.

Now, Professor James's aversion to this type of theology is not, apparently, due solely to the fact that such a doctrine conflicts with the fundamental presupposition of which I have spoken. There is another characteristic conviction of his—also appearing in some of his earliest papers—which, if it does not serve of itself to confute the monistic theology, at least establishes on both ethical and logical grounds a serious presumption against it. This is the conviction that the rather prevalent fashion of intellectually playing fast and loose with evil—of calling in the religious consciousness to bless what the moral consciousness has pronounced accursed—is not, in the long run, compatible with either logical or moral integrity. Especially since the time of Hegel, and partly as a result of the diffusion of Hegelian ideas, this sort of book-keeping by double entry has become exceedingly common, even among those having little acquaintance with philosophical systems; the very essence of religion has seemed to some to consist in the affirmation that there is a higher point of view, a superior plane of insight, at which the stubborn differences of things—and, among others, the difference between the good and the bad—disappear in a transcendent synthesis where all is unity and all is good. Of this tendency Professor James has been the lifelong opponent; he has stood stoutly as the defender of what he has called "the chastity of the intellect," insisting that differences do not disappear by being ignored, and that, in particular, evil is neither annulled nor absolutely compensated by being—as it happily may be—passed beyond or even utilized to further future good. The point has been well-expressed by a sane and admirable humanist of our time, who makes small pretensions to technical philosophy:

> Evil comes from the gods, no doubt; but so do all things; and to extract good from it—the great Prometheus-feat of man—is not to evil's credit, but to the credit of good. The contrary doctrine is a poison to the spirit, though a poison or medicinal use in moments of anguish, a bromide or an opiate.[9]

[9] Vernon Lee in *Hortus Vitae* (1907).

To a mind thus deeply impressed with the necessity of keeping distinct things distinct, and above all of honestly facing the irresolvable evilness of evil, and loyally maintaining the rigorous dualism of the moral judgment, the monistic system must inevitably appear suspect. For in that system the point of view represented as highest—the point of view of the Absolute Consciousness—transcends and confounds the ethical distinction. The Sinner, if he be also a monist clear-headed enough to see the implications of his own metaphysical belief, may always have the consolation of considering that he in his sin, no less than the saint in his virtue, is contributing an indispensable ingredient in that strange compound of Being which his God has from all eternity willed and in which is his everlasting delight.

But the ultimate ground of objection to the monistic theology lies, I think, for the philosopher of pragmatism, in the fact that—if it be construed literally—it takes away from our "present" moments of action that character of real, determinative responsibility, and from the future that character of possessing real and undetermined possibilities, the presupposition of which is inexpugnably implicit in the act of conscious and purposive volition. "The essential contrast," he writes, "between pragmatism and rationalism [really between the opposing metaphysical conceptions of pluralism and monism] is that for rationalism reality is ready-made and complete from all eternity, while for pragmatism it is still in the making, and awaits part of its complexion from the future." According to the latter view, in our cognitive as well as in our active life we are creative. "We *add*, both to the subject and to the predicate part of reality.

The world stands really malleable, waiting to receive its final touches at our hands. Like the kingdom of heaven, it suffers violence willingly. Man *engenders* truths upon it." [10]

The conception of the universe which is implied by this doctrine is radically new in at least this sense, that it has rarely been taken seriously and whole-heartedly by either theology or the general religious consciousness. It runs counter to what is perhaps the strongest and most characteristic religious tendency of the present generation—the craving for the consolations and the mystical intoxications of thoroughgoing monism and unqualified optimism. It is, for example, essentially uncongenial to what appears to be the metaphysical side of that somewhat confused medley of conceptions now exercising the minds of the English churches under the name of the New Theology. And it is almost as little in harmony with what may be considered the dominant (though far from the unique) strain in the greater part of the theological thought of the past. For (as a paper in this Journal by the present writer sought to show several years ago [11]) theology has rarely taken the reality of the time-process, of the temporal aspect of human experience seriously; it has always been in haste to fix itself upon the eternities. But the doctrine of the pragmatistic philosopher takes the time-process so seriously as to imply that all the reality of which we have any possible knowledge is

[10] James, *op. cit.*, pp. 257, 256. The philosophical reader will observe that this doctrine, though not really based upon the pragmatist epistemology as formulated by James, does undoubtedly imply a reconstruction of certain parts of epistemology. That, however, is a matter lying beyond the scope of this paper.

[11] *The American Journal of Theology*, VI, 3 (1902), p. 439.

strictly temporal and processive in character. Religious emotion, too, in the past (even when most conjoined with the ethical temper) has often been prone to seek the opiate of an eventual optimism, to demand a final assurance against all real loss, to cultivate the confidence that all things (even their own sins) work together for good to them that love God. The doctrine of the pragmatist, if it has its encouraging and its bracing aspect, has also its drastic aspect; and it is unable to give any such assurance. There are, in its universe, indefensible evils and uncompensated losses. Our business with these is not to harmonize them, or even to explain how they came to be there; our business is to get rid of them, and to devote our powers to eliminating them from the world that is to be. And even in that future we may expect obstacles and we must face risks. The salvation of the world, says James, is no absolutely predictable certainty. So far as we have knowledge, it appears to be a world "the perfection of which is potential merely, the condition being that each several agent does its own 'level best.' . . . The world's safety is unwarranted. It is a real adventure, with real danger, yet it may win through. It is a social scheme of co-operative work genuinely to be done."

Such a doctrine, while it rejects the arguments for theism offered by the monistic philosophy, finds the theistic faith a reasonable and a needful postulate. It has a natural affinity for the belief in a power not ourselves that makes for righteousness, and from whose abounding supplies we may, in the ways known to religious experience, draw reinforcement of our own spiritual energies. It is, perhaps, in this hidden and mysterious source of moral power empirically known in the inner life of men that James himself is chiefly interested. But from his general doctrine there follow certain consequences in regard to the conception of God, in so far as that relates not only to a power that functions in our experience, but also to a being of whom we may have some sort of intellectual representation. Such a philosophy as that of the pragmatist sees no reason for belief in the reality of an idle perfection, however sublime, having no real contact with the mud and dust of things, no truly militant part and no vital stake in the battle which for us is often so full of hazard and of desperate seriousness. Its God must be a God having an existence in the temporal world which alone is real to us, and therefore one having his own perfection of being and his own triumph still to achieve—with us, and through our loyalty in that vast, co-operative work in which we have every reason to think that the universe consists.

It must suffice for the present to have recapitulated this conception and to have disengaged it from the ambiguous and unconvincing epistemological theories with which it has needlessly been involved. The conception, it is fairly manifest, is still far from being fully worked out; and it suggests some serious questions which it does not answer. It is doubtless something less than the whole truth of the rational theology of the future. But it contains, I think, truth to which the theology of the future will find it necessary to give a place among the fundamentals. The greater number of the theologians and the philosophers of the past have sought the solution of their problems by taking the considerations that lead to the monistic type of thought as their starting-point.

By this time, any who will consent to think clearly may, as it seems to me, see that the result of these efforts is, and must be, a doctrine struck through with inevitable self-contradiction on its logical side, and on its ethical side, tending to the eventual divorce of the religious from the moral consciousness. In this situation, it is from the way of thinking that has as yet scarcely ever been fairly tried that we have most reason to expect light.

IV

WILLIAM JAMES AS PHILOSOPHER *

When the memory of such a human being as William James is still vivid in the minds of all, and a sense of personal loss is strong in all who ever came under the spell of that large and ardent personality—which means, in some degree, nearly all who ever read any of his writing—the moment is hardly suitable for a purely impersonal analysis of his philosophical reasonings. On the other hand, the portrait of the man behind the philosophy, especially in the more intimate relations of colleague and neighbor and familiar friend, must be drawn by those who had the good fortune of knowing him in those relations. But besides the man and the philosophy, there is the philosopher, the man *in* the philosophy. And it is upon the relation between some of the distinguishing traits of William James's mind and the character of his doctrines that I should like to dwell. The first task which the ending of the work of so highly individual a thinker imposes upon the generation he taught is that of endeavoring to see clearly and justly what manner of man he was as he philosophized, to which of the many real aspects of the world his nature was peculiarly inclined to

* First published in *International Journal of Ethics* 21 (1911), pp. 125–53; reprinted here with some omissions and additions.

respond, and how the content and the emphases, and also the limitations, of his teaching were affected by the special aptitudes of his intellect and by the characteristic temper of his personality.

"Any author," said James somewhere in *A Pluralistic Universe*, "is easy if you can catch the center of his vision." But, whatever the metaphor may imply, it is not to be assumed that the personal vision of a richly endowed mind, singularly sensitive to the variety and complexity of things, will be focused with such clearness and steadiness that its true center must be at once apparent to casual observation; we need not expect to find such a mind's view of the world a perfectly simple and uncomplicated thing. It is certain that the distinctive traits of James's philosophic outlook are not to be apprehended without some effort of discrimination. There seem to be many who conceive that because he is always easy and delightful to read he must therefore be easy to understand. As a matter of fact, there have been few recent philosophical writers whose meaning it has been so easy to mistake. The qualities which gave to his writing its vivacity and charm also made it a somewhat uncertain medium for conveying what was, in reality, a tolerably complicated and many-sided, even a rather delicately-balanced, scheme of ideas. This is indicated, though not proved, by the frequency with which of late years James had occasion to complain of radical misunderstandings on the part of other philosophers not sharing his views. Some of this may have been due to the inherent elusiveness of philosophical conceptions as such, some of it to what James once described as an innate "inability almost pathetic" of some of his critics to understand him; but some of it also must, it seems clear, be ascribed to certain difficulties in his own exposition of it. There was, indeed, in James's philosophic teaching nothing that need remain an unfathomable mystery to anyone who would consent to compare one part of that teaching with another, to reflect with a little patience upon the meaning of the whole, and to refrain from a meticulous literalism in construing occasional detached passages in which the vehemence of the philosopher's temperament had led him to overstate his own case, or his generosity had led him to make too liberal concessions to his adversaries. But the concreteness of his mode of expression and the apparently impetuous rush of his thought gave to many of his readers the impression that, with *this* philosopher, at least, all such precautions were unnecessary. He who ran, therefore, might—and did—read the author of *Pragmatism* abundantly; but he was not unlikely to read amiss, to suppose the doctrine to be a good deal simpler and more unambiguous than it was.

The needfulness of some circumspection in interpreting James is illustrated by the diversity of types of philosopher which he has been supposed to be, and the corresponding diversity of tendencies of opinion to which, by his writings, he gave—or has been declared to give—aid and comfort. He has been taken for a hard-headed utilitarian, the embodiment of the supposed "American spirit" of calculating practicality, who would reduce divine philosophy to a meager *Nützlichkeitskrämerei;* and he has been taken for the discoverer of a new basis for theology in the realities of inner spiritual experience. An influential English religious leader rejects pragmatism as inadequate because he has always "thought of it as the expression on the side of philosophy of the habit of mind engendered by the inductive method and the empiricism of modern science"; a French critic rejects pragmatism because "it means that we can at our leisure deny all science." And as James's doctrine repelled different men for opposite reasons, so it attracted different men for opposite reasons. Many "naturalistic" men of science found satisfaction in his philosophy because it seemed to some of them simply a generalization of the method of scientific positivism, or to others simply an application of Darwinism to the definition of truth; and many troubled clergymen found satisfaction in his philosophy because it seemed to them to issue to everybody a general license to believe what he liked or found "helpful" and to establish his belief upon whatever he might be pleased to call a judgment of value, without too much deference to either logical canons or physical facts. All this cannot, without analysis, be assumed to imply an equal inconsistency in James's own doctrine; but it at any rate implies, if not a many-sidedness, at least a several-sidedness, in his thought. And the problem remains of determining his characteristic personal position and real sympathies amid these diversities of tendency. It might, perhaps, appear sufficient to say that the personally distinctive thing was the catholicity which led him to unify—or to seek to unify—these diverse elements into a single philosophy. There would be some truth in such an observation; but there would also be something misleading. There have been a number of philosophers in the past who have been temperamental peace-makers, determined to make the lion and the lamb lie down together harmoniously in their systems, anxious somehow to find room there for all the tendencies of opinion that normally arise among men. Leibniz was such a philosopher; Hegel in a different way was another. And to such philosophers it not unnaturally happens that their systems, in the hands of their disciples, break up again into the original diversity and discord of their elements. But William James was by temperament no lover either of amiable compromises or of higher syntheses; in matters of belief, as in affairs—so he wrote in a characteristic early paper—we are ever confronted with "mutually exclusive alternatives, of which only one can be true at once. The wrench is absolute: 'Either—or!' "

The tendency of James's mode of self-expression to convey certain false impressions, not only about his opinions but about himself, *quâ* philosopher, is in nothing more strikingly shown than in a widely prevalent conception concerning his manner of arriving at his philosophy. He has, of course, done much to give currency to the idea that any philosopher's doctrines are wholly predetermined by the idiosyncrasies of his personal taste in universes. He has repeatedly observed that the really illuminating thing to ask about any philosophy is not on what professed "grounds" its author believes it to be true, but why he wishes it to be true. In one of his latest volumes he declared that "the history of philosophy largely bears out" the saying of an eighteenth-century writer, that reason was given to men chiefly "to enable them to find reasons for what they *want* to think and do." With such passages in mind, Mr. J. A. Hobson has dubbed pragmatism the "go-as-you-please philosophy." The natural inference has been drawn by many, from the same passages, that the inventor of pragmatism was a go-as-you-please philosopher, caring little how his conclusions were arrived at, if only they were in themselves "satisfactory." But the fact—patent to everyone who will read James's last two volumes in their entirety—is that there has probably been no philosopher in our time—indeed, I can think of but few since Kant—who reached his eventual doctrinal position through a longer or more patient struggle with purely logical difficulties, after a more honest submission to the leading of the argument as he understood it. The stages in James's approach to his final view—which he reached only in his sixties, after at least thirty years of pretty steady philosophical reading and reflection—are marked by the solution of definite problems or the elimination of specific false premises; the intervening periods seem to have been filled with painful but undiscouraged flounderings amid unresolved antinomies. James even seems (by his own account, which probably is, characteristically, a little too generous) to have owed the discovery of the way through, at each critical transition, to the insights of others. Thus his revulsion from absolute idealism is arrested for a time by an argument of a younger colleague which he sees no way of controverting; nine years later an article by a friend and former pupil shows him that this argument is not so cogent as it had seemed.[1] For many years, again, his principal objection to idealistic monism, e.g., that of his colleague Royce lay in a difficulty based upon grounds of purely "intellectualist" logic: the difficulty of conceiving how "many consciousnesses can be at one and the same time one consciousness." "I had," he writes, "yielded to these objections against my 'will to be-

[1] William James, *The Meaning of Truth* (1909), p. 22.

lieve' out of pure logical scrupulosity. The absolutists, professing to loathe the will to believe and to follow purest rationality, had simply ignored the objections. . . . My own conscience would permit me no such license." Yet the rationality gained by loyalty to this "intellectualist" principle seemed to be at the cost of irrationality at other points. "Sincerely and patiently as I could, I struggled with the problem for years, covering hundreds of sheets of paper with notes and memoranda and discussions with myself over the difficulty." Then Bergson, as James for a time conceived, revealed to him the possibility of cutting the Gordian knot.

This tenacious and laborious (even if frequently confused) thinker it is who has been supposed to be the embodiment of intellectual self-pleasing and logical irresponsibility; an eminent English writer has said of him that "abstract argumentation appeared to him futile, and subjects which require it were therefore uncongenial to him. His mind worked by flashes of brilliant insight." In spite of all the hard sayings that may be quoted from him against "abstract argumentation," James in fact devoted much the greater part of his life to precisely that employment; and, on the more fundamental and technical philosophic questions, at least, his "brilliant flashes" were preceded by arduous efforts of analytical reasoning. So far may a man's way of expressing his convictions give a false impression of the processes which he has gone through before arriving at those convictions. Whatever be thought of the actual consistency and tenability of James's opinions, it is the simple truth that few philosophers have ever tried to play the game more fairly, with less evasion of troublesome objections, with less haste to arrive at a "system" by illicit short-cuts.[2] His seriousness and good faith as a philosopher are again shown by his exceptionally wide reading in *contemporary* philosophy, by his readiness at all times to enter the lists of technical disputation in behalf of his opinions, and by his willingness to modify the details of his doctrines, to supplement or to qualify them, in response to criticism. At an age when he was entitled to enter upon the ease of the veteran, and after he had come to be in the eyes of the world the foremost intellectual figure in America, and perhaps the most widely read of English-speaking philosophers, he continued not merely to write philosophy but—what is a very different thing—to philosophize; he would cross lances on equal terms with the youngest dialectician of them all, and—though often impatient and a little irritated at what he (perhaps too hastily) regarded as wanton miscomprehension—he accepted correction, when he could see its pertinency, from any quarter, not only cheerfully, but with the handsomest acknowledgments. To some eminent philosophers a system, once shaped and polished, has served chiefly as a pedestal whereon they might mount, to stand there as their own monument in dignified immobility, undisturbed by the current controversies of the philosophic forum round about them. James was incapable of enjoying the monumental posture; he bore his part in the melee to the last.

It is to be observed, moreover, that James's final philosophy on its practically most significant side, his personal re-

[2] This is well-illustrated by James's struggles and alternations of opinion on the metaphysical "problem of time" in his posthumously published *Some Problems of Philosophy* (1911).

ligious hypothesis, was avowedly *not* perfectly satisfying to all the cravings of religious feeling; it was not arbitrarily put together so as to embrace all the propositions which it is congenial to human nature to believe, but was the product of a deliberate choice between alternatives recognized as logically exclusive of one another. A "finite God" or gods exercising a restricted power—a struggle of this power, and of our hopes and ideals, against inexplicable obstructions—but a fair fighting chance of victory, a working probability that they that be for us are stronger than they that be against us: this dualistic religious philosophy is not the creed of one who would have scorned to let a little matter of logical consistency stand in the way of the gratification of his religious cravings. James, it is true, was one of those minds that care more that the fight be genuine and strenuous, and therefore of not wholly predetermined outcome, than that the triumph be assured; to whose spiritual taste a universe without the biting tang of real risk would seem flat and unpalatable. But he was not insusceptible of the other moods of religious feeling: to the pleasures of the "moral holiday" enjoyable at will by the "healthy-minded" optimist who believes that because God's in his heaven, *all's* well with the world; to the subtler ecstasy in the mystic's sense of utter oneness with the Infinite One. What is significant about James is that, with an exceptional sensitiveness to all these phases of religious emotion, his logical scrupulosity forbade his fashioning an ontology which should profess to justify them all. And in this he shows a degree of intellectual integrity extremely rare among those philosophers of the nineteenth century who have shown any sensitiveness at all to the religious emotions. The English Hegelians, in particular, ostensible and even ostentatious rationalists though they have been, have nearly always shown an insatiable determination to eat their cake and have it too; have insisted upon combining thorough-going optimism with moral seriousness (than which no two things are logically more incongruous), a sort of evolutionism with the assertion of the perfection and timelessness of ultimate reality, monism with the freedom and responsibility of the individual, a theistic backing for our moral preferences with a conception of the Absolute which makes that entity a mere unselective summary of all the empirical facts that have turned out or may turn out to exist. James's actual examples as a philosopher—whatever be said of some of his detached utterances—so far from being an incitement to this sort of spiritual promiscuity, is a standing protest against it. He heard and obeyed, as few so many-sided and abundant natures have obeyed, the voice of that jealous god, the Understanding, with its constant demand for a choice between incompatible alternatives, its "Choose ye this day whom ye will serve!"

To say, however, that James's philosophical conclusions were not reached without much persistent, open-minded, and intellectually scrupulous reasoning is not to represent his philosophy as a mere impersonal product ground out by the automatic working of dialectical machinery upon a given mass of raw material. All philosophies—and it is this that makes the study of the history of philosophy the richest and the most typically humane of the humanities—are the result of the interaction of a temperament (itself partly molded by a historical situation) with impersonal logical considerations arising out of the nature of the problems with which man's reason is confronted. Even the most rigorous reasoner must needs have premises; and not even the most conscientious reasoner is likely to see all the premises that there are which are pertinent to so large an argument as that concerning the general nature of things. What each sees will depend upon his personal vision. The impersonal "necessities of thought," or seeming necessities, by which epistemologies and ontologies are actuated, are not, as they at first present themselves to different minds, manifest parts of a single scheme; perhaps they may ultimately be harmonized, but primarily they are quite distinct; and one type of mind will seize first upon one, another upon another, for the motive power for its speculative machinery. The fact, then, that William James's philosophy was attained through "objective" reflection upon the logical issues involved in the problems with which he dealt, does not imply that it was not also in large measure an expression of the traits of his personality. There were, in fact, two or three characteristics of his mind which gave to his reasonings their starting point and their lines or directions, and thus went far to predetermine the character of his doctrine. These several tendencies, however, when reflectively developed, led to results not always harmonious with one another. A certain degree of inner discord must be recognized in the original predispositions of his thought, which accounts both for the nature of some of the logical difficulties with which he found occasion to grapple in the course of his reflection and for some residual incongruities which, as it seems to me, remained even in the outcome.

It is perhaps not altogether fanciful to see in that species of elusiveness which, as has been said, belongs to James's style as a writer, a manifestation of the same tendency of mind which constituted the most characteristic and remarkable trait in his endowment as a philosopher. His doctrine is sometimes easy to misapprehend from precisely the same cause which makes his writing easy to read, and from just the contrary cause to that which often makes Kant's writing hard either to read or to apprehend. Kant, it has sometimes been said, tried to crowd his whole system into each sentence that he wrote, in fear lest the numerous considerations supplementing and qualifying the point which he was at the moment expounding should be even transiently forgotten by his readers. James, on the contrary, was himself prone, in his enthusiasm for the point which he was at the moment expounding, to forget the qualifying considerations which he elsewhere plainly enough acknowledged or even emphatically affirmed. It cannot, I suppose, be denied that he was likely sometimes to overstate the truth immediately before his mind, especially if it seemed to him a truth that had been shabbily treated, a deserving philosophical waif that had been arrogantly turned away from the doors of all the respectable and established doctrines. To adversaries who were disposed to make the most of his detached utterances he thus offered many an opening for plausible criticisms which yet were, in reality, beside the mark as criticisms of his real—and not unascertainable—meaning. But if this peculiarity of his manner of exposition sometimes aroused unjustified opposition to his doctrines, it also probably gave to his doctrines—or, at any rate, to pragmatism—a certain appearance of sensational novelty that was not wholly justified either. When the pragmatist formulas about the meaning of concepts or the criteria of truth were set down with all of their qualifying and explanatory clauses explicitly attached to them, they proved to be a good deal less startling and revolutionary than they at first looked; and pragmatism appeared to be not very much more than what its author frankly and modestly called it, "a new name for some old ways of thinking." The assertion, for example, that the true is "the satisfactory," or that which "gives the maximal combination of satisfactions," naturally seemed (according to one's temperament) a repellent or an engaging paradox; but when it turned out that there are certain "theoretic" satisfactions and "logical demands" which may, when we are bent upon truth, rightly claim precedence of all others, the paradox seemed to have deflated almost to the shape of a platitude. Much of James's argumentation for pragmatism seems to me to have consisted in repeatedly moving back and forth from the one aspect of that doctrine to the other, first stating the formula *simpliciter*, in its paradoxical guise, then —especially under the challenge of criticism—indicating the qualifications and amplifications which he had meant to be tacitly understood from the start. This procedure, however, was certainly not a rhetorical artifice on his part; he always seemed, indeed, to be a little bewildered and vexed by the bewilderment which it caused in some other men's minds. It was, I cannot but think, one manifestation (in itself not a fortunate manifestation) of that quality of mind which fitted and predestined him to be the great spokesman of pluralism in philosophy. Just as the Kantian or Hegelian type of philosophic mind cannot bear to let the individual proposition stand by itself, but must ever modify and attenuate or sublate it through its relation to other propositions, so James could not quite bear to spoil the sharpness and distinctness, the actual individualness, of the individual proposition by immediately huddling it up in the qualifications and provisos and related considerations which he nonetheless was prepared to recognize on occasion. For though he was very far from blind to the relatedness and reciprocal implications of things, he was also, almost beyond any recorded philosopher, sensitive to the actual aspects of separateness and uniqueness in them; he was not one who believed that any real entity or real truth can be defined wholly in terms of the sum of its relations to other entities or other truths.

There is a quality of physical perception which painters, who much desire it, are, I believe, accustomed to call "purity of eye." To most of us red is red and blue is blue; and the brick wall yonder, once recognized as a red brick wall, shows to our perception thereafter pretty much the same unvarying shade. But (we are told) to the eye that has retained, or through systematic training has in some degree recaptured, the primitive responsiveness to the actual diversity of color stimuli, even a red wall is scarcely twice quite the same, but all day long moves through an exquisitely graduated and astonishingly wide gamut of shifting hues. William James brought, not to the physical world, but to human nature and the world of ideas, the artist's freshness and purity of vision. He came to each concrete bit of existence with an unspoiled power of *seeing* the thing as it was, in its unique differentness from other things. Man's ability to classify the objects of his experience is assuredly a convenient faculty; but it also makes for the blunting of his perceptions, since for most of us to recognize an object as belonging to a familiar class is forthwith to become more or less inattentive to all the characteristics of the object beyond those few flat, hackneyed, generalized ones which enable us to identify the class; it is often, also, to assume that the similarity of the particular object to the rest of the class extends farther than it really does. James's genius lay chiefly in this, that he had by nature, and retained undiminished to the end of his life, an extraordinary immunity to the deadening influence of those intellectual processes of classification and generalization in which, in one form or another, scientific and philosophical reasoning largely consist. He kept an unweakened sense for the particularity of the particular—a sense which the occupations of the philosophical system-builder ordinarily tend to atrophy. Thus he was always prepared to see in each individual person, each separate fact, each immediately present aspect of experience, even in each distinct logical category, something unique, unshared, irreducible, ineffably individuated. And toward each new, not-yet-fully-examined fact he always maintained an attitude of liberal expectancy; because it was enough like certain other facts to be classified with them was no reason for assuming that it might not, if given a fair chance, develop wholly novel and admirable qualities and potencies of its own. Uniformities were to be recognized so far as they actually exhibited themselves; but they were not to be allowed wholly to prejudice the case of "the unclassified residuum"; and it was in the unclassified residuum that James's greater interest lay. He was thus predestined by the possession of what may be called a particularist mind to be a pluralistic philosopher.

Here, no doubt, more nearly than in any other single point of view, lies the center of William James's personal vision. The temper of mind which I have tried to indicate appeared in his character as a social being as plainly as in his tendencies as a philosopher, as truly in his attitude toward his fellows as in his attitude toward the universe. The most large-hearted and tenderhearted of men, he showed the characteristic quality of his generosity not so much in his bestowal of material kindnesses, large and constant and delicately considerate though those were, as in his unquenchable *interest* in all sorts and conditions of individuals, his wholehearted appreciation of other men's qualities, and his indefatigable encouragement of their work. This interest in others was not at all the generalized and regularized benevolence of the philosophical "altruist," loving mankind in the abstract upon principle; it was not the interest of the moralist, sedulous to edify and to improve; it was only in part the interest of the sympathetic hedonist, rejoicing in the spectacle of the happiness of others or pained at their griefs. It was essentially the interest of a lover of human nature in the concrete and of the richness of its individual manifestations—especially of the diversity of its intellectual-emotional reactions upon the common data of experience. James's capacity for admiration of the intellectual performances of others was astonishing in its range and in its heartiness; not only his old pupils, but utter strangers, neglected Spinozas of the ghetto or Hegels budding unobserved in provincial newspapers, were likely at any moment to receive a letter, or one of his characteristic post cards, with a few, or sometimes many, words of heartening applause—applause often too liberal, but not undiscriminating—evoked by the reading of some piece of work that seemed to him to have in it something of freshness or individuality. The least sign of the emergence in American philosophy, or, indeed, anywhere, of a mind having a quality of its own, possessing novel or distinctive and strongly-marked powers, caused in him a joy like that of a man who had found the pearl of great price. I can even recall once hearing him exclaim with admiring wonder over some examination papers of Harvard undergraduates which he had been reading. It was not that those productions as a rule betrayed any extraordinary familiarity on the part of their authors with the subjects with which they were supposed to deal. But the ready ingenuity of these American youth who could, upon so slender a basis of actual acquaintance with the matter in hand, fill so many pages of blue book with stuff so plausible—and often conveying such surprising novelties even of misapprehension—that, to James, was after all a delightful and not altogether unadmirable manifestation of the possibilities of the human mind. All this generosity in appreciation, no doubt, sometimes led him into extravagances; originality was, to him, a mantle that sometimes covered completely a rather great multitude of sins. But this "characteristic excess" of James's was not only the excess characteristic of a singularly magnanimous mind; it was also the excess of a mind singularly alert to the real differences, the personal and unique traits of the reactions upon life of other minds. Even where he could not share or directly sympathize with those reactions, they had, if honest and serious and not illiberal, scarcely less value in his eyes.

It is, of course, a natural consequence of this that one of the two traits by which James's more directly ethical writings are chiefly distinguished is an exceptionally vivid feeling for the underived and intrinsic value of almost all distinctive and spontaneous manifestations of human nature, the indefeasible validity of each personal point of view not itself merely negative and destructive of others, the inner significance *for itself,* when lived simply and heartily, of every separate pulse of vital experience. This gospel had been, in a different fashion, powerfully preached before James preached it, by Whitman and by Stevenson—two lay moralists who, by reason of natural affinity of mind, seem to have influenced him not a little. In the domain of practical ethics the most characteristic thing, as it seems to me, that James ever wrote is the essay "On a Certain Blindness in Human Beings," the kernel of which consists in certain very happily chosen passages from those writers. But to him, since he was not simply a lay moralist but a philosopher, the teachings of that essay were merely one practical application of a more general way of thinking. He himself took pains in the preface to the volume containing the essay to insist upon the larger implications of the ideas expressed in it:

> The address "On a Certain Blindness in Human Beings" . . . is more than the mere piece of sentimentalism which it may seem to some readers. It connects itself with a definite view of the world and of our moral relations to the same, . . . I mean the pluralistic or individualistic philosophy. According to that philosophy, the truth is too great

> for any one actual mind, even though that mind be dubbed "the Absolute," to know the whole of it. . . . There is no point of view absolutely public and universal. Private and incommunicable perceptions always remain over, and the worst of it is that those who look at them only from the outside never know *where*.

In this passage is manifest the very process of transition in James's thought from the intense feeling for the individual and the particular characteristic of the innermost temper of his mind to the generalization and formulation of that feeling in a metaphysical doctrine. On the practical side—to dwell for a moment longer upon that aspect of the pluralistic spirit—the outcome of this characteristic of James's was that, whenever occasion arose, he always stood as the champion of a "democratic respect for the sacredness of individuality" and of "the outward tolerance of whatever is not itself intolerant." To these phrases, now become somewhat empty and ineffective through much vain repetition, he sought to restore "a passionate inner meaning." It was almost inevitable that one of this temper, in facing the especially difficult contemporary casuistical problem of the treatment of the backward by the "civilized" races, should be a stout anti-imperialist. He once exclaimed in a certain amazed impatience over the inability of most "Anglo-Saxons" to see that these "new-caught, sullen peoples" "really had insides of their own." The consideration from which he could himself never escape was that all manner of individuated entities—races, persons, ideas, types of religious experience—have "insides of their own" never wholly to be identified with any aspect which they may present on the outside; that "no one elementary bit of reality is eclipsed from the next bit's point of view, if only we take reality sensibly and in small enough pulses."

There are, however, it is worth-while to note, certain tendencies in modern thought, two or three different phases of individualism, to which these pluralistic preconceptions of James's might seem to point, but into which they did not in fact carry him. The special differentiae of his own sort of "individualistic philosophy" ought not to be overlooked. One familiar type of pluralism in recent philosophy, for example, has been the monadism, or "multi-personal idealism," represented by such writers as Renouvier, Thomas Davidson, Mr. Sturt, Professor Howison, and, in his earlier phase, Mr. E. D. Fawcett. These men, too, may be said to have developed the spirit of democracy into a metaphysics; for them also there is no single center of reality that is "absolutely public and universal," and "the facts and truths of life need many cognizers to take them in." But the metaphysics of James can hardly be described as a monadology. The motives which lead to that sort of pluralism he did not, for the most part, strongly feel; and the pluralistic inclinations which he did feel did not seem to him to lead to just that sort of pluralism. The independence of the action of each human self from all external causation, its "cut-off" character and its consequent personal responsibility, an idea which has, for example, presented itself to Howison very forcibly, was to James hardly a congenial idea. This was partly because his pluralism was combined in his mind with another tendency yet to be mentioned, his "temporalism." He was, if I may so put it, even more essentially a "length-wise" than a "cross-wise" pluralist; it was primarily and more frequently the uniqueness and the creative efficacy of the passing phases in each flowing stream of consciousness that he had in mind, rather than the timeless discreteness and inaccessibility to external influences of any windowless monads.[3] Discreteness, indeed, was not a category under which it was easy for his mind to represent any concrete entity; though he was, as has been said, peculiarly ready to recognize qualitative diversity and a certain incommensurability in things, he was also prone to think of them as imperceptibly passing into one another and in constant interplay with one another, as somehow immersed, though never dissolved, in a larger stream of being from which a constant endosmosis takes place. How far this combination of a special sensitiveness to the unique individuating differences of things with a disposition (shown in a predilection for metaphors drawn from the properties of fluids) to think in terms of a continuum, led to actual contradiction in James's philosophy, I do not here wish to discuss; but it was, I think, the combination distinctive of his personal type of pluralism.

Just this combination, however, might perhaps have been expected to produce certain other tendencies of thought in James, to which, once more, he did not in any exceptional degree incline. On the side of his appreciative attitudes, for example, his moral and aesthetic likings and dislikings, it might have led to that exaggeration of catholicity in sympathy and admiration which, as it showed itself in a Whit-

[3] It is perhaps proper to mention that, in a letter to the writer, James himself once adopted this antithesis: "I would also call myself a length-wise pluralist."

man, amounted to virtual indifferentism, to the professed feeling that each aspect and fragment of reality, as it happens to turn up, is as good as any other—and a bit better; or that, if any choice at all is to be made, the preference must always go to mere bigness or mere intensity of emotion. This "democratic" spirit toward the diverse elements of human life, as they are manifested in one's self or in others, this doctrine of the intrinsic equality of all the phases of existence is, unless offset by other tendencies, hardly likely to promote the fighter's temper or the reformer's zeal. But from this large, loose, and sprawling attitude of unselective acceptance of things, James was delivered by certain complementary features of his temperament. He had, indeed, as has been sufficiently remarked, an extraordinarily wide capacity for appreciation and sympathy; his first impulse, in the presence of a novel type of fact or person, was to seek to understand and to admire. But he had also a somewhat choleric nature. He had not many, but he had a few strong, temperamental aversions and disgusts; Plato's "spirited part of the soul" was well-developed in him. His tolerance—as a phrase I have already quoted from him intimates—did not extend to the toleration of intolerance; anything that savored of cruelty, overbearance, narrowness, awoke in him a hot indignation; for soft and relaxed ways of thinking and ways of living he had a keen dislike; and for overblown intellectual pretense and the spiritual emptiness of a great part of the world's respectabilities he had a penetrating vision and a humorous contempt. Various and intense as was his response to the manifold interestingness of existence, great as was his power to find value in things commonly unconsidered or despised, life presented itself to him, in the last analysis, in a dualistic, a Manichaean, guise—as a field of combat rather than as merely a source for the promiscuous enrichment of experience or an object of undiscriminating aesthetic appreciation. With all the exceptional breadth and geniality of his nature, there remained a touch of Puritan austerity in him. He had a temperamental need of a certain hardness and opposition in his environment. The world he found a place in which a man is imperatively called upon to take sides.

Nor is there in this any real incongruity with that catholic sense for the distinctive quality of each particular phase of reality which was his dominant characteristic. The dualistic aspect, the fighting edge in James's view of life was rather an evidence of his power of recognizing real differences. For the very essence of the inwardness of certain items of existence is their antagonism to certain other items. To accept and affirm all reality and call it good is after all to deny some parts of it, for the inner meaning of some parts lies in their negations. To sympathize equally with powers bent upon the destruction of one another, to be on the side of both Ormuzd and Ahriman, to be one with the red slayer and the slain is in reality to fail to understand the "inside" aspect of either. The attempt to harmonize such opposites can commend itself only to minds whose vision for the inner distinctiveness of other individual existences has become at least a little blurred through the habit of thinking of things in lumps, who rise so easily to "higher points of view" that they quite forget that the higher point never truly reveals the observed object's situation as it appears at the object's own level. James's position with respect to the problem of evil was thus a manifestation of that same trait of his nature which was also the source of his pluralistic tendencies. At least some evils—the sufferings of animals, for example, or certain monstrosities of moral perversion—seemed to him simply intrinsically and irreducibly bad. They may be triumphed over, they may even be made instrumental to good; but the badness that was in them can never be *aufgehoben*, nullified, or even perfectly compensated. Readers of *The Varieties of Religious Experience* must recall the nightmare-like horror of a passage in which James's extraordinary sense for the reality of the individual is turned upon this aspect of the world:

> Our civilization is founded upon the shambles, and every individual existence goes out in a lonely spasm of helpless agony. If you protest, my friend, wait until you arrive there yourself! To believe in the carnivorous reptiles of geologic time is hard for our imaginations,—they seem too much like mere museum specimens. Yet there is no tooth in any one of those museum-skulls that did not daily through long years of the foretime hold fast to the body struggling in despair of some living victim. Forms of horror just as dreadful to their victims, if on a smaller spatial scale, fill the world about us to-day. Here on our hearths and in our gardens the infernal cat plays with the panting mouse, or holds the hot bird fluttering in her jaws. Crocodiles and rattlesnakes and pythons are at this moment vessels of life as real as we are; their loathsome existence fills every minute of every day that drags its length along; and whenever they or other wild beasts clutch their living prey, the deadly horror which an agitated melancholiac feels is the literally right reaction on the situation.

This, as a reading of animal psychology, is perhaps somewhat overdrawn; but the passage is singularly typical of the vividness in James of what a psychologist might call the ejective imagination. When things of this sort are once seen as palpitating, individuated facts there is nothing to be done, James wrote in one of his early essays, but to cry out against all such aspects of reality Carlyle's "Everlasting No." James has sometimes been compared to Emerson, chiefly for the reason that the two have been the most influential American writers on philosophical themes, and the only two who have had a wide international hearing. But in one important respect James is the antithesis to Emerson. That bland disregard for "those unconcerning things, matters of fact," which has been said to be the root of Emerson's optimism, was impossible to a man with James's type of vision. And since this pleasant Emersonian nearsightedness has become in certain quarters a contagious and a noxious spiritual disease, it is fortunate that from the original center of that infection so potent a corrective has of late been dispensed. James was, to be sure, no pessimist; and the sort of utterance that I have last quoted was never the last word with him. But it expressed a side of the real world which he was convinced was not to be denied nor rationalized away. And the universe could therefore never appear to him, in any final reckoning, as wholly good or as rational through-and-through, but rather as of a mixed character, and above all, of a character largely yet to be formed. That process of formation involved, to his mind, purgation and elimination as well as enlargement and enrichment. And both results depended for their realization in great, perhaps in a decisive, measure upon the present and future loyalty of human agents to the not-yet-attained ideals which they mysteriously find within themselves, to "the demands which the self of one day makes on the self of another," to the "imperative goods" whose "nature it is to be cruel to their rivals."

These last considerations, however, already bring to mind a second (not wholly separate) characteristic trait of James's personal mode of apprehension of reality—the only other such characteristic which it will be possible to consider here.[4] He was one of those in our day who have most fully

[4] It would have been worth-while, if space had permitted, to note the influence of James's "particularistic" sort of intellectual vision in some of his more special and technical metaphysical doctrines, especially in his earlier view (which, for reasons briefly indicated later in this paper, he eventually abandoned) of the impossibility of "compounding" states of consciousness, and in his logical theory of the "externality of relations" which seems to have had an important part in the development of the "new realism." There was a third strain in James's thought—less potent, yet significant—which should at least be mentioned: the nominalistic and simplifying temper, the desire to translate abstractions into "concrete particulars of somebody's experience," the demand for the rigorous elimination of all obscure and redundant notions. On one side of him, James continued the succession of the great British nominalistic empiricists, the prophets of the law of intellectual parsimony, such as William of Ockham, Berkeley, Hume. In certain moods of his reflection he became, incongruously, very much what the French call an *esprit simpliste.* Thus he seeks to reduce the concepts of "God," "freedom" and "immortality" to their "positive experienceable operation" and so finds that "they all mean the same thing, *viz.*, the presence of 'promise' in the world." This trait is not strictly contradictory to James's dominant characteristic; it is rather the negative side of the same sense for concrete, particularized reality. Yet it tended, unquestionably, to work against the pluralistic spirit; for it naturally predisposes to the nullification of real differ-

and clearly realized that the primary peculiarity of conscious experience is its flowing temporally successive character; that this ("time of inner experience") is a unique *quality* of existence, not to be reduced to anything else nor described in terms of anything else; and that no philosophy can be adequate which virtually ignores (as most of the historic philosophers have ignored) the primacy of the temporal quality of experience as a starting point for the interpretation of the nature of reality and the meaning of truth. Readers of James's earliest philosophical essays must already have seen what aspect of human existence, what sort of moment in life, presented itself to him as the central and illuminating fact, the point at which we have reason to suppose that the inner nature of reality is most directly revealed to us. This is the moment in which a man looks before and after, faces the future *as* future, and knows that that future, as yet a field of alternative possibilities, is to be defined and shaped, that certain of those alternatives are to be forever shut out from real existence by the decision now in process of forming itself in his mind. Now, just as the dominant methods and preoccupations of both science and philosophy have tended to lead thought away from the particular to the generalized, so they have tended to lead thought away from the truly temporal—from the uniqueness of the unprecedented and unrepeatable single moment in the time-flow—to fix it upon the eternal or the immutable or the identically

---

ences and the too speedy reduction of multiplicity to unity. James's "particularism" gave birth to two children, the pluralistic and the nominalistic tendency; and these two sometimes came to be at variance in his mind.

recurrent. Logic has been interested in changeless concepts, metaphysics in the absolute and eternal, science in unvarying laws, in qualitatively immutable "primary" properties of bodies, in quantitatively constant sums of matter and energy, in "causes" conceived as capable of presenting themselves as the "same" over and over again in perfect indifference to mere diversities of date as such. Except by certain idealistic metaphysicians, the "reality" of time has not been denied; but most that makes up the actual temporality of time and its significance in our inner experience has been commonly disregarded not only by philosophy and science, but even by theology and religion. James's vision of the distinctiveness and the validity of the "particular" point of view was complemented by—or rather implied—an equally keen sense of the validity and the distinctiveness of the temporal point of view. And his task as a philosopher was that of stirring up his contemporaries to do justice to these two primary yet neglected aspects of existence.

This "temporalism" showed itself in a number of items of James's philosophy, though, until he became interested in the work of Bergson, he hardly seems to have been so explicitly conscious of the decisive part it played in his own thinking as he was of that played by his pluralistic preconceptions. It was already apparent, however, in the *Psychology*, and in some of his early untechnical essays. The core of the *Psychology*, and the part of it having the most general theoretical significance, lay in the chapter on "the stream of consciousness"; and that chapter (which contains the germ of a considerable part of James's subsequent philosophy), together with the chapter on "the sense of time," was primarily an attempt to penetrate by means of an introspective analysis—as Bergson in his earliest work was at the same time seeking to penetrate—to the essential differentia of our time-experience. James's chief originality as an empirical psychologist lay in his emphasis upon the transitive character of mental states and his abandonment of all "static" psychological "elements." In him, again, as in Bergson, the predominance of the temporal point of view led at once to the affirmation of a somewhat new form of indeterminism and to more or less new arguments for it. The "Dilemma of Determinism," for example, expresses primarily these contentions (though they are, perhaps, not wholly disentangled from other considerations): that, if two alternatives present themselves as equally possible before a choice is made, it is pure dogmatism to say that this beforehand-view of the facts is any less valid than the *post-factum* view which regards all save the *fait accompli* as *having been* impossible, since the two views are merely the natural products of two different temporal situations; that, further, if we *are* to ask which view is the truer, the one which exhibits to us more correctly the nature of things, we have reason to give the preference to the beforehand-view, since not only the whole meaning of our active life, but also the one legitimate escape from a pessimistic despair of the universe, depends upon the maintenance of the absolute distinction between the possible and the necessary and of the reality of possibilities which are as yet *mere* possibilities. In the same essay James vigorously attacked the neo-Hegelian conception of a timeless, all-knowing mind and made the pregnant remark that "to say that time is an illusory appearance is only a round-about manner of saying that there is no real plurality, and that the frame of things is an absolute unit. *Admit plurality, and time may be its form.*"

Pragmatism itself, though it was many other things also, was primarily epistemological temporalism. It proposed to define "meaning" and "truth" in terms of intertemporal relations between successive phases of experience. They had usually been defined in terms which either ignored temporal distinctions of before and after or expressly professed to transcend all such distinctions. Some sort of "cross-wise" relation had been taken to constitute the nature of truth, some correspondence of a judgment with its object or with the eternal knowledge of an absolute intelligence; James undertook to make the whole matter one of "lengthwise" relations. A judgment made by a human being, he insisted, is always and essentially an act of a creature standing at a specific moment in the time-flow, facing the future, preparing in some way for that future by means of the activity of judging, and himself moving forward into the future even while he judges. So greatly, indeed, was James impressed by this aspect of the judging-process, that he occasionally seemed to forget the fact that the past and the simultaneous are also phases of the temporal, and that it obviously will not do to define the import of a judgment or the nature of truth in a way which prevents judgments from truly referring to these phases, which tries to metamorphose the whole meaning of pastness and contemporaneity into pure futurity. The passages in which James expresses himself to this effect must, I think, be regarded as exaggerations and partial misapprehensions of his own insight into the significance for epistemology of the temporal and mainly forward-facing and anticipatory character of our thinking. But it does not belong to the purpose of this paper to enter into a discussion of pragmatism. As illustrations of James's temporalistic way of envisaging things his overstatements of his insight are even more pertinent than any more qualified expression of it.

It was, finally, through his own and through Bergson's reflections upon the paradoxes involved in the nature of temporal process that James was chiefly led to that extreme form of "anti-intellectualism" which characterized one phase of his thinking—to the doctrine of the radical incongruity between "conceptual thought" and the nature of reality as immediately apprehended in our time-consciousness. This outcome of his temporalism (as I have elsewhere suggested) was a rather striking departure from one of the earliest manifestations of his pluralism. At the beginning of his career he was the most vigorous of representatives of the good old eighteenth-century respect for the principle of contradiction, which Hegelianism seemed to be undermining. The categories and fundamental notions of our mind were each distinct and unsublated; they did *not* become "their own others." Again, states of consciousness of two finite centers could not be metaphysically compounded so as to make one unified consciousness. But in the later chapters of *A Pluralistic Universe,* James seemed to recant the logical doctrine of the essay "On Some Hegelianisms" and to imply that reality may be not merely opaque to the intellect, but even self-contradictory. It should be said, however, that this matter James seems to have regarded as not definitively clarified and formulated in his own mind.[5]

It is time to conclude. In the light of this consideration of James's characteristic traits as a philosopher, it is perhaps possible to determine in some degree the significance and the historic place of his contribution to philosophy. Doubtless the chief service which he rendered to those of his contemporaries, especially in England and America, to whom philosophy was a serious concern was of a sort so general and pervasive that it is not easy to define. It lay in the bracing, stimulating, and mind-enlarging influence of his personality, in the contagion of openness of view and simplicity of utterance, of intellectual courage and intellectual candor, that proceeded from him; in the example of his constitutional inability to wear any bandages of either scientific or philosophic dogmatism over that vision turned straight to the face of immediate experience, of "raw, unverbalized life" in all its manifoldness and concreteness and richness of

[5] This seems to be shown by some sentences of his own on the point, in reply to some comments of the sort that have been set down above: "I think you take an extravagantly exaggerated view of my anti-logicality. . . . I imagine that much war will be waged by many combatants in print before Bergson's thesis gets settled to general satisfaction. All that I contend for is that things *are* as continuous as they seem to be and that the intellectualist arraignment of experience as self-contradictory and impossible won't pass. If continuity and flow mean logical self-contradiction, then logic must go." Some of the recent mathematical logicians, James added, consider that they have "saved logic by the 'new' infinite. Perhaps they have, and if so, the better. But I wait to be convinced." What this shows is that, unlike some philosophers, James did not positively *like* paradoxes and contradictions, but would reluctantly accept them if the only alternative was to deny the "continuity and flow" experience.

unexcluded possibilities. He touched nothing which he did not vitalize; and more than one ancient discipline and age-withered problem, upon contact with the robust and hearty piece of human nature that he was, took on new life, as by a transfusion of blood. But the more specific and perhaps the more permanent significance of his contribution to philosophy consists, as it seems to me, chiefly in this, that he brought to the vocation of the philosopher an almost unequaled power of *seeing* these two generic aspects of reality: the uniqueness and inwardly self-authenticating character of concrete individual existences, the irreducibility of their being and their natures to any mere external relations to the wholes with which they may be connected; and the uniqueness and the primacy of the temporal quality of experience, the impossibility of translating this *quale* into any nontemporal categories, or of ever truly describing the innermost nature of reality as we know it by means of such categories. Now, philosophy begins with things seen, with *aperçus*, not with things inferred; I do not mean, of course, with physical observation, but with the direct *noticing* of some general and logically pregnant trait of the conditions of experience or the data of thought. It does not, indeed, end with *aperçus;* nor did James's activity as a philosopher so end. He devoted himself, as I have already said, conscientiously and laboriously for many years to the work of focusing his vision more sharply upon these aspects of reality, of following out their implications, of correlating them in a logically definite manner with one another and with older and more familiar philosophical ideas which he recognized as considerations not to be neglected. The success of this attempt at precise formulation and elaboration could be suitably discussed only after a lengthy technical examination. However great or small its success, it is not in it that James's more notable service as a philosopher has been rendered. The growing points in the history of thought come when a man arrives upon the scene with a new or a neglected *aperçu*—and the power to tell about it. James belongs among the philosophers of fresh vision, of distinctive personal insight into fundamentally significant aspects of the facts of our experience. His work may very well prove to have opened a highly important new chapter in the history of philosophy, at least among peoples of English speech. For—as he himself said, speaking in praise of another—"originality in men dates from nothing previous, other things date from it, rather."

V

JAMES'S DOES CONSCIOUSNESS EXIST? *

I

The advocates of epistemological monism in the last half-century were not, in all cases, also advocates of a thoroughgoing psychophysical monism. Their theory of knowledge was sometimes based upon a dualistic metaphysical premise. For they thought it essential to distinguish between the phenomenon of being aware of objects and the objects of which one is aware—between the *-ings* and the *-eds,* which they regarded as the two necessary components in any cognitive act. The objects which we think of, which our judgments are about, exist independently of our thinking of them or our perception of them. Yet it would obviously be self-contradictory for a realistic philosopher to assert that no object can at any time exist unless and in so far as it is at the same time perceived or thought of by somebody. The existence of physical objects and their being perceived must therefore be two essentially different kinds of facts; only by a Berkeleian idealist can the *esse* of things be, without self-contradiction, said to be identical with their *percipi.*

* Printed here for the first time.

What, then, happens when a physical object *is* perceived? Many realists of recent times have answered that nothing happens to the object—*it* is not changed in any way—but that a conscious organism simply perceives, thinks of, or in some manner becomes aware of, the object. This event—someone perceiving something—is not an event in the physical world to which the object belongs; it occurs only in the consciousness of the percipient organism. Thus it is that one group of contemporary physical realists finds it necessary to hold that "consciousness"—the state of or process of "being conscious"—must be admitted to be a fact in our actual experience, though they also maintain that all the things of which we can thus be conscious are "true parts of the physical world." In short, with regard to what are commonly called the *contents* of consciousness—sense-data, percepts, etc.—these philosophers are epistemological monists, but consciousness itself they assume to be a non-physical or "mental" phenomenon.

The relevance of all this to the topic of the present paper lies in the fact that William James in his celebrated essay "Does Consciousness Exist?" [1] sought to show that "consciousness" is a nonentity; the term stands for nothing that is actually present in or presupposed by such events in the life of human or other organisms as perceiving, thinking, feeling. The traditional view, which had been accepted as evident by many philosophers and psychologists whose doctrines on other matters were wholly discordant—realists, idealists of various schools, even some pragmatists—was ex-

[1] First published in *The Journal of Philosophy* (1904); reprinted in *Essays in Radical Empiricism* (1912), pp. 1–38.

pressed in the following passage by a distinguished Kantian idealist:

> Consciousness (*Bewusstheit*) is inexplicable and hardly describable. While . . . it is the only thing which distinguishes a conscious content from any sort of being that might exist without anyone's being conscious of it, yet this only ground of the distinction defies all closer explanations. The existence of consciousness, although it is the fundamental fact of psychology, can indeed be posited as certain, can be brought out by analysis, but can neither be defined nor deduced from anything else."[2]

[2] Paul Natorp, *Einleitung in die Psychologie* (1888), pp. 14, 112; the passage is quoted by James in "Does Consciousness Exist?" A similar affirmation of the existence of consciousness had been recently (1903) published by G. E. Moore, and is also quoted by James; however, Moore was not an idealist but a monistic realist with regard to the contents of consciousness. Not long after 1904 several well-known psychologists who believed the "content" of experience to be physical, also insisted that there is no experiencing of any contents apart from consciousness, and had done so for the reason already indicated—that though objects exist without being objects of consciousness, they cannot be known or apprehended without any (non-physical) consciousness of them on the part of the knower. I cite a few typical examples. L. T. Troland in *The Mystery of Mind* (1920), p. 26: "Consciousness is the most real and certain of all facts, but the last to attract attention." R. S. Woodworth, *Psychology* (1921), p. 8: "For all the objections, it remains true that the *typical* matter for psychological study is conscious. 'Unconscious mental processes' are distinguished from the unconscious activity of such organs as the liver by being somehow *like* the conscious mental process. It would be correct, then, to limit psychology to the study of conscious activities and of activities akin to these." Knight Dunlap, *Social Psychology* (1925), pp. 16–17: "The 'consciousness' with which psychology is concerned is not a thing, or system of things, forces, or objective entities such as the 'ideas' of Malebranche and Locke, or the 'sensations,' 'images,'

It was because the truth of this was generally admitted in the early eighteen-nineties, as it had been for centuries before, that many zealous champions of epistemological monism had deemed it impossible to defend that thesis, or even to formulate it intelligibly, without admitting an element of psychophysical dualism: *objects,* physical or other, can be known without the interposition of "ideas" or mental images, but we cannot know them without being conscious of them, and being conscious of anything is not a state or a process describable in physical terms.

It was, then, the assumption expressed in the passage quoted from Natorp, but often accepted also by neo-realists, that James was attacking in this essay of 1904. "My contention," he wrote,

> *is exactly the reverse of this. Experience, I believe, has no such inner duplicity; and the separation of it into consciousness and content, comes not by way of subtraction but by way of addition*—the addition to a given concrete piece of it [i.e., of experience] of other sets of experiences. . . . A given undivided portion of experience, taken in conjunction with one context of associates, may play the part of a knower, of a state of mind, of a state of "consciousness," while in a different context the same undivided bit of experience plays the part of a thing known, of an "objective" content. In a word, in one group it figures as a thought, in another group as a thing. And since it can figure in both groups simultaneously we have

---

and 'feelings' which later philosophers substituted for the 'ideas.' . . . 'Consciousness' for psychology, as in popular usage, is the awareness, or the being aware, of whatever things in the world one may be aware of. It is the observing, and not the thing or object observed."

> every right to speak of it as subjective and objective both at once.[3]

Such was James's formulation of the thesis which he intended to prove.

The formulation may perhaps seem to some readers, upon careful analysis, to be not altogether perspicuous. That it is a denial of the existence of "consciousness" in the traditional sense of the word is, of course, perfectly clear; and it thus apparently denies that anyone can be meaningfully said ever to be "conscious"—or to be "conscious *of*" anything. But James's statement of his thesis is not limited to these negations. It also proffers a certain substitute for the nonexistent "consciousness," which, James believed, performs the "same function" that consciousness had been supposed to perform. That substitute is "experience," and its "function" is said to consist in an object's becoming a bit of someone's "experience"—or, as it is otherwise phrased, a part of someone's "personal biography." We can, then, "experience" objects or events without being "conscious" of them; upon this distinction between the meaning of two terms—or rather, upon the assumption that one of them has meaning and the other no meaning—James's argument for the nonexistence of consciousness rests. But "experience," at least, is admitted by him to have meaning; what, then, *is* its meaning? He admits that we have experiences intelligibly designated, in the English language, as having sensations, perceiving objects, believing some propositions to be true, thinking of not-now-

[3] "Does Consciousness Exist?" (1904), hereafter referred to as D.C.E., in *Essays in Radical Empiricism* (*E.R.E.*, for short) pp. 9–10; italics in original.

existing objects, reasoning from the truth or falsity of one proposition to the truth or falsity of another; but he cannot consistently admit that we are "conscious" of having any such experiences. What, then, in James's terminology, does having these experiences mean and what does an object's *being* experienced mean? I do not here attempt to answer this question; in fact, I find it an extremely difficult question to answer. I only suggest that, until the question is answered, the essay here under consideration has no comprehensible meaning.

However, at this stage of our analysis of this essay we must not hastily assume that James does *not* answer this question, i.e., does not explain how one can "experience" an object or event without being conscious or aware of it. Possibly he may be using the word "experience" in a sense of his own, in which it does not connote any awareness of what is experienced; for example, he may choose to say that any process or state in my bodily organism is "experienced" if it actually takes place, without my knowing at the time that it is taking place. Many such events do, of course, take place without my knowledge of their occurrence, e.g., the processes of metabolism (when I am not suffering from dyspepsia). Or conceivably he may have also designated as "my experiences" any events which, though not perceived by me, are causally related to changes in my bodily condition, as an alteration of the velocity or temperature of wind blowing from the Arctic region may cause me to feel chilly. Many such events, either in my body or affecting my body, certainly are important factors in my "personal biography," and if they are to be called "my experiences," then *some* of my experiences are not accompanied by anything that would commonly be called "consciousness." But in English usage the term "experience" has no such wide denotation; and I do not really suppose that it did for William James. I am only suggesting that if "experience" was *not* employed by him in this unusual sense, it still remains unexplained how he distinguished between, e.g., the bodily processes which go on in me without my knowledge and the events which I see or feel going on in my body, or the external objects which I am said to perceive. Simply to call them all alike "concrete bits of experience" is not merely to misuse the noun "experience"; it is to ignore the fact that between the two sorts of so-called "experiences" there is a manifest and highly important difference—precisely the difference between the existents of which we are, or may be, conscious, and those of which, though they are held by realists to be parts of our biographies as animal organisms, are not by us "experienced" at all—the difference, in short, between my perceiving a piece of toast on my breakfast table, and my subsequently digesting it—and thereby unconsciously transforming it into the flesh and blood of an animate body.

II

But let us now pass over for the present the question whether James in this essay does not tacitly admit the existence of consciousness under another name—"experience"—

and examine the argument by which he endeavors to show that consciousness "does not exist." When we do so, we find that most of his reasoning is not directed to proving the nonexistence of "*consciousness*" but to a quite different conclusion—namely, the nonexistence of "*content*" of "consciousness," as distinct from physical objects. In other words, the argument, if valid, would not prove anything about consciousness, as such, but only that the entities which we "experience"—our percepts, concepts (and also our hallucinations)—are existentially identical with "real" objects, the objects which, as realists believe, exist independently of any one's experience. It is an argument for epistemological monism with respect to such indubitably "experienced" things as the table I am writing on, the house I see across the street, the moon, or the satellites of Jupiter. When, as James would put it, I "experience" such things, I experience them, he maintained, "immediately," not through "representations" or (partial) simulacra of them. But, as we have seen, epistemological monism with respect to what were commonly called "contents of consciousness"—in James's terminology, "bits of experience"—is not inconsistent with a psychophysically dualistic view about the "function" or phenomenon of being aware of them; and, as we have also seen, some philosophers who are resolute defenders of the thesis that all experienced contents are identical with true parts of the physical world have thought it necessary to assume that—since their merely *existing* is obviously not the same as their being experienced—some event or process must be occurring in the organism to account for this difference.

III

It should, I think, be already apparent that in the essay in question James was confusing two issues, and offering arguments pertinent to one of them which are not pertinent to the other—to the one with which he supposed himself to be dealing. But lest this fact be not yet evident to everyone, I will quote more fully James's own statement of the argument:

> The dualism connoted by such double-barreled terms as "experience," "phenomenon," "datum," *Vorfindung* . . . is still preserved in [my] account, but reinterpreted, so that instead of being mysterious and elusive, it becomes verifiable and concrete. It is an affair of relations, and falls inside, not outside, the single experience considered, and can always be particularized and defined.

A single thing, in short, may be related in a certain manner to one set of other things and not be related in that manner to another set of other things. A building at the intersection of Broadway and Fifth Avenue has one set of spatial relations to a certain set of buildings on Broadway and a different set to other buildings on Fifth Avenue; it may be westward of the former and eastward of the latter. Such a building may be said to exemplify the compatibility of existential identity with differentness of relations; and it is this concept that James uses in his argument to show that there is no existential duality of "thing" and "thought," but only a difference of relational "context." But just what are the things of which he proposes to prove the existential identity, in spite of their relational "duplicity" by means of this "crossroads concept," as we may call it? And what are the relations concerned—since, of course, they are not spatial relations? James is not telling us that a building at the intersection of two streets is for *that* reason a bit of experience, a "thought," while buildings not so situated are not experienced, are not objects of thought.

James answers these questions simply by asking us to examine our own experiences. "Let the reader begin with a perceptual experience, the 'presentation,' so-called, of a physical object, his actual field of vision, the room he sits in, with the book [he holds in his hand] as its center." But the reader, James assumes—and this is the crucial and question-begging assumption of the entire argument—will be a psychophysical monist, will conceive of the room and the book "in the commonsense way as being 'really' what they seem to be, namely, physical things cut out from an environing world of other physical things with which *these* physical things have actual or potential relations. Now it is just *those selfsame things* which his mind, as we say, perceives." Thus is solved "the puzzle of how the one identical room can be in two places. It is at bottom just the puzzle of how one identical point can be on two lines. It can, if it be situated at their intersection." The one room "has so many relations to the rest of experience that you can . . . treat it as belonging with opposite contexts. . . . One of these contexts is . . . the reader's personal biography, the other is the history of the house of which the room is part." But it "enters both contexts in its wholeness, giving no pretext for being said to attach itself to consciousness by one of its parts or aspects and to outer reality by another." Thus, James concludes, is happily ended the "long wrangle" which has gone on within "the philosophy of perception from Democritus's time downwards, over the paradox that what is evidently one reality should be in two places at once, both in outer space and in a person's mind."

James's use of words in the argument ending with this triumphant *Q.E.D.* is, the reader will note, manifestly confused and is inconsistent with the conclusion. The "intersection" of which he speaks is not a spatial intersection of two lines; it is a temporal intersection—the occurrence at a given moment of an event which has two different series of other events preceding it in time. The two contexts in question are admittedly different contexts—my past experiences and the past physical history of the room; and the fact, supposing it to be a fact, that an event "belonging in" the one context (i.e., in my personal biography) happens at the same time as an event in the history of the room is no evidence that an event in the one series is identical with an event in the other series. If the intersection were a spatial intersection—if the event in my biography happened simultaneously at the same *place* as the event in the history of the room—the two *would* be one and the same, and both physical; assuming that two physical things cannot occupy the same space at the same time. But this is not James's argument; he is saying that the simultaneity of the time of occurrence of my percept of the room and the time of occurrence of something in the physical history of the room proves that the percept and the room perceived cannot be two realities but one. Yet he constantly speaks of this coincidence in time as equivalent to "being in the same place."

The epistemological dualists (with respect to what they called "content of consciousness") whose theory of perception James was attacking did not, of course, hold that my percept of the room I sit in or the book I am reading is "in two *places* at once." The dualists assumed that nothing can be in two places at once; it was for this reason, among others, that they argued that a star, billions of light-years distant and possibly now extinct, cannot be existentially identical with the bright object that an astronomer sees tonight. Doubtless, the astronomer's percept of that object may be said to be "a bit of his personal biography"; but it obviously is not the "self-same thing" as the vastly distant and now nonexistent star that he is, in colloquial terms, said to be now perceiving. But James ignores this and all the numerous other familiar arguments of the dualists to justify their thesis that we cannot know physical objects immediately through the literal presence of those objects, without duplication, in our perceptual fields. James's only reply to these arguments of the dualists is the following:

> "Representative" theories of perception avoid the logical paradox, but on the other hand they violate the reader's sense of life, which knows no intervening mental image but seems to see the room and the book immediately just as they actually are.[4]

It is generally assumed, however, that one does *not* see the book, room, etc., "just as they actually are," but as they appear through his organs of vision from the position at which

[4] *E.R.E.*, pp. 11–12.

he sits. He has learned that if one looks from a certain angle at a penny which he believes to be actually round, the perceived penny will be elliptical; that when he looks along a railway line, the tracks "seem" convergent at a distance, though they are really parallel. Realistic epistemological monists (with respect to perceptual content) have tried to devise ingenious ways of reconciling these discrepancies between our visual percepts and real objects; but none of them, so far as I know, have simply invoked their "sense of life" as a sufficient reason for disregarding these apparent discrepancies.

But even if James's argument were sound, it would still be an argument for the wrong conclusion; that is to say, it was not the conclusion that he had announced that he intended to demonstrate and believed he had demonstrated. It was an argument which, if valid, proved that what were usually called "thoughts" or "percepts" of physical things were really physical things themselves, that the house which was standing across the street long before I ever saw it is the same existent as the physical object I "see" when I look across the street—the existent which dualistic philosophers and psychologists were wont to call my percept of the house. But this conclusion, if it *had* been demonstrated, would, as we have seen, have left the question of the existence of consciousness completely untouched: one could, and many psychologists did, without inconsistency accept, in agreement with James, the thesis of the physicality of the *contents* of our fields of perception, and for just that reason were convinced that consciousness *must* exist, as the necessary condition of our experiencing, being aware of, these external realities.

IV

In the concluding passage of his essay, James abruptly drops his argument—which we have seen to be irrelevant to his nominal theme—the argument for the identity of the objects we sensibly or otherwise experience with extra-experiential purely physical things. He turns, at last, to the question with which he supposed he had been dealing throughout, viz., the question whether "consciousness" exists. He now seems to recognize—not, indeed, that most of his preceding arguments *were* irrelevant to that question—but at least what the believers in the existence of consciousness *meant* by the word, and why they held that belief. They meant, as James puts it, by "consciousness" something "flowing within us, in *absolute contrast with the objects which it so unremittingly escorts.*" And they believed in its existence because we [that is, presumably, all men] have an "immediate intuition of it." We "feel our thought flowing within us. The dualism is a fundamental datum."

Now James agrees that we *do* feel *something* going on within us which incessantly accompanies all our thoughts. But it is not "consciousness"; it is a movement of matter. James "greatly grieves that his last word will to many sound materialistic." But he too has his "intuitions and must obey them."

> I am as confident as I am of anything that, in myself, the stream of thinking (which I recognize emphatically as a phenomenon) is only a careless name for what, when scru-

tinized, reveals itself to consist chiefly of the stream of my breathing. The "I think" which Kant said must be able to accompany all my objects, is the "I breathe" which actually does accompany them. . . . Breath, which was ever the original of "spirit," breath moving outwards between the glottis and the nostrils, is, I am persuaded, the essence out of which philosophers have constructed the entity known to them as consciousness. *That entity is fictitious, while thoughts in the concrete are fully real. But thoughts in the concrete are made of the same stuff as things are.*[5]

This, of course, *was* materialism—double-barreled materialism; neither consciousness nor thoughts exist as non-physical entities. And one can only admire the forthrightness and clarity with which James in the last two sentences states his conviction. It was, if true, a far more important doctrine than the pragmatism which most readers apparently suppose to be his principal and most distinctive thesis. But does he in his "last word," the brief passage just quoted, refute the belief in the existence of consciousness?

The reasoning he here offered in support of this negative proposition has three logical peculiarities.

1. It assumes that *if* consciousness *does* exist, one must be conscious of the consciousness at the same moment at which one is conscious of the object—i.e., that consciousness at that moment must itself be one of the objects of consciousness. But this assumption was not made by those who asserted the existence of consciousness; recall the statements already quoted from Natorp and others.[6] Such psychologists usually

[5] *E.R.K.*, p. 37; italics in original.
[6] Above, p. 116.

held that when one is thinking of, e.g., the star Sirius, one is not *at that instant* also necessarily thinking "I am now thinking of that star." Such an assumption would, obviously, entail an infinite regress: "I am thinking that I am thinking of the star; therefore I am thinking of my thinking of my thinking of the star; therefore I am thinking . . . ," and so on ad infinitum. The distinction between the act or event of being conscious and that of which one is conscious was fundamental in the theory that James was seeking to refute, but its exponents did not assert or imply that when I usually perceive a star I also must be thinking of myself and of an infinite number of similar percepts.

2. James's basic reason for denying that consciousness exists is, he says, a subjective "intuition" of his own—his "certainty" that it does not exist. Such a mere declaration that one does not accept a view accepted by many other psychologists who have reflected on the question at issue is hardly likely, by itself, to be convincing to the others.

3. James does, however, finally give another sort of reason for his rejection of the belief in consciousness—though it too is a personal conviction not previously held by anyone else. He has, he tells his readers, discovered how other people (including, of course, psychologists and philosophers) have been led to adopt that erroneous belief. He is, he declares, "as certain as he is of anything" that the notion of consciousness has arisen through a failure to scrutinize with sufficient care a certain physical phenomenon which invariably accompanies all our thinking and does what "consciousness" is said to do. Whenever we experience objects, "*breathing*" is compresent with all our thoughts [*sic*] and from

the failure to bear this fact in mind, "consciousness" was invented to serve as the incessant companion of the thoughts. It is upon this premise, namely, that breathing performs all the functions that consciousness had been supposed to perform, that James's ultimate proof of his contention is made to rest. We must therefore, before concluding, do some "scrutinizing" for ourselves. *Does* "breathing" adequately perform the function of consciousness?

The answer, of course, is obvious—so obvious that it seems absurd to state it. *1*. Breathing, the continuous aeration of the blood through alternate inhalation and exhalation, is a process within the body that is indispensable to the existence of a living organism; when breathing is stopped, life stops. *2*. Being thus necessary for life, it "accompanies" all processes or events occurring during life—among them, the "stream of thinking," which James "recognizes emphatically as a phenomenon." *3*. But though there is no thinking unaccompanied by breathing, there *is* breathing unaccompanied by thinking—i.e., the organism may still live and breathe when unconscious, as in coma, fainting, dreamless sleep. The fact that a phenomenon, A, always accompanies a certain phenomenon, B, when B occurs, is no proof that A *is* B; and the fact that while A is going on without interruption, B frequently does not go on, is proof of the contrary. *4*. The function which "consciousness" had been invoked to perform—that of making possible, *inter alia,* sensible experiences of all kinds of physical objects and qualities—certainly is not performed by breathing. Movements of air in our noses are doubtless needed in our olfactory sensations; there is no reason to suppose that they are prerequisites to our having visual or auditory sensations—except insofar as they are prerequisites to the continuance of all organic functions. Though I may, in a sense, be said to smell flowers through my nose, I cannot in any sense be said to see lightning or hear thunder through my nose. 5. Most obviously of all, the concept of exhalation does not include or imply or in any way refer to such experiences as thinking of distant stars, of the square root of minus-one, of the thoughts or emotions of other men, of past events in my own life, and of events yet to come. (Of the last, surely, a pragmatist should, of all men, be most certain that he thinks, since pragmatism, whatever more it may be, is the doctrine that much, if not all, of our thinking is directed toward the future.)

James's certainty that we think through our noses was not shared even by the contemporary philosophers whose doctrines on some matters were somewhat akin to his. C. S. Peirce, whom James had always generously credited with the origination of pragmatism, on receiving the article on consciousness, jocosely replied that in his own experience the reverse of James's assumption was true: "many people, of whom I am one, involuntarily hold their breath while thinking. . . . If I have got to believe that I think with my lungs, I will take as my equation, *Ich denke* = I don't breathe." And James Ward wrote: "It has long been a favorite notion of mine that the word 'consciousness' is exactly the most treacherous weapon in the philosopher's armoury, but I have never known it serve anybody so badly as it seems to me to have served you." [7]

[7] Quotations from Peirce and Ward in Perry's *The Thought and Character of William James* (1935), II, pp. 432 and 653.

There are two other oddities to be noted in this essay. One of them is James's neglect to consider the class of phenomena called "emotions." The empirical and logical considerations pertinent here are quite different from those pertinent to the epistemological questions whether ideas or consciousness exist. And most people who deny that they have ideas and that they are conscious of anything would, I imagine, be very reluctant to admit that they never felt any emotions—affection or love, dislike or hatred, happiness or joy, melancholy or grief. William James, being a man of strong natural affections, of a much more than average capacity for sympathy with the feelings of others, and also notably capable of a *saeva indignatio* over any cruelties inflicted upon other men or upon animals—could such a man be conceived to have believed that neither he nor anyone else ever experienced an emotion? But can one be unconsciously angry or sorrowful or happy? Or are these emotions simply variations in the volume or velocity of the air passing through one's nose? James apparently never realized that these were questions which he was logically bound to answer before his thesis could be held to have been adequately "scrutinized." The other curious omission in the essay, also especially surprising in the case of William James, was the total disregard of the known facts concerning the relation of processes in the nervous system and the cerebral cortex to the phenomena of memory, of normal perception, and of illusions and hallucinations. James, of course, knew these facts thoroughly—probably more thoroughly than most psychologists of the period. He simply failed to see their relevance to the two theses, or rather, the two negations—nonexistence of consciousness, nonexistence of visual images and concepts—which, in that phase of his philosophizing, he accepted and thought it possible to prove.

I think it doubtful that this phase was lasting. Certainly it seems irreconcilable with any of the other theses which James propounded.

VI

PRAGMATISM VERSUS *THE PRAGMATIST* *

I shall in this essay inquire into the logical relations of the doctrine known as pragmatism to the principal philosophical problems under consideration in this volume. Does pragmatism imply the truth of realism, or of idealism, or of neither? If it is in any sense realistic, is it so in a monistic, or a dualistic, or in some third sense? Does it, expressly or by implication, affirm, or admit, or deny, the existence of "consciousness," or "mental states," or "psychical entities"? These are the questions to which answers are to be sought.

Pragmatism is not a thing of which one can safely draw the definition from one's inner consciousness. It is, primarily, a historic complex of opinions which have been or are held by certain recent or contemporary writers, and of the arguments by which those writers have supported their opinions. It is not the product of a single logical motive or generating insight—though this is a proposition which will require proof, since many pragmatists would probably deny

* First published in Durant Drake and others, *Essays in Critical Realism: A Cooperative Study of the Problem of Knowledge.* (London: Macmillan and Company, Ltd., 1920), p. 35–81.

it. We must, therefore, at least begin our inquiry into the bearing of the pragmatist theory upon these problems by noting carefully what pragmatists themselves have had to say upon them. And since pragmatist writers are fairly many and rather various, we shall do well to devote our attention in the main to the reasonings of one representative of the school. I shall, therefore, in this paper, be concerned chiefly, though not quite exclusively, with the writings of Professor John Dewey. Mr. Dewey not only is the most eminent and influential of the living spokesmen of the pragmatic doctrine, but he also has dealt more directly and abundantly than any other with the particular issues that interest us here; and his personal variant of the doctrine contains certain elements, or at any rate certain emphases, which are of especial significance in the present connection.

It is not a purely expository treatment of the subject that I shall attempt. We may at least entertain as an hypothesis to be tested the supposition that some of the theses of pragmatist writers are more closely related to their central conceptions, are more genuinely "pragmatic," than others; and we may thus be able, in the course of the analysis, to arrive at a species of rectified pragmatism which will at least have the interest and value of internal simplicity and consistency. Nor need we limit our efforts, either critical or reconstructive, to the detection and elimination of inner incongruities or redundancies. In great part the pragmatist proffers what purport to be, not simple deductions from an antecedently defined dogma, but independent "considerations," capable of being judged upon their own merits, and bearing directly upon the problems of this book. A critical appraisal of the force and pertinency of those considerations is therefore necessary, as an indispensable part of any comprehensive discussion of such problems in the light of contemporary philosophy.

It is perhaps only fair to give notice to the reader in advance that the quest to be undertaken will be neither simple nor straightforward in its course. He will perhaps find it exasperatingly devious, hesitant, full of false starts, and of revisions or reversals of results provisionally arrived at. I can only ask him to believe, or to observe for himself, that these peculiarities of the analysis are not arbitrary, and attributable to the taste of the analyst, but arise inevitably from the nature of the questions asked, taken in conjunction with the nature of the material available for answering them. A guide is not held responsible for the character of the country over which he conducts the traveller.

I

Pragmatism, Realism, and Idealism

Though a philosopher evades formal definitions always at the peril of confusion and misunderstanding, it nevertheless seems hardly necessary in this case to begin with a definition of pragmatism in general, irrespective of the specific aspects of it here to be considered. The customary formulas are presumably known to all persons who are at all likely to read this volume; and any attempt to review those formulas, to analyze their meanings, and to rid them of the ambiguities in which they abound would itself be a large undertaking.[1] Pragmatism began as a theory concerning the conditions under which concepts and propositions may be said to possess meaning, and concerning the nature of that in which all meanings must consist. From this there developed a theory of knowledge, a theory of the meaning of truth, a theory of the criterion of truth, a theory of the limits of legitimate philosophical discussion, and the rudiments of a metaphysical theory. All of these have been expressed in various, and not always obviously synonymous, terms; and if we were to examine and seek to unify all of these we should hardly get, in the space here available, beyond the vestibule of our inquiry. We may, then, proceed at once to the first question to be considered and interrogate the writings of Professor Dewey with a view to determining how pragmatism stands related to realism and to idealism—as these have been elsewhere defined in this book.[2]

1. Let me first cite what seem to be definite pronounce-

[1] How large, the present writer has quite inadequately shown in a previous essay on the subject, "The Thirteen Pragmatisms," *Journal of Philosophy*, V (1908).

[2] A similar question has been illuminatingly discussed by Professor W. P. Montague in a series of articles in the *Journal of Philosophy* ("May a Realist be a Pragmatist?" VI, 1909). It is, however, as Mr. Montague's formulation of it makes evident, not quite the same question as is here raised, and it is not dealt with by the same method, since no extensive review of pragmatist discussions of the subject forms a part of Mr. Montague's plan of treatment. So far as the same ground is covered, however, the conclusions of this paper are substantially the same as those expressed by Mr. Montague—though the reasons for these conclusions are, in the main, different.

ments by our chosen representative of pragmatism in favor of thorough-going realism.[3]

> What experience suggests about itself is a genuinely objective world which enters into the actions and sufferings of men and undergoes modifications through their responses (*C.I.* 7).

> According to pragmatism, ideas (judgments and reasonings being included for convenience in this term) are attitudes of response taken toward extra-ideal, extra-mental things (*D.P.* 155).

> Reflection must discover; it must find out; it must detect; it must inventory what is there. All this, or else it will never know what the matter is; the human being will not find out "what struck him," and will have no idea where to seek for a remedy (*E.L.* 23).

> There are always some "facts which are misconstrued by any statement which makes the existence of the world problematic" (*E.L.* 297).

> One of the curiosities of orthodox empiricism is that its outstanding problem is the existence of an "external world." For in accordance with the notion that experience is attached to a private subject as its exclusive possession,

[3] Writings of Professor Dewey here referred to will be cited by the following abbreviations: *D.P.—The Influence of Darwin upon Philosophy and Other Essays in Contemporary Thought, 1910; E.L.—Essays in Experimental Logic, 1916; C.I.—Creative Intelligence: Essays in the Pragmatic Attitude, 1917.* In the last-named volume, only the opening essay, "The Need for a Recovery of Philosophy," is by Professor Dewey.

> a world like the one in which we appear to live must be "external" to experience, instead of being its subject-matter. Ignorance which is fatal; disappointment; the need of adjusting means and ends to the course of nature, would seem to be facts sufficiently characterizing empirical situations as to render the existence of an external world indubitable (*C.I.* 25).

> Speaking of the matter only for myself, the presuppositions and tendencies of pragmatism are distinctly realistic; not idealistic in any sense in which idealism connotes or is connoted by the theory of knowledge. . . . Pragmatism believes that in knowledge as a fact, an accomplished matter, things are "representative of one another." Ideas, sensations, mental states are, in their cognitive significance, media of so adjusting things to one another that they *become* representative of one another. When this is accomplished, they drop out; and things are present to the agent in the most naïvely realistic fashion. . . . Pragmatism gives necessarily a thorough reinterpretation of all the cognitive machinery—sensations, ideas, concepts, etc.; one which inevitably tends to take these things in a much more literal and physically realistic fashion than is current (*Journal of Philosophy*, 324–326).

Nor are these mere casual dicta unsupported by argument. On the contrary, Mr. Dewey devotes almost an entire essay to what appears to be a dialectical demonstration of the self-contradictory character of even a problematical idealism. True, he describes his argument, at the outset, as if it were a proof of quite another conclusion. He announces it as a demonstration that the question of the existence of an external world is one which cannot logically be asked—that it is "not a question at all."[4] And this might naturally be taken for a contention as adverse to the realist as to the subjectivist. It suggests that, since the question is meaningless, any answer to it must also be meaningless. And in another paper precisely this consequence seems to be drawn from the same contention. "On the supposition of the ubiquity of the knowledge-relation," we are told, "realism and idealism exhaust the alternatives; if [as pragmatism holds] the ubiquity of the relation is a myth, both doctrines are unreal, because there is no problem of which they are the solution."[5] From this one would gather that realism and idealism in all their forms stand equally condemned, and that the pragmatist has discovered a third way of thinking, radically different from either.

But when we inquire why (in the essay especially devoted to this topic) Mr. Dewey regards the "problem of the existence of the world" as a "meaningless" one, we discover that what he asserts is merely that the problem cannot be intelligibly formulated without *implying an affirmative answer*. It is in a statement of the question by Mr. Bertrand Russell that Mr. Dewey's discussion takes its point of departure. And Mr. Russell's question was quite unequivocally the question of physical realism. "Can we know that objects of sense . . . exist at times when we are not perceiving them?" "Can the existence of anything other than our own hard data be inferred from the existence of those data?" What Mr. Dewey undertakes to show is that each of Mr. Russell's ways of putting this inquiry includes terms which

[4] "The Existence of the World as a Logical Problem," *E.L.*, p. 283.
[5] *E.L.*, p. 266.

"involve an explicit acknowledgment of an external world." [6] Pointing out a whole series of assumptions involved—and necessarily involved—in the statement of the question, Mr. Dewey remarks: "How this differs from the external world of common sense I am totally unable to see." "Never," he concludes, "in any actual procedure of inquiry do we throw the existence of the world into doubt, nor can we do so without self-contradiction. We doubt some received piece of 'knowledge' about some specific thing of that world, and then set to work as best we can to verify it." [7] No realist could ask for better. All that he finds his seeming critic urging against him is that his answer to the question is indubitable.[8] The problem is called "meaningless" in the sense—the rather peculiar sense—that its solution is certain and easy.

2. Yet what seem equally plain expressions of idealism—of a "multipersonal" and temporalistic type of idealism—are also to be found in Mr. Dewey's expositions of the bearing of the pragmatic logic upon this old controversy. Nor can any one be surprised at this who is mindful of the historic lineage of pragmatism (as traced by William James),[9] and remembers the part played in it—especially in James's early formulations of it—by such a logical motive as the principle of parsimony and by the general temper and method in philosophy to which James gave the name of

[6] *E.L.*, p. 291.

[7] *E.L.*, p. 302.

[8] I do not think it needful at this point to examine in detail the arguments of the essay on "The Existence of the World as a Logical Problem" in behalf of its unqualifiedly realistic conclusion.

[9] *E.R.E.*, pp. 41–45.

"radical empiricism"—i.e., the principle that philosophy "*must neither admit into its constructions any element that is not directly experienced,* nor exclude from them any element that is directly experienced."[10] James again and again reiterates that pragmatism can recognize no objects or relations that are "altogether trans-experiential."[11] At times he intimates that the pragmatist does not dogmatically deny the abstract possibility of things-in-themselves, or assert the "intrinsic absurdity of trans-empirical objects."[12] But he at any rate admits no possibility of *knowing* their existence, or of making any use of them even for logical or explanatory purposes; so that, to all significant intents and purposes, he excludes them from his universe altogether. The reality of intertemporal "pointings" within experience, and consequently of a kind of "transcendence" of an idea by its "object" or objective, he not only admits but insists upon. "At every moment we can continue to believe in an existing *beyond*"; but "the beyond must, of course, always in our philosophy be itself of an experiential nature." And James adds that if the pragmatist is to assign any extra-perceptual reality whatever to the physical universe—if the "beyond" is anything more than "a future experience of our own or a present one of our neighbour"—it must be conceived as "an experience for itself whose relations to other things we translate into the action of molecules, ether-waves, or whatever else the physical symbols may be." It is, in

[10] *Ibid.*, p. 42.
[11] James's, *The Meaning of Truth*, xvii.
[12] *E.R.E.*, p. 239.

short, intimated by James that if the pragmatist is not a pure Berkeleian idealist, he must at least be a panpsychist.[13]

This idealistic strain in the make-up of pragmatism is, as I have said, abundantly manifest in Mr. Dewey's reasonings:

> Like knowledge, truth is an experienced relation of things, and it has no meaning apart from such relation (*D.P.* 95).

> "Sensationalistic empiricism" and "transcendentalism" are both alike in error because "both of these systems fall back on something which is defined in non-directly-experienced terms in order to justify that which is directly experienced" (*D.P.* 227).

> The presentative realist [erroneously] substitutes for irreducibility and unambiguity of logical function (use in inference) physical and metaphysical isolation and elementariness (*E.L.* 45).

> "The [pragmatic] empiricist doesn't have any non-empirical realities," such as " 'things-in-themselves,' 'atoms,' 'sensations,' 'transcendental unities,' " etc. (*D.P.* 230).

[13] *Ibid.*, p. 88. There is, however, in James the same strange conjunction of realistic with idealistic utterances that we find in Dewey. Cf. e.g., for the realistic side in James, the following:

"Practically our minds meet in a world of objects which they share in common, which would still be there, if one or several [Query: 'or all'?] of the minds were destroyed" (*E.R.E.*, p. 79). "The greatest common-sense achievement, after the discovery of one Time and one Space, is probably the concept of permanently existing things. However a Berkeley, a Mill, or a Cornelius may criticize it, it *works;* and in practical life we never think of going back upon it, or reading our incoming experience in any other terms" (*Meaning of Truth*, p. 63). "Radical empiricism has more affinity with natural realism than with the views of Berkeley or of Mill" (*E.R.E.*, p. 76).

> The belief in the *metaphysical* transcendence of the object of knowledge seems to have its origin in an empirical transcendence of a very specific and describable sort. The thing meaning is one thing; the thing meant is another thing, and is a thing presented as not given in the same way as the thing which means. It is something *to be* so given [i.e. to be subsequently experienced directly]. . . . Error as well as truth is a necessary function of knowing. But the non-empirical account of this transcendent (or beyond) relationship puts *all* the error in one place (our knowledge) and all the truth in another (absolute consciousness or else a thing-in-itself) (*D.P.* 103).

Here, then, we have the typical pragmatic subjectivism—the recognition of an intertemporal, but the denial of a transsubjective, reference in either perception or reflective thought. The interpretation suggested by these brief passages is confirmed by an examination of the argument of an essay in which our pragmatist explains at length the meaning of his "immediate empiricism." This doctrine, represented as an essential part of the pragmatism, "postulates that *things are what they are experienced as. Hence if one wishes to describe anything truly, his task is to tell what it is experienced as being.*"[14] Such an empiricism recognizes "a contrast, not between a Reality and various approximations to, or phenomenal representations of, Reality, but between different reals of experience." Take, says Mr. Dewey, the case of an experience of "an out-and-out illusion, say of Zöllner's lines. These are experienced as convergents; they are 'truly' parallel. If things are what they are experienced as being,

[14] *D.P.*, p. 228, "The Postulate of Immediate Empiricism."

how can the distinction be drawn between illusion and the true state of the case?" The immediate empiricist replies that the distinction is at any rate not one between a reality and a nonreality, nor even between degrees of reality. The experience of the lines as divergent must in the most uncompromising fashion be called "real"; the later experience into which the first develops is another real related to the first in a particular experienced manner.

> The question of truth is not as to whether Being or Non-Being, Reality or *mere* Appearance, is experienced, but as to the *worth* of a certain concretely experienced thing. It is because this thing afterwards adjudged false is a concrete *that*, that it develops into a corrected experience (that is, experience of a corrected thing—we reform things just as we reform ourselves or a bad boy) whose full content is not a whit more real, but is true, or truer.[15]

Similar passages might be cited from other members of the school. Thus we find in Professor A. W. Moore's contribution to *Creative Intelligence* what can only be described as a subjectivistic definition of "objectivity" itself. To the pragmatist, he observes, there is "no ground for anxiety concerning the objectivity of hypotheses," for a hypothesis "is objective in so far as it accomplishes the work whereunto it is called—the removal of conflict, ambiguity, and in-

[15] *D.P.*, p. 235. I am, I confess, unable to reconcile the language of this passage with that of the following: "The Greeks were wholly right in feeling that the questions of good and ill, as far as they fall within human control, are bound up with discrimination of the genuine from the spurious, of 'being' from what only pretends to be" (*C.I.*, p. 56–57).

hibition in conduct and affection."[16] These conflicts, inhibitions, etc., and the removal of them are, it will be observed, phases of the experience of individual minds, or, if the pragmatist dislikes that word, of individual organisms; so that everything implied by "objectivity" is, in the pragmatic theory of knowledge, to be found within the limits of individual experience.

3. When one discovers in the utterances of a philosopher such apparent contradictions as subsist between the two sets of expressions cited above from Professor Dewey, one is bound to examine the philosopher's text more closely to see if he does not somewhere suggest a means of removing or softening the contradiction—if, for example, the appearance of it is not due to some oddity in his use of terms. When we thus interrogate the writings of Mr. Dewey, we do, in fact, find certain intimations of means of reconciling his two seemingly antithetic positions. We note, for example—as bearing upon the statement, already quoted, that ideas have to do "with extra-mental things"—that Mr. Dewey defines "mental" in a sense of his own:

> We may, if we please, say that the smell of a rose, when involving conscious meaning or intention, is mental; but this term "mental" does not denote some separate type of existence—existence as a state of consciousness. It denotes only the fact that the smell, a real and non-psychical fact, now exercises an intellectual function. . . . To be in the mind means to be in a situation in which the function of intending is directly concerned (*D.P.* 104).

[16] *C.I.*, p. 97.

> When a cry of fire suggests the advisability of flight, we may, in a sense we must, call the suggestion "mental." But it is important to note what is meant by this term. Fire, and running, and getting burned are not mental; they are physical. But in their status of being suggested they may be called mental when we recognize this distinctive status (*E.L.* 50).

Here, then, we seem at first to get some help. When Mr. Dewey asserts that there are "extra-mental things," and that our ideas are conversant with them, he must, according to the definition cited, be understood to mean only that there are experienced things which do not (at a given moment) have the "distinctive status" of either "suggesting" other things or being suggested by them.

But does this make the assertion realistic or idealistic in its import? The answer must be that it *permits* us to take this seemingly realistic utterance of Mr. Dewey's in an idealistic sense. For the "extra-mental things," the things which are not at the moment performing an "intellectual function," may, it is obvious, still be intraexperiential things. It is one of the favorite contentions of Mr. Dewey that a large part of "experience" is, in fact, noncognitive; that "to much the greater portion of sensory stimuli we react in a wholly noncognitive way." [17] And it would be in keeping with his definition of "mental" to take "extra-mental" as synonymous

[17] *C.I.*, p. 49. But, as a further illustration of the difficulties to be met with in the attempt to construct a harmony of the pragmatic gospels, cf. the following (which I shall have occasion to cite again below) : "Experience is full of inference. There is apparently no conscious experience without inference; reflection is native and constant" (*ibid.*, p. 8).

with "the non-cognitive portion of experience." The definition, I have said, permits us to take his meaning so; it does not, perhaps, strictly require us to do so. But if we do not so take it, we have done nothing to reconcile Mr. Dewey's declaration that pragmatism believes in "extra-ideal, extra-mental things" with the idealistic expressions which have been quoted from him. Either, then, the one passage contradicts the others, or else a harmony is to be reached by construing the realistic-sounding passage, in the light of Mr. Dewey's definition of "mental," as of idealistic import. Meanwhile the conclusion and arguments of the essay on "The Existence of the World" remain unaffected by this harmonizing measure; they still appear to be hopelessly at variance with Mr. Dewey's "immediate empiricism."

There is, however, another suggestion offered for the alleviation of the seeming contradiction. It is hinted at in a phrase cited in the preceding paragraph, but is more fully developed elsewhere—best perhaps in the following passage:

> That the pragmatist is (by his denial of transcendence) landed in pure subjectivism or the reduction of every existence to the purely mental, follows only if experience means only mental states. The critic appears to hold the Humian doctrine that experience is made up of states of mind, of sensations and ideas. It is then for *him* to decide how, on *his* basis, he escapes subjective idealism, or "mentalism." The pragmatist starts from a much more commonplace notion of experience, that of the plain man who never dreams that to experience a thing is first to destroy the thing and then to substitute a mental state for it. More particularly, the pragmatist has insisted that experience is a matter of functions and habits, of active adjustments and

> readjustments, of co-ordinations and activities, rather than of states of consciousness. To criticize the pragmatist by reading into him exactly the notion of experience that he denies and replaces . . . is hardly "intellectual" (*D.P.* 157).

Here we have an explanation which seems to swing our interpretation of the pragmatist's position wholly over to the realistic side—and, indeed, to the neorealistic side. He appears in this passage as an adherent of what has been named (by an unhappy verbal coinage) "pan-objectivism"—as one who denies the existence of states of consciousness altogether. An experience—such seems to be his present thesis—is not made up of a special kind of "experiential" stuff; it is simply a selected fragment of the world of "things," taken as they exist, without duplication. The question of "transcendent" or "trans-subjective" reality does not arise in such a philosophy, for the simple reason that there is, for it, no realm of *subjective* reality for things to be "beyond."

We have come upon a feature of Mr. Dewey's philosophy so significant, especially in relation to the purposes of this volume, that it requires extended examination on its own account. To such examination the next section of this paper will be devoted; pending it, we cannot reach a conclusion as to the bearing of this thesis upon our attempt to decide where, in the last analysis, the pragmatist stands upon the question at issue between the realist and the idealist. Yet, meanwhile, one remark is already pertinent to the passage last cited. To say that experience is made up simply of things having no distinctively psychical character does not amount to realism—monistic or other—unless it implies that there also exist things which do not, at any given moment, figure in the selective groupings which at one moment is in the context called "my experience" and may at other moments exist while absent from that or any similar context. But this last would amount to a very definite assertion of what Mr. Dewey calls "transempiricals." If, then, he means the passage last cited to be taken in the only sense in which it would serve the purpose for which it is obviously intended (namely, as a repudiation of "subjectivism"), why does he elsewhere ridicule the hypothesis of "transempiricals"? Taking the passage to mean what it clearly seems intended to say, we have not found here any means of harmonizing Mr. Dewey's realistic and idealistic utterances; we have merely found an additional contradiction of his idealistic utterances.

II

Pragmatism and the Existence of Mental Entities

I turn to consider at length, both for its own sake and for its bearing upon the matter already discussed, the pragmatist's view upon the question so much debated in recent philosophy, of the reality of "psychic" existences, of "consciousness," of "mental states," and of percepts and ideas regarded as distinct, numerically and in their manner of being, from the external objects of which they are supposed to afford knowledge. The answer given to this question by any philosophy will obviously depend primarily upon its conception of the kind of situation in which knowledge consists. The two opposing views upon this question may be named "immediatism" and "mediatism." According to the former, whatever kind of entity be the object of knowledge, that object must be actually given, must be itself the directly experienced datum. According to the latter view it is of the essence of the cognitive process that it is mediate, the object never being reached directly and, so to say, where it lives, but always through some essence or entity distinguishable from it, though related to it in a special manner. Both the idealist and the monistic realist are thus "immediatists"; to both of them—and this is the plausible consideration which makes the immediatist view a natural phase of philosophic thought—it seems unintelligible that anything deserving the name of knowledge should be possible at all, if the object supposedly known is never itself "got at," but is always at the remote end of a complicated process of causal action and of "substitution" or representation.

We have already seen one passage in which Mr. Dewey appeared to pronounce in favor of immediatism, and specifically, as it seemed, of a monistic realism, on the ground that "experience" does not consist of "mental states" which duplicate "things," but simply of "things." The passage is typical of many others. The "presentative theory" of knowledge, with its implication of the division of entities into the two classes of "psychical" and "physical," seems to arouse in the pragmatist even more than ordinary detestation. Mr. Dewey repudiates as a "fundamental misstatement" of the facts "the conception of experience as directly and primarily 'inner' and psychical." [18]

> There are many who hold that hallucinations, dreams, and errors cannot be accounted for at all except on the theory that a self (or "consciousness") exercises a modifying influence upon the "real object." The logical assumption is that consciousness is outside of the real object, is something different in kind and therefore has the power of changing reality into appearances, of introducing "relativities" into things as they are in themselves—in short, of infecting real things with subjectivity. Such writers seem unaware of the fact that this assumption makes consciousness supernatural in the literal sense of the word; and that, to say the least, the conception can be accepted by one who accepts the doctrine of biological continuity only after every other way of dealing with the facts has been exhausted.[19]

To the pragmatist, knowing or apprehending, or whatever it be called, is a "natural event"; it is "no change of a reality into an unreality, of an object into something subjective; it is no secret, illicit or epistemological transformation." Indeed, Mr. Dewey's very conspicuous dislike for what he calls "epistemology" seems to be directed in reality against the dualistic doctrine only; for he makes it a part of his characterization of epistemology that it assumes "that the organ or instrument of knowledge is not a natural object, but some ready-made state of mind or consciousness, something purely 'subjective,' a peculiar kind of existence which lives,

[18] *C.I.*, p. 18.
[19] *C.I.*, p. 35.

moves, and has its being in a realm different from things to be known."[20] "Only the epistemological predicament leads to 'presentations' of things being regarded as cognitions of things previously unrepresented."[21]

Against the dualistic conception of knowledge the pragmatist argues, like the idealist and the monistic realist, that it is a conception which, so far from rendering knowledge intelligible, makes it inconceivable that "the mind," shut within the circle of its own ideas, should ever make the acquaintance of an "external" world at all. "Will not some one," asks Mr. Dewey, "who believes that the knowing experience is *ab origine* a strictly 'mental' thing, explain how, as a matter of fact, it does get a specific extra-mental reference, capable of being tested, confirmed, or refuted?"[22] In truth, "the things that pass for epistemology all assume that knowledge is not a natural function or event, but a mystery"; and "the mystery is increased by the fact that the conditions back of knowledge are so defined as to be incompatible with knowledge."[23]

Here, at last—the reader will perhaps say—we have a position clearly enough defined and unequivocally asserted; and from it we may proceed confidently in the interpretation of the other and more obscure parts of the pragmatist's doctrine. Whatever else he may admit, he is emphatically opposed to epistemological dualism. Knowledge for him is no affair of "representation," and "truth" never means the

[20] *D.P.*, p. 98.
[21] *C.I.*, p. 51.
[22] *D.P.*, p. 104.
[23] *D.P.*, p. 97.

"correspondence of an idea with an existence external to it." And he wishes his fundamental immediatism to be taken in a realistic, not in an idealistic, sense. Of the two parts of the traditional dualism, it is not, with Bishop Berkeley or his like, the "objects without the mind" that he eliminates from his universe, but rather the supposed mind over against the objects.

And yet it is easy to establish from Mr. Dewey's own text the exact opposite to all this; to find him arguing in effect, not only (as we have already seen) that a thorough-going physical realism is inadmissible, but also that a *monistic* realism is peculiarly untenable; that if one were to be a realist (as the term has ordinarily been understood) one must needs also accept a "presentative" and dualistic theory of knowledge. I shall show this first by an examination of two of Mr. Dewey's most extensive and carefully reasoned passages on this subject.

1. The literally presentative character of at least one type of knowledge—namely, *anticipatory* knowledge—could hardly be more insisted upon than by Mr. Dewey. "We have an experience which is *cognitional*" when we have one "which is contemporaneously aware of meaning something beyond itself. Both the meaning and the thing meant are elements in the same situation. Both are present, but both are not present in the same way. In fact, one is present as not-present-in-the-same-way-in-which-the-other-is. . . . We must not balk at a purely verbal difficulty. It suggests a verbal inconsistency to speak of a thing present-as-absent. But all ideal contents, all aims (that is, things aimed at) are present in just such fashion. Things can be presented as

absent, just as they can be presented as hard or soft, black or white." "In the experimental sense, the object of any given meaning is always beyond or outside of the cognitional thing that means it." [24]

All this, so far as it goes, is an admirable phrasing of a dualistic epistemology. Here we have *two ways* in which data are present at the moment of cognitive experience, and one of the ways is "presence-as-absent." But this is precisely what "epistemology" has always meant by "representation." And if it is in any sense true that the dualist has ever described knowledge as a "mystery," or as other than a "natural event," it is only because he observes that a thing's presence-as-absent—even the presentation of a future physical experience, at a moment when it is not itself a physical experience—is a distinctive and highly *peculiar* event, to which the rest of nature seemingly presents no analogue.

But Mr. Dewey's recognition of the reality of presentational knowledge is, in the important essay under examina-

[24] *D.P.*, pp. 88, 103. While some of the phrases above cited clearly imply the full idea of representation, i.e., of an evocation of the represented object in idea, Mr. Dewey tends to substitute for this the notion of mere suggestion by association, as when "smoke" suggests "fire" and this prompts the act of telephoning to the fire department. There are really, in all cases of "meaning," three elements: the original sense-datum, or "cue," which initiates the process (e.g., the smell of smoke); the imagery thereby aroused, through which not-present *qualia* get actually, though more or less imperfectly, "presented," and presented-as-absent; and the external (e.g., future) things which they represent. The first two of these seem to me to become often blurred and confused with one another in pragmatist analysis of the knowledge-experience. Indeed, the existence of images and concepts is a fact which the pragmatist psychology is curiously prone to forget.

tion,[25] subject to two restrictions which are not justified by his argument.

a. He apparently makes it a part of every anticipatory or prospective "meaning" that it shall involve a reference to an "operation" to be set up with a view to its own fulfilment. This amounts to an assertion that we never anticipate without proposing to ourselves some course of action with reference to the thing anticipated—an assertion which I take to be a false psychological generalization. The original pragmatic formula of James recognized "passive" as well as "active" future experiences "which an object may involve," as consistent with the pragmatist theory of meaning; and in this he did less violence than Mr. Dewey to facts which any man, I take it, can verify for himself. To dream of some windfall of fortune which one can do nothing—and therefore intends to do nothing—to bring about is surely a common enough human experience. Even our forward-looking thoughts may at moments be purely contemplative.

b. A more significant error, and one, as I think it possible to show, which is inconsistent with a true instrumentalist logic is Mr. Dewey's limitation of the "knowledge-experience" *exclusively* to forward-looking thoughts. While in this essay he actually describes all knowledge as representative or substi-

[25] That on "The Experimental Theory of Knowledge," in *D.P.*, pp. 77–111.

tutional, he does so only because he identifies all knowledge with anticipation. An intention-to-be-fulfilled-through-an-operation is part of his very definition of knowledge.[26]

Now, no doubt, a philosopher must be given license to define words as he will. It is not, however, as an arbitrary verbal definition, but as a piece of descriptive psychology that Mr. Dewey puts forward this formula. And as such it manifestly tells only half the story, at best. It ignores the patent empirical fact that many of our "meanings" are retrospective, and the specifically "pragmatic" fact that such meanings are indispensable in the planning of action. The scent of an unseen rose may beget in me an anticipation of the experience of finding and seeing the rose; but it may, quite as naturally, beget in me a reminiscence of an experience of childhood with which the same odor was associated. In the one case as in the other, the olfactory sensation does not, in itself, "represent" anything; it merely serves as the

[26] "An experience is knowledge, if, in its *quale,* there is an experienced distinction and connection of two elements of the following sort: one means or intends the presence of the other in the same fashion in which itself is already present, while the other is that which, while not present in the same fashion, *must become so present if the meaning or intention of its companion or yoke-fellow is to be fulfilled through the operation it sets up*" (*D.P.*, p. 90).

It is to be borne in mind—and has been in the above discussion—that Mr. Dewey is not here defining knowledge in the "eulogistic" sense—i.e., in the sense of valid judgment. He is stating, as observable facts, the generic marks of any experience "which is for itself, contemporaneously with its occurrence, a cognition, not something called knowledge by another and from without. . . . What we want is just something which takes itself as knowledge, rightly or wrongly" (*ibid.*, 76).

cue which evokes the representation of something else. In both cases alike, the something else is present-as-absent; but in the latter case it is no part of the meaning of the experience that the thing meant shall ever itself "*become* present" in the fashion in which the other elements of the experience (whether the memory-evoking odor or the memory-image) are now present. That there can be no such thing as truly "instrumental" or practically serviceable cognition without such genuine representation of the past, I shall show at some length elsewhere in this paper; for the moment I am content merely to cite Mr. Dewey's testimony (in another of his essays) to the same effect. "Imaginative recovery of the bygone," he observes in *Creative Intelligence,* "is indispensable to successful invasion of the future." [27]

We thus see that intertemporal cognition, the reference of one moment's experience to that of another moment—which is the mode of cognition with which the pragmatist is especially preoccupied—is essentially mediate and representative; and that the pragmatist himself, when he addresses himself to a plain descriptive analysis of the knowledge-situation, especially in its practical functioning, is compelled to acknowledge that it has this character. Whatever the prejudice against "presentative theories" in general which the pragmatist may share with the neorealist, he, at least, cannot deny the occurrence of "pre-presentative" (not to speak now of "re-presentative") cognitions. Whatever his antipathy to epistemological dualism, from the dualism of anticipation (and of reminiscence) he cannot escape.

[27] *C.I.*, p. 14.

2. In one of his *Essays in Experimental Logic*, Mr. Dewey deals directly with the question of the relative logical merits of "naïve" and "presentative" realism.[28] Here, as in many other cases, he assumes toward the believer in representative knowledge and in mental entities the kindly office of the prophet Balaam. He has at the outset an alarming air of having come to curse the camp of the dualists, but in the end he remains to bless it. He begins with an apparent confutation of certain arguments supposed to be used in proof of the psychical character of perceptual data. Many "idealists"—the word is here manifestly equivalent to "believers in the existence of subjective or psychical entities as factors in experience"—have, Mr. Dewey observes, "adduced in behalf of idealism certain facts having an obvious physical nature and explanation." The visible convergence of the railway tracks, for example, is cited as evidence that what is seen is a "mental content." So it is with the whole series of natural illusions, and the general fact of the relativity to the spectator of the shapes and colors of visible objects, etc. All of these are taken as "proof that what one sees is a psychical, private, isolated somewhat." In reality, all these diversities of appearance of a given object are merely diverse physical effects produced by its interaction with other physical things at different points in space. The image of the railway tracks is as convergent on a camera-plate as on the retina; the round table assumes a variety of elliptical shapes in a series of mirrors placed at different positions as truly as in the "sensations" of diversely placed percipients. Shall we then classify cameras and mirrors as "mental"? "Take a

[28] *E.L.*, pp. 250–263.

lump of wax and subject it to the same heat, located at different positions; now the wax is solid, now liquid—it might even be gaseous. How 'psychical' these phenomena!" "Taking one-and-the-same-object, the table presenting *its* different surfaces and reflections of light to different real organisms, the idealist eliminates the one-table-in-its-different-relations in behalf of a multitude of totally separate psychical tables. The logic reminds us of the countryman who, after gazing at the giraffe, remarked, 'There ain't no such animal!' " To use the diversities in the physical relations and consequences of things as proofs of their "psychical nature is also to prove that the trail the rocket stick leaves behind is psychical, or that the flower which comes in a continuity of process from a seed is mental."

So far Mr. Dewey would seem to be pleasantly making game of the dualist, to the amused applause of the neorealist. But the real point of the jest is quite other than it seems. In the first place the argument from illusions, from the relativity of perceptions, and the like has, so far as I can recall, never been used by those who believe in "mental existences" to support the conclusion which Mr. Dewey represents them as seeking to prove by it. They employ these facts to quite a different purpose—and to a purpose which they serve exceedingly well. That purpose is the *disproof* of *monistic* realism—i.e., of the thesis that the percept as actually given is identical, qualitatively and numerically, with the specific object which is its cause and which is supposed to be cognized by (or, rather, in) it. For the monistic realist does *not* say that the "real object directly given in perception" is, e.g., the image on my retina; he says it is the remote and "public" object to which my optical apparatus is reacting in its proper and undeniably physical manner. He is thereby involved in the absurdity of maintaining that, though what is present in my experience is an ellipse, and what is present in my neighbor's experience is a circle, nevertheless exactly the same entity, without duplication or diversity, *is* my neighbor's percept and mine. It is needless to dwell here upon this difficulty in monistic realism, since it is fully set forth elsewhere in this book. The point is that Mr. Dewey's ridicule applies to a wholly imaginary use of these considerations and does naught to aid monistic realism to escape the force of the dualist's real argument.

What is more, Mr. Dewey himself adopts the very same argument and directs it skilfully against the neorealistic position. For he goes on to insist that, *in so far as perception is taken as having a cognitive value,* a "knowledge status," the percept and the thing known in perception can never be regarded as identical; so that the "idealistic (*sc.* dualistic) interpretation" of *knowledge* is justified. The thesis of monistic realism that "the perceived object is the real object" is in conflict with the facts of the situation, and with its own assumptions.

> It assumes that there is *the* real object. . . . (But) since it is easily demonstrable that there is a numerical duplicity between the astronomocial star and its effect of visible light, the latter evidently, when the former is dubbed "*the*" real object, stands in disparaging contrast with its reality. If it is a case of knowledge, the knowledge refers to the star; and yet, not the star, but something more or less unreal (that is, if the star be "the" real object) is known.

> . . . Moreover, the thing known by perception is by this hypothesis in relation to a knower, while the physical cause is not. Is not the most plausible account of the difference between the physical cause of the perceptive knowledge and what the latter presents precisely this difference —namely, presentation to a knower? . . . Thus, when the realist conceives the perceptual occurrence as an intrinsic cause of knowledge to a mind or knower, he lets the nose of the idealist camel into the tent. He has then no great cause for surprise when the camel comes in and devours the tent.[29]

And, referring specifically to his earlier remarks on the physical explicability of illusions, etc., Mr. Dewey now adds: "This (physical) explanation, though wholly adequate as long as we conceive the perception to be itself simply a natural event, is not at all available when we conceive it to be an attempt at knowing its cause."

Whatever else he is, then, our pragmatist is *not* a monistic realist. For such a realist is after all epistemologically minded; he believes that our percepts make us acquainted with a real world outside of our skins—i.e., beyond the peripheral termini of our sensory nerves. And whoever believes this must, according to Mr. Dewey's argument, admit the numerical duality of the sensory data and the objects to which they are assumed to introduce us.

The pragmatist himself, however, it is to be remarked, professes to repudiate that belief. He escapes dualism—so the foregoing argument would seem to suggest—by rejecting the premise common to *both* kinds of realists, the premise

[29] *E.L.*, pp. 254–255.

which, when accepted, gives the dualist the best of that family quarrel. We seem once more—the pragmatist is constantly giving us these exciting moments—to be on the point of finding in pragmatism a *tertium quid*, a new insight which will enable us to escape from both horns of the traditional dilemmas. Once realize that perceptions are *not* "cases of knowledge," but are simply "natural events"—no more, no less—and your speculative worries are ended. You recapture the happy innocence, the "genuine naïveté," of the "plain man." "The plain man, of a surety, does not regard noises heard, lights seen, etc., as mental existences; but neither does he regard them as things *known*. That they are just things is good enough for him. By this I mean more than that the formulae of epistemology are foreign to him; I mean that his attitude to these things *as* things involves their *not* being in relation to him as a mind or a knower. He is in the attitude of a liker or hater, a doer or an appreciator." To the much harassed neorealist, otherwise hopeless of deliverance from the dualistic logic, this avenue of escape is especially pressingly commended. "Once depart from thorough *naïveté* and substitute for it the psychological theory that perception is a cognitive presentation to a mind of a causal object, and the first step is taken on the road which leads to an idealistic system." [30]

Perhaps the hopeful reader now takes courage and exclaims, "Here, finally, is the heart of the pragmatist's mystery! He is *neither* monistic nor dualistic realist; indeed, he is neither realist nor idealist, in the usual senses of those terms. By the simple device of *regarding perception as non-*

[30] *E.L.*, p. 258.

cognitive he transcends these ancient antitheses, and reaches a higher point of view from which the old controversies appear irrelevant. The Rousseau of the metaphysical world, he offers philosophy salvation from its troubles and an end to its quarrels through a return to the (intellectually) simple life."

Unhappily the reader will find this hope of speculative salvation speedily dashed by Mr. Dewey himself. One has but to read to the end of the same essay on "Naïve and Presentative Realism" to discover the author of it undoing all that he had seemed to do, by making evident the philosophical irrelevancy of the thesis that "perceptions are not cases of knowledge." For, in the closing pages of the essay, it appears that "by 'second intention' perceptions acquire a knowledge status." For example, "the visible light is a necessary part of the evidence on the basis of which we infer the *existence*, place, and structure of the astronomical star." Thus, since the body of propositions that forms natural science hangs upon perceptions, "*for scientific purposes* their nature *as* evidence, *as* signs, entirely overshadows their natural status, that of being simply natural events. . . . *For practical purposes* many perceptual events are cases of knowledge; that is, they have been *used* as such so often that the habit of so using them is established or automatic."[31] A man, in short, "takes the attitude of knower" as soon as he "begins to inquire"; and all of us, it would seem, depart from "thorough *naïveté*" almost as soon as we depart from our nativity. Indeed, Mr. Dewey's qualification of his assertion of the noncognitive character of (human) perception

[31] *E.L.*, pp. 261–262.

amounts in some cases to a denial of it. "Experience," he writes, in a passage already cited in another connection, "taken free of the restrictions imposed by the older concept, is full of inference. *There is apparently no conscious experience without inference; reflection is native and constant.*" And again, in another essay: "Some element of reflection may be required in any situation to which the term 'experience' is applicable in any sense which contrasts with, say, the experience of an oyster or a growing bean vine. Men experience illness; . . . it is quite possible that what makes illness into a *conscious* experience is precisely the intellectual elements which intervene—a certain taking of some things as representative of other things."[32] Mr. Dewey hereupon adds, it is true, that "even in such cases the intellectual element is set in a context which is noncognitive." But this, after what immediately precedes, can scarcely mean more than that the raw material of human cognition consists of bare sensory data which might by themselves very well resemble the "experience of the oyster or the growing bean vine." *Qua* conscious and *qua* human, experience admittedly is—if not exclusively made up of—at least natively and constantly shot through with reflection; is irremediably addicted to the habit of taking present data as disclosures of the existence and nature of things other than themselves.

Thus it appears that the "thorough *naïveté*" which, a few pages back, we saw commended to the neorealist as his only means of escape from dualism, demands of that philosopher a feat of a certain difficulty for one of his intellectual parts. Not even by becoming, intellectually, as a little child shall he

[32] *E.L.*, pp. 3–4.

be saved; no *naïveté* less thorough than that of the oyster or the bean vine will really serve him. Meanwhile, we have but to put together the two pragmatic theses which our analysis, in this section of our inquiry, has disclosed, to determine where the pragmatist himself stands—or should stand, if he would but adhere steadfastly to his own doctrines. *In so far* as our perceptual experience is taken as cognitive (we have seen Mr. Dewey maintaining), it must be dualistically interpreted; for, if perception is a case of knowing, "the doctrine that the perceived object is the real object" cannot be justified. But (as Mr. Dewey equally maintains) for the purposes of reflection our perceptual experience *must* be taken as cognitive. Percepts *become* cases of knowledge; and all distinctively human experience is reflective, using sensory materials as signs and evidences of existences lying beyond the immediate data. Thus the upshot of the argument as a whole is a vindication of the general epistemological view which I have called mediatism.

But (it may still be asked), even granting that—if Mr. Dewey is a representative pragmatist—the pragmatic theory of the knowledge-relation is thus dualistic (though apparently not in such a way as to prevent the pragmatist from now and then asserting the contrary view), why should this dualism be construed as justifying the belief in the existence of "mental" or "psychical" entities? The question might be answered in an *ad hominem* way by quoting again Mr. Dewey's remarks about the consequences of letting the nose of the "idealistic camel" into the tent. But it can better be answered by considering the implications of the type of cognition of which the pragmatist is surest—namely, intertemporal cognitions—the representation at one moment of the experience of another moment. In such cognitions, as we have seen, the bit of experience which knows is existentially (because temporally) distinct from the future or past bit of experience that is the object of knowledge. There is a representation and a somewhat represented, and no possibility of reducing them to identity.[33] Of these two, at least the one which is the representation must, in a perfectly definite sense and for plain reasons, be described as a "psychical" or "mental" existent. It is such, namely, in the sense that it is not physical—that room cannot be found for it in the physical order of nature as conceived by science. Just as the objects of a hallucination cannot be assigned to the points in "real space" at which, to the victim of the hallucination, they appear to exist, so future or past experience or experienced objects, when now represented in imagination, cannot, as such, be assigned to *any* place in *present* space. There is no mystery about the signification of the adjectives "mental" and "psychical," as I am here using them; they simply designate *anything which is an indubitable bit of experience, but either cannot be described in physical terms or cannot be located in the single, objective, or "public," spatial system, free from self-contradictory attributes, to which the objects dealt with by physical science belong.* Anything which is "present-as-absent" (when absent is used in a temporal sense) is manifestly thus psychical; for physical things, the entities of physical science, are never present in that way. A momentary cross-section of the physical universe,

[33] The two have, of course, a common character or essence and are thus "essentially" one, without detriment to their existential duality.

as science conceives it, would disclose merely a present. This present, though apprehended by us as the effect of yesterday and the preparation of tomorrow, would show us nowhere the actual content of yesterday and tomorrow; nor would it show us the content of our false memories or of our hopes destined to disappointment. And, most evidently of all, it would nowhere exhibit to us pastness or futurity as actual *attributes* of any of the things that it contained. Yet of certain contents of our experience those attributes are of the very essence. "All ideal contents, all aims (that is, things aimed at)" are, as Mr. Dewey has remarked, present in just such fashion—i.e., they have the paradoxical status of presence-as-absent which is unknown to the categories of physical description. The pragmatist or instrumentalist is in no position to deny the existence of entities "psychical" in the sense indicated, since he is insistent upon the reality of "aims" and "ideal contents" in their true character as genuinely external to their objectives and fulfillments. The only way in which he can escape from acknowledging two classes of existents, mental as well as physical, lies in acknowledging that the one class which actually exists is "mental." He cannot (while recognizing the reality of intertemporal cognitions) set up a real physical world, and then find room in it for the ideal contents which admittedly belong to such cognitions; but he can reject the hypothesis of an independent physical world altogether, in which case he is left with *nothing but* mental—i.e., sensibly experienced—entities in his universe. That, then, is the alternative to which he is limited—*either* idealism or else dualism, both in the psychophysical and the epistemological sense of the latter term.

A conception of knowledge which should be at once realistic and monistic is barred to him. So much, at least, seems to be a conclusion which we may regard as definitely established. I do not mean that it is a conclusion which the pragmatist can be depended upon to admit, or, at any rate, to refrain from contradicting on occasion. I mean that it is a consequence which can be seen to be implied in his most indispensable premise—namely, that we have thoughts of the future—as soon as it is also recognized that (as Mr. Dewey justly insists) these thoughts include contents which are present-as-absent, and that such contents (as he does not appear to note) are necessarily nonphysical.

In this last conclusion, however, we have already gone beyond the pragmatist's text and have drawn inferences from his premises which he himself neglects or refuses to draw. Throughout the remainder of this paper we shall be chiefly occupied in rectifying and reconstructing the pragmatic doctrine of knowledge, and in noting how such a rectified pragmatism bears upon the problems mentioned at the outset. This does not mean that we shall make up a new doctrine out of our own heads and name it pragmatism. We shall in every case reason from principles actually held, and insisted upon, by writers of this school. But we shall find that these principles are incongruous with certain other principles, or at any rate with certain modes of argument and certain specific conclusions which are put forward by the same writers. We shall discover a deep inner conflict in the "pragmatism" of the pragmatists, an opposition of underlying logical motives, from which the ambiguities and contradictions that we have already noted in their utterances naturally enough arise. This conflict, we shall see, is incapable of adjustment; one of the opposing principles or the other must simply be abandoned. And we shall find reasons for holding that one of these principles is not only sound in fact, but is also, in a quite definite sense, the more profoundly and distinctively "pragmatic."

III

Pragmatism and Knowledge of the Past

The pragmatist, as has been observed earlier in this paper, manifests a curious aversion from admitting that we have knowledge, and "true" knowledge, about the past. I have already cited from Mr. Dewey a formal definition of knowledge" which excludes from the denotation of the term everything except judgments of anticipation. What are the reasons for this strange disinclination to acknowledge the immense importance of retrospection in the processes by which our practical knowledge is built up, and to recognize the possibility of veridical retrospection? Three reasons seem distinguishable; the third of them is the one of chief significance for our present purpose.

1. The first reason is suggested in such passages as the following:

> The finished and done-with is of import as affecting the future, not on its own account; in short, because it is not wholly done with. Anticipation is therefore more primary than recollection; projection than summoning of the past;

> the prospective than the retrospective. Given a world like that we live in, . . . and experience is bound to be prospective in import. Success and giving it the eulogistic name of knowledge, is to substitute the reminiscence of old age for effective intelligence (*ibid.* 14).

Here there appears to be a confusion between import and importance, signification and significance. Doubtless what makes the past important to us is chiefly its serviceableness as a guide in our efforts to shape the future; but this does not in the least imply that what we require to know, precisely for the sake of that service, is not an actual past. We may, and in fact do, need to "*isolate* the past" provisionally, not for its own sake, but because only so we can get from it the material for processes of inference which, when completed, may enable us to construct the future in anticipation. The outcome of these processes is usually a generalization about the habits or uniform sequences of nature. These generalizations or laws, when formulated as such, doubtless contain an implicit reference to the future, but they also contain an implicit reference to the past; and to discover them, we must first look the past straight in the face to see what it *was,* without first assuming the generalization (and thereby the future reference) which our retrospective inquiry may eventually justify. As Mr. Dewey himself has remarked in the same context: "Detached and impartial study of the past is the only alternative to luck in assuring success to passion." Why, then, deny to such study "the eulogistic name of knowledge," while permitting anticipation to claim that name? Why deny to the fruits of such study, at its best, the name of truth? The only answer to these questions intimated in the sentences thus far quoted is the wholly irrelevant one that retrospection is not impossible or invalid, but under certain circumstances, useless and undesirable. What, in short, we have here is a sort of moral appraisal masquerading as a logical analysis.

2. A second reason why retrospection is the Cinderella of the pragmatic theory of knowledge is apparently to be found in the fact that the pragmatist desires to look "upon the goal and context of knowledge" not "as a fixed, ready-made thing," but as one "which has organic connections with the origin, purposes, and growth of the attempt to know it." [34] He finds it difficult to see how the data which serve in an inference can be unaffected by the intent of the inference and by the character of the particular situation in which the need for inquiry and inference originates, how "the terms of the logical analysis" can be "there prior to analysis" as "independent given ultimates." [35] But the past notoriously fails to exhibit the characteristics which the pragmatist thus desiderates in the object of knowledge. It is just blankly *there*, unmodifiable, irremediably external to the "present concrete situation," inaccessible to action either present or prospective. It consists exclusively of "independent given ultimates." It is therefore a region of existence naturally uncongenial to a philosopher determined to look upon all the contents of his universe as somehow "organically" related to his purposes and as material for the exercise of his active powers. Yet the proper inference from this uncongeniality would not seem to be that the past is not an object of knowledge,

[34] *D.P.*, p. 9.
[35] *E.L.*, pp. 38–39.

or that true judgments about it are impossible, but rather that the universe is not altogether such as the philosopher has supposed.

3. The principal reason, however, for the pragmatist's unwillingness to classify retrospection as true knowledge is plainly to be found in that subjectivistic strain in his thought of which we have already seen examples. The status of my past experience, from the point of view of a present judgment or inquiry concerning it, is precisely the same as the status of a contemporaneous but extra-subjective reality. Neither the one nor the other can now or hereafter be directly experienced; of neither is the reality accessible to verification. If, then, truth is an experienced relation, true judgments about the bygone are as impossible as true judgments about such "transempirical" objects as "things-in-themselves, atoms," etc.; for the past term of the relation is also, *qua* past, a kind of "transempirical." Just as Royce and other idealists have argued with a good deal of dialectical force that, if the object of my judgment is wholly alien to and independent of my purpose or meaning, it is not clear how my judgment can be known to mean *that particular object,* so Mr. Dewey argues with respect to the past:

> Since the judgment is as a matter of fact subsequent to the event, how can its truth consist in the kind of blank, wholesale relationship the intellectualist contends for? How can the present belief jump out of its present skin, dive into the past, and land upon just the one event (that *as* past is gone for ever) which, by definition, constitutes its truth? I do not wonder the intellectualist has much to say about "transcendence" when he comes to dealing with the truth of

> judgments about the past; but why does he not tell us how we manage to know when one thought lands straight on the devoted head of something past and gone, while another thought comes down on the wrong thing in the past? (*D.P.* 160).

The parallel with the traditional "refutations of realism" is complete. The past cannot be known because, since it is *ex hypothesi* now inaccessible to us, we can never compare it with our idea of it, nor determine which of our ideas of it are true and which false.

Mr. Dewey is not unaware of the obvious objection to this: the "Pupil" in the philosophical catechism from which I have last quoted points out that objection plainly enough. "When I say it is true that it rained yesterday, surely the object of my judgment is something past, while pragmatism makes all objects of judgment future." [36] The pragmatist "Teacher" replies with a *distinguo:* the "content" of a judgment, he observes, must not be confused with "the *reference* of that content." "The content of any idea about yesterday's rain certainly involves past time, but the distinctive or characteristic aim of judgment is none the less to give this content a future reference and function." Both the falsity and the irrelevancy of this distinction escape the "Pupil," but will not escape the critical reader. Even if it were true (which it is not) that, as a matter of descriptive psychology, every judgment about the past contains, or is accompanied by, a reference to the future,[37] nevertheless the judgment is pri-

[36] *D.P.*, p. 161.

[37] Even Mr. Dewey concedes that there is such a thing as "the reminiscence of old age" which is pure retrospection.

marily *about* the past. The content which is "present-as-absent" in my "idea about yesterday's rain" is, more specifically, present-as-past. Not only is it past content, but the direction in which the judgment "points" is backward. It is yesterday that I "mean," and not tomorrow, and no logical hocus-pocus can transubstantiate the meaning "yesterday" into the meaning "tomorrow." No future object of experience could fulfill *that specific meaning;* it is, in very truth, a meaning intrinsically incapable of directly-experienced fulfillment. And yet it is a meaning without which our thought is unable to operate, and in the lack of which the intelligent framing of a "plan of action" would be altogether impossible. Without ever actually experiencing the fulfillment of these meanings, we nevertheless have an irresistible propensity to believe that some of them are in fact valid meanings; that they "point" at something which truly *was,* and that the qualities which belong to the given content when it is present-as-past also belonged to the actually past content for which it presents itself as standing. We have even developed a technique by means of which we believe ourselves able to distinguish certain of these representations of the past as false and others as true.

But, of course, the pragmatist finds a difficulty in the fact of the unverifiability of such beliefs. By what right, he asks, do we affirm the "truth" of a retrospective belief, in the sense of some sort of present correspondence of present data with past data, when in the same breath we admit that the alleged correspondence cannot be "verified," since the two terms of it can never be brought together for actual comparison in the same experience (i.e., in the same *moment* of experience)? "If," says Mr. Dewey, "an idea about a past event is already true because of some mysterious static correspondence that it possesses to that past event, how in the world can its truth be *proved* by the *future consequences* of the idea?" [38] In other words, only upon the assumption that the idea *meant* the future in the first place, and that its supposed "truth" meant a particular kind of future experience conceivably serve as evidence of the fulfillment of that meaning, as the mark of the idea's truth. And yet, even for the "intellectualist" (a term which here evidently signifies a believer in the possible truth of retrospective judgments as such) all verification of such judgments is present or future—at any rate, subsequent to the past content of the judgment. To suppose that we can actually "know" what the past *qua* past *was* by ascertaining at some future time what the then present is, seems to the pragmatist much like supposing that we can prove the other side of the moon to be made of green cheese by showing that grass is green and can be converted into cheese.

Here, no doubt, is the most effective and plausible part of the pragmatist's dialectical reasoning against the possibility of strictly retrospective "knowledge." Fantastic paradox though the negation of such knowledge, taken by itself, must appear to common sense, it is now evident that the paradox is embraced in the attempt to escape from a real difficulty, or at any rate from what intelligibly may appear as a difficulty, in the contrary view. Yet, that there is no escape here will become apparent if we remember that the essential thing about a verification, after all, is not *when* it occurs, but

[38] *D.P.*, p. 162; italics in the original.

what it is that is verified. Now the matter to be verified is determined by the actual "meaning" of the particular antecedent judgment with which the verification is concerned. A judgment is its own master in deciding what it means, though not in deciding as to the fulfillment of its meanings; and a process of verification must therefore verify what the original judgment *knew itself* to mean, or else it is without pertinency to that judgment. However singular may appear the fact that a judgment about the past should find the *locus* of its verification in the future, the singularity of the fact does not entitle us to argue backward and declare that the judgment could not have meant what it expressly presented itself as meaning—and *what the verification actually presents itself as proving.* When I point to this morning's puddles as proof that it rained last night, the puddles are the means of proof, but not the thing proved. For verification-purposes their sole interest to me is not in themselves, but in what they permit me to infer about last night's weather. If some one shows that they were made by the watering-cart, they become irrelevant to the subject-matter of my inquiry—though the same proposition about the future, "there will be puddles in the street," is still fulfilled by them. It is tedious to reiterate considerations so obvious; but they are considerations which it is necessary to recall, in order to show how inverted is the logic by which the pragmatist seeks to persuade us of the truth of his paradox concerning retrospective knowledge.

What leads him into this paradox—and, in so far as he is consistent with his radical empiricism, into others involving the same principle—is his unwillingness to concede that a belief can ever be adequately validated indirectly, i.e., without the fulfillment of the belief's meaning in actual experience, the presentation as immediate data of the matters to which it relates. Yet in rejecting indirect verification as such, he is endeavoring to transcend one of the commonest and most unescapable limitations of human thought. And he does this only because he is not pragmatist enough. A consistent application of what Mr. Dewey, at least in his most characteristic passages, seems to mean by the "pragmatic method" would require him to place himself resolutely at the point of view of the moment of practical reflection—to stand, as it were, inside that phase of experience in which the intelligent agent is seeking means of coping with a practical problem which has arisen. A truly "pragmatic logic" would first of all be a faithful analysis of what is given and involved in that situation; and such an analysis would include an enumeration of the not-immediately-given things which it is *needful for the effective agent, at that moment, to believe or assume*—the things which, in fact, he habitually does assume—if the process of reflection is to be of any service to him in the framing of an effective plan of action. Within the limits of this deliberative moment the agent stands gazing out, as through windows, upon a whole worldful of things lying beyond those limits; and he will never act at all unless he accepts, instinctively or as a conscious assumption, various beliefs whose "meanings" are not and could not conceivably be fulfilled, whose truth is not and cannot be empirically verified, inside of that moment. If he is to plan a course of action in the future, he must know to some degree what the sequences and concomitances of things have been in the past. But at the moment at which he practically needs this knowledge he cannot "get at" that past; he must trust either his personal memory or the recorded results of empirical science. He also must assume that knowledge about the past is equivalent, within limits, to prediction about the future; but this, as Hume rightly showed, is a belief which is not itself susceptible of any empirical verification. The planner of action, furthermore, must assume that there is to *be* a future for him to act in; and he must believe that the future moment in which his present belief would find verification will in fact come. And this belief, be it noted, is from the point of view of the moment of practical reflection as destitute of strict "verification" as a belief about the past, or about the uniformity of natural processes in past and present. The practical judgment points two ways, forward and backward; and, in so far as it *is* practical, it has to do with the not-directly-verified as much when it points forward as when it points backward. For the future moment when a given belief about a happening *shall have been* verified will not be a moment of practical deliberation with respect to that happening. The happening, as soon as the judgment that referred to it is "empirically" verified, is already a past thing, without pragmatic importance except as material for a retrospective judgment from which an inference reading forward into a new future may be derived.

Thus, all strictly "pragmatic" verification is indirect verification, based either upon instinctive assumptions or upon inference from explicit postulates; for only such verification is attainable within the limits of the moment of practical reflection, the moment in which the intelligent agent, looking before and after, seeks to determine what present course of action will give him the future experience that he desires. The pragmatist or instrumentalist logician should be the last man in the world to doubt that a given bit of direct experience can contain cognitions and make "true" judgments about things external to that direct experience; for the only judgments that are "instrumental" are those which relate to the not-experienced, and knowledge is "practical" only if it is proleptic and transcendent of the given.

Let me now, at the cost of some repetition, make clear the bearing of all this upon our main theme, by summing up in somewhat formal fashion the results of the argument of this section. Epistemologically speaking, knowledge of the past, if actual, is analogous to a knowledge of transempirical realities; for it must necessarily consist in a present *factual* correspondence of an idea or representation with an object "pointed at" by that representation, which object, however, never is and never can be directly experienced, and therefore can never be directly compared with the idea of it. Observing this analogy, the pragmatist, under the influence of the strain of "radical empiricism" in his thought, excludes judgments about the past from his definition of "knowledge"—even when knowledge is not used in a "eulogistic" sense—and also maintains that no such judgment can properly be called "true." In this he is entirely consistent with the principle of radical empiricism; however paradoxical the conclusion, it truly follows from *that* premise. But the arguments and distinctions by which the pragmatist seeks to justify or to soften this paradox have been seen to be unsuccessful, and to be especially out of keeping with certain features of Mr. Dewey's own account of the pragmatic logic. The pragmatist, therefore, must acknowledge that there can be cognitions of past existents, and true judgments about those existents; that in the case of retrospection, as in that of anticipation, not only can we experience things present-as-absent, but also can meaningfully *believe* that the characters which as present they bear are the same characters which they bear as absent. It follows from this conclusion about retrospective knowledge that the pragmatist has no reason for denying *in principle* the possibility of a knowledge of "transempiricals." The whole series of arguments which pragmatist writers have taken over from the idealists to show that knowledge cannot consist in a "static" correspondence of a representative datum with a not-present reality is essentially foreign to the pragmatic method. If we can have meaningful and legitimate beliefs about past (or future) events now inaccessible to direct experience, we may conceivably hold meaningful and legitimate beliefs about contemporaneous existents inaccessible to direct experience. Whether we have equally good reasons for, or an equally irresistible propensity to, the latter belief is another question. We shall get a partial answer to that question in the next section, where we shall find the pragmatists agreeing with the greater part of mankind in the belief in at least one sort of contemporaneous existent essentially inaccessible to the direct experience of the believer.

IV

Pragmatism and Knowledge of Other Selves

We have seen Mr. Dewey making use in his idealistic-sounding passages, and especially in his formulation of "immediate empiricism," of a distinction between "transcendent" or "non-empirical" objects (which pragmatism is in these passages declared to repudiate) and "that which is directly experienced." This distinction, however, remains ambiguous until we ask whose experience is referred to. Knowledge, it will presumably be agreed by the pragmatist, is a thing achieved by and belonging primarily to individual persons or organisms. Psychologically considered, the knowledge-experience is a private experience, however public be the objects with which it deals; and noncognitive experience would seem to be even more obviously multiple and discrete. When, then, the pragmatist repudiates "trans-empiricals," does he refer to entities which transcend *my* direct experience (past, present, and future) or to those which transcend *everybody's* direct experience?

The latter is, of course, what he really intends. Pragmatists have always been admirably mindful of the fact that man is a social animal and have looked upon this fact as one which philosophy cannot afford to regard as irrelevant to its problems, even to its so-called theoretical problems. Mr. Dewey's philosophy has aimed not only at a logic of action and "operation," but also at a logic of social interaction and co-operation. The pragmatist, then, would not deny—would, in fact, affirm—that in a knowledge-experience of my own there may be "present-as-absent"—i.e., may be represented —the knowledge-experience, or the non-cognitive experiences, of others.

Yet this admission of the reality of a knowledge of experiences never directly experienced by the organism which does the knowing is incongruous with the logic of "immediate empiricism." Upon his empiricist principles, what the pragmatist *ought* to mean by his rejection of all "transempiricals" is a denial of the possibility of knowing existents which transcend the experience of the knower. For, once more, the pragmatist's immediate empiricism purports to be an account of what is involved in a cognitive situation. It is, in spite of the pragmatist's dislike of the word "epistemology," essentially an epistemological doctrine. It is, indeed, open to the pragmatist to add to this doctrine a metaphysical spiritualism, if he so desire; he may, for example, as James suggested, be a panpsychist. But it is not by a direct or a legitimate inference from his radical empiricism that he will be led to the metaphysical generalization that all existents are of a psychic nature. On the contrary, such a generalization implies a claim to a kind of knowledge which radical empiricism should declare to be impossible; it implies that A's experience can "mean" realities which *he* neither now nor at any time experienced directly, and that he can make true judgments which he can never directly verify. If Peter can know Paul, though Paul is never merely an experience of Peter's, then there is no reason, *so far as the nature of knowing goes*, why Peter should not know "atoms" or any other entities which are existentially other than his experience, or Paul's, or anybody's.

If Mr. Dewey had applied the logic of immediate empiricism as consistently to the question of the knowledge of other minds and their experiences as to the question of knowledge of the past, we should have found him raising the same difficulties in the one case as in the other. He would have asked: "Since Peter's judgment about Paul is as a matter of fact external to Paul's existence, how can its truth consist in the kind of blank wholesale relationship the intellectualist contends for? How can Peter's belief jump out of his skin—physical or psychological—and land upon just the one Other Self which, by definition, constitutes its truth?" It would have appeared evident to a consistent "immediate empiricist" of a pragmatic type, that the only Paul that Peter could "mean" was a Paul existing wholly within Peter's experience, and existing wholly as a means, or obstacle, to the future realization of Peter's plan of action. The really "radical" empiricist would have professed that an "automatic sweetheart" was good enough for him; or he would have followed the neorealist in the attempt to show that somehow, when Peter is thinking of Paul, Peter and Paul become so far forth identical. But, in point of fact, Mr. Dewey has far too profound a sense of the real nature of social experience to carry out his "immediate empiricism" consistently. He knows well that such experience presupposes the genuine existential otherness of the social fellow, and that distinctively social action begins only when I look upon my neighbor, not merely as a means or obstacle to my own ends, but as an end in himself.

Here again, then, we find the pragmatist committed to a position which is, in its epistemological principle, both realistic and dualistic.

V

Summary: The Epistemology of a Consistent Pragmatism

If space permitted, it would now be in order to go on to examine into the implications of a rectified and consistent pragmatism with respect to a specifically *physical* realism. That, however, is a question which it is impossible to discuss adequately within the limits of the space still remaining to me. For the present occasion, then, I must be content with the results, in relation to the questions set down at the beginning, which have thus far been reached. And the most significant of those results may now be summed up in a sentence. *A consistent pragmatism must recognize:*

a. That all "instrumental" knowledge is, or at least includes and requires, "presentative" knowledge, a representation of not-present existents by present data;

b. That, pragmatically considered, knowledge is thus necessarily and constantly conversant with entities which are existentially "transcendent" of the knowing experience, and frequently with entities which transcend the total experience of the knower;

c. That is, if a real physical world having the characteristics set forth by natural science is assumed, certain of the contents of experience, and specifically the contents of anticipation and retrospection, cannot be assigned to that world, and must therefore be called "psychical" (i.e., experienced but not physical) entities;

d. That knowledge is mediated through such psychical existences and would be impossible without them.

VI

The True Pragmatism and the False

It would, perhaps, be too sanguine to hope that this essay may serve to convert some pragmatists to pragmatism, and thereby to an acceptance of the four propositions just given. History affords but few examples of mature philosophers converted by the reasonings of other philosophers. Yet such a hope will possibly have a slightly greater chance of realization if, before concluding, I set down in more general terms and in a more connected manner the meaning and grounds of that distinction between "true" pragmatism and its aberrations which I have already suggested, especially in the discussion of the pragmatist's treatment of retrospective judgments. I will therefore state first what I conceive to be the fundamental and essential insight of pragmatism, at least of that form of it which we owe chiefly to Professor Dewey; and I will then show through what process this was distorted into its own implicit negation.

Pragmatism seeks to be a *philosophy of man as agent, and as reflective agent, in a physical and social environment.* That man is, in fact, such an agent and is such specifically in his cognitive capacity, it perceives to be the distinctive presupposition of human experience; and in this presupposition it finds a fixed point from which philosophical inquiry may set out and a criterion by which the tenability of other philosophical hypotheses may be judged. To deny this assumption, to maintain that consciousness, even when it takes the form that we call planning, is only "a lyric cry in the midst of business," is, as the pragmatist sees it, to contradict what is implicitly taken for granted in every reflective activity of man; it is to deny what is necessarily assumed by every farmer, every physician, every engineer, every statesman, and every social reformer. That knowing is "functional," that it "makes a difference," and does so by virtue of those characteristics which are distinctive of it *as* knowing; [39] and that, on the other hand, its character and method cannot be understood without a consideration of its functional significance; these seem to me the deepest-lying premises of the philosophy of Mr. Dewey and of some other pragmatists.

To have formulated the starting-point and a guiding principle (I do not say *the* guiding principle) of philosophy in this way is to have done a notable service to philosophical thought. For this is in truth an essentially new way of ap-

[39] It is, for example, on the ground of the principle indicated that Mr. Dewey repudiates absolute idealism and every "eternalistic" sort of doctrine about the nature and function of thought. "A world already in its intrinsic structure dominated by thought, is not a world in which, save by contradiction of premises, thought has anything to do. . . . A doctrine which exalts thought in name, while ignoring its efficacy in fact (that is, its use in bettering life), is a doctrine which cannot be entertained or thought without serious peril" (*C.I.*, pp. 27–28).

proaching many old problems, especially the problem of knowledge; and, subject to certain qualifications, it is, in my opinion, a sound and fruitful way. Only, as I cannot but think, the pragmatists themselves have as a rule, at a rather early stage of their reasonings, wandered from that way into very different and less trustworthy paths.

One of the earliest [40] and the most serious of these aberrations consisted in the identification of the pragmatic principle—in its bearing upon the problem of knowledge—with the "principle of radical empiricism." It would be easy to show the natural confusions of ideas through which this identification took place; but it is not necessary to our present purpose. That the two principles, so far from being identical with or inferrible from one another, are essentially antipathetic and lead to contrary conclusions on ulterior questions has been illustrated in the foregoing pages by several specific examples. A truly pragmatic method applied to the problem of knowledge would inquire how thought or knowledge is to be construed when it is regarded as a factor acting upon and interactive with a physical and social environment. And the first step in the procedure would be to sharpen, to make precise, the time-distinctions pertinent to this inquiry. For the pragmatic method is necessarily a special form of what I have elsewhere referred to as the "temporalistic method"; and to this aspect of pragmatism

[40] Not the only one, nor perhaps the earliest of all. At least four other latent or explicit logical motives distinct from the genuine pragmatic principle and tending to pervert or to contradict it, are distinguishable in Mr. Dewey's reasonings alone—and several more in the writings of other pragmatists. But a complete enumeration of these is not indispensable here.

Mr. Dewey on occasion has given clear expression. "A philosophical discussion of the distinctions and relations which figure most largely in logical theories depends upon a proper placing of them in their temporal context; and in default of such placing, we are prone to transfer the traits of the subject-matter of one phase to that of another, with a confusing outcome."[41] This is a golden saying; and, as I have said, it is a proper consequence of the primary pragmatic insight. To define knowledge in terms of the elements of the situation in which the reflective agent, or would-be agent, finds himself is to focus the attention of the logician upon a situation in which time-relations and time-distinctions are of the essence.

"Radical empiricism," however, is a doctrine about knowledge which, when consistent, characteristically ignores time and temporal distinctions. It is a philosophy of the instantaneous. The moving spring of its dialectic is a feeling that knowledge means immediacy, that an existent is strictly "known" only in so far as it is given, present, actually possessed in a definite bit of concrete experience. If we apply the demand for temporalistic precision to this assumption, we are obliged to construe it as meaning that a thing is known at a given moment of cognition only if it is both existent and immediately experienced *within the time-limits of that moment*. But to demand in this sense that philosophy shall "admit into its constructions only what is directly experienced" is to forbid philosophy to admit into its "construction" of the knowledge-situation precisely the things

[41] *E.L.*, p. 1. Cf. Mr. Dewey's comment on the great service rendered by William James "in calling attention to the fundamental importance of considerations of time for the problems of life and mind."

that are observably most characteristic of and indispensable to that situation, *qua* functional—and also *qua* social. For the moment of practical deliberation is concerned chiefly with things external to the *direct* experience of that moment. What these things specifically are we have seen in part; they consist of the various sorts of content which must be "present-as-absent"—such as representations of the future, of a past that truly *was*, of experiences not-directly-experienced (i.e., the experiences of others); and they consist, further, of judgments, with respect to these types of content, which must be assumed and can never be directly verified (in the radical-empiricist sense of verification) at the moment of their use.

What has befallen pragmatism, then, is that, under the influence of "radical empiricism," the pragmatist philosophers have confounded their temporal categories. A "proper placing" of the knowledge-situation "in its temporal context" (and, I may add, in its social context) is precisely what they have neglected. They "transfer to one phase of experience the traits of another phase." Their primary concern, as I have already remarked, should be with that particular moment in which the reflective agent is, in fact, reflecting, i.e., seeking by means of knowledge to deal with a practical exigency, looking for the mode of action which can be depended upon to bring about a desired future result. But the pragmatists have failed to segregate sharply, for the purposes of their analysis, this moment, or phase, of practical inquiry and forecast. They have sometimes tended to read into it the traits of the moment of answer or fulfilment; and they have sometimes strangely confused its traits with those of what is by definition a nonreflective and precognitive phase of experience. More singularly still, they have persistently blurred the contrast between the retrospective and prospective reference of judgments, insisting that because a judgment about the past can be verified only indirectly and in the future, it therefore "refers" only to the future. Most pregnant, perhaps, of all these confusions, they have declared that truth must be "an *experienced* relation," without asking the essential questions: experienced *when* and *by whom?* For if they had definitely raised these questions, they would have recognized that this account of truth gets its seeming plausibility only if taken as meaning: "a relation of which both terms are given at the same time and in the same sense in the experience of the same experiencer." But a "truth" really corresponding to such a definition would speedily have been discovered to be the least "instrumental," the least "pragmatic," of all possible possessions. Of these primary confusions of temporal distinctions and points of view, most of the contradictions and infirmities of logical purpose which we have earlier noted in pragmatist reasoning are the results.

Thus the doctrine commonly put forward as "pragmatism" may be said to be a changeling, substituted almost in the cradle. I have here had the privilege of proclaiming the rightful heir and of pointing out the marks of identity. I invite all loyal retainers to return to their true allegiance. If they will do so, they will, I think, find that there need be—and, over the issues which have been here considered, can be—no quarrel between their house and that of critical realism.

VII

PRAGMATISM AS INTERACTIONISM *

The doctrine of pragmatism began as a theory about what thinking is; it has of late come to be chiefly a theory about what thinking does. Its point of de-departure lay in the provinces of logic and epistemology. The earliest formulation of the doctrine, we have seen, was an attempt to define the conditions under which ideas and judgments possess meaning, and to formulate the generic nature of all "meanings." This soon developed into a theory concerning the nature of knowing, and the meaning, and consequently the criterion, of truth; and from this followed certain conclusions as to the scope of possible knowledge and the limits of genuinely significant philosophical discussion. These epistemological preoccupations, though not absent, seem distinctly subordinate in the latest collective manifesto of our American pragmatists, the volume of essays entitled *Creative Intelligence.* The outstanding thesis of that volume appears to be the one indicated in its title, that man's "intelligence" is genuinely efficacious and "creative." The

* First appeared in *The Journal of Philosophy, Psychology and Scientific Methods,* Vol. XVII, No. 22, Oct. 21, 1920; printed here with some omissions and additions.

several contributors (it is intimated in the prefatory note), while by no means professing any complete identity of doctrine, "agree in the idea of the genuineness of the future, and of intelligence as the organ for determining the quality of the future, so far as it can come within human control."

Thus the significance of this form of pragmatism, "instrumentalism," lies in its bearings, not upon logic or epistemology, but upon metaphysics, and, more specifically, upon the philosophy of nature. Its principal quarrel—little as some pragmatists seem able to distinguish their enemies from their friends—should be with mechanistic "naturalism," the dogma that the laws of the more complex and later-evolved processes of nature can be "reduced" to, and may eventually be deduced from the laws of the simpler processes—that "consciousness" is nothing but movements of the muscles, that muscular movements are wholly explicable by the principles of physiology, that the categories and explanatory principles of physiology can be "fetched back" to those of chemistry, these be resolved into the dynamics of the molecule, and the entire spectacle of nature, despite its seeming variety, finally be shown to be nothing but the manifestation of a few simple laws of the relative motion of particles or of mass-points. The opposition of pragmatism to this type of doctrine is evident from its denial of an essential part of the mechanistic creed—its denial, namely, of parallelism and all other forms of epiphenomenalism. Against whom but the epiphenomenalist does pragmatism need (in Professor Dewey's words) to "enforce the pivotal position of intelligence in the world and thereby in control of human fortunes (so far as they are manageable)"? Is it not the familiar mechanistic doctrine that

> The first morning of creation wrote
> What the last dawn of reckoning shall read,

that is described by Professor Dewey in the following terms: "Thinking was treated as lacking in constructive power; even its organizing capacity was but simulated, being in truth nothing but arbitrary pigeon-holing. Genuine projection of the novel, deliberate variation and invention, are idle fictions in such a version of experience. If there ever was creation, it all took place at a remote period."[1] But to this doctrine Professor Dewey tells us that the antagonism of his own philosophy is absolute. Similar protest against the "block-world" of naturalism is made by nearly all the writers in *Creative Intelligence;* the following passage, by Professor G. H. Mead, is typical: "The individual in his experience is continually creating a world which becomes real through his discovery. In so far as new conduct arises under the conditions made possible by his experience and his hypotheses the world . . . has been modified and enlarged."[2]

In an earlier volume Professor Dewey even more plainly indicated the import of his own philosophy by an express repudiation of Mr. Santayana's familiar and striking formulation of epiphenomenalism, first printed in this Journal.[3] The belief "which attributes to thought a power, by virtue of its intent, to bring about what it calls for, as an incanta-

[1] B. H. Bode, *Creative Intelligence* (hereafter cited as *C.I.*), p. 23.
[2] *C.I.*, p. 225.
[3] *Journal of Philosophy*, III (1906), p. 412.

tion or exorcism might do," seemed to Mr. Santayana merely "a superstition clung to by the unreconciled childishness of man." "The consequences of reflection," he wrote, "are due to its causes, to the competitive impulses in the body, not to the wistful lucubration itself; for this is mere poetry. . . . Consciousness is a lyric cry in the midst of business." On the contrary, writes Mr. Dewey, "if one understands by consciousness the function of effective reflection, then consciousness is a business—even in the midst of writing or singing lyrics." [4] The essential thesis of the volume of *Essays in Experimental Logic* is "that intelligence is not an otiose affair nor a mere preliminary to a spectator-like apprehension of terms and propositions." In the eyes of a pragmatist, "faith in the creative competency of intelligence was the redeeming feature of the historic idealisms." [5]

In view of such dicta as these, one naturally looks to pragmatist writers for a connected and comprehensive discussion of the problem of interaction and of the older types of doctrine concerning the psychophysical relation. The passages which have been quoted from Professor Dewey and others, and many more like them, fairly bristle with suggestions of questions to which one desiderates answers from the same philosophers. What is this "intelligence" which the pragmatist apparently credits not only with the ability to push molecules about, but also with the power to enrich the universe with new contents? Does it or does it not include any entities or any processes not definable in ordinary physical

[4] John Dewey, *Essays in Experimental Logic* (hereafter cited as *E.L.*), p. 18.

[5] *E.L.*, p. 30.

categories? When matter is moved by "intelligence," is the intelligence itself matter? or a motion of matter? or a form of energy which must find its place in the equations of thermodynamics? or something other than any of these? How is the thesis of its efficacy in the physical world to be adjusted to the generalizations of physical science about the motion of masses and particles? Does that thesis presuppose such views about natural laws and their logical relations as have been set forth by Boutroux in his *Contingence des lois de la nature,* or a doctrine of the "heterogeneity and discontinuity of phenomena" such as is defended by Boex-Borel in his *Le Pluralisme?*

To these questions the representatives of pragmatism offer less direct and less thorough and connected answers than could be desired; but we are not left wholly without light upon the matter. The nearest approach, so far as I can recall, to a fairly full treatment of this issue from the pragmatist's point of view, is to be found in Professor B. H. Bode's essay in *Creative Intelligence.* Here we get a somewhat extended statement of reasons for rejecting the "doctrine that conscious behavior is nothing more than a complicated form of reflex, which goes on without any interference on the part of mind or intelligence." According to parallelism, in Bode's words "intelligence adds nothing to the situation except itself. The psychic correlate is permitted to 'tag along,' but the explanations of response remain the same in kind as before they reached the level of consciousness. . . . The explanation of behavior, is to be given wholly in terms of neural organization." [6]

[6] *C.I.*, p. 251.

Such a view, Professor Bode contends, is inadmissible because it conflicts with clear empirical evidence; "some facts persistently refuse to conform to the type of mechanism, unless they are previously clubbed into submission." What are these facts? Professor Bode enumerates three: "foresight," "the sense of obligation," and the process of reasoning. The two former "must learn to regard themselves as nothing more than an interesting indication of the way in which the neural machinery is operating, before they will fit into the [parallelistic] scheme." Mr. Bode does not develop his argument here as fully as one could wish; he merely points out these two implications of epiphenomenalism and assumes that, once stated, they will immediately be recognized by the reader as absurdities. But the argument based upon the occurrence of reasoning in man is somewhat more explicitly stated; it seems to consist in the observation that, if parallelism (or a mechanistic behaviorism) were accepted, the notion of validity, of truth and error, would become meaningless. By the mechanistic theory "the progress of an argument is in no way controlled or directed by the end in view, or by considerations of logical coherence, but by the impact of causation. Ideas lose their power to guide conduct by prevision of the future, and truth and error consequently lose their significance, save perhaps as manifestations of cerebral operations. . . . [In] a description of this kind everything that is distinctive in the facts is left out of account, and we are forced to the conclusion that no conclusion has any logical significance or value." [7]

It is interesting thus to observe a pragmatist vindicating

[7] *C.I.*, p. 257.

the most important thesis in his doctrine by a method which has most frequently been employed in recent philosophy by the partisans of epistemological dualism or idealism—the method, namely, of testing a metaphysical theorem by inquiring whether it is consistent with the postulate of the possibility of error, and whether it leaves room for a "world of values." Concerning the cogency of this or the other suggested arguments against epiphenomenalism I shall not, at this point, inquire; it is more to my present purpose to point out that, while thus attacking parallelism, Professor Bode apparently conceives that he can avoid falling into any position properly to be described as interactionism. By the latter theory, he observes, "a certain importance is indeed secured to mental facts"; but "so far as purposive action is concerned we are no better off than we were before." For "the mental is simply another kind of cause; it has as little option regarding its physical effect as the physical cause has with regard to its mental effect. Non-mechanical behavior is again ruled out, or else a vain attempt is made to secure a place for it through the introduction of an independent psychic agency." [8] "The only difference between the two doctrines"—and to Professor Bode this is apparently an unimportant difference—is "the question whether it is necessary or permissible to interpolate mental links into the causal chain." [9]

I am not certain that I understand either the criticism of the doctrine of interaction which these sentences are meant to convey, or the nature of the *tertium quid*—neither inter-

[8] *C.I.*, p. 253.
[9] *C.I.*, p. 251.

actionism nor parallelism, as usually understood—which Professor Bode intends to propound. But if I at all follow him, his objections to admitting interaction are two, involving quite distinct considerations. (*a*) The first objection would seem to be based upon the assumption of a sort of indeterminism. Even the theory of interaction assigns "mental" causes for physical events; and Mr. Bode seems to imply that the recognition of *any* kind of cause "which has no option with regard to its effects" amounts to a denial of the "creative" efficacy of consciousness. Behavior is apparently still too "mechanical" if it is subject to any uniform determination whatever. Here we have the Romantic, the ultra-Bergsonian view, which rejects both mechanism and ordinary interactionism for ultimately one and the same reason, *viz.*, that they both seem to exclude "invention," pure innovation, true freedom. (*b*) But Professor Bode's other suggested objection to interactionism appears to be brought from quite another quarter of the philosophical horizon. It is that the interactionist attributes efficacy to a "psychic agency," whereas nothing "psychic" exists, either as an active or an otiose element in reality. This, at least, I take to be the point of a passage of Professor Bode's in which he explains the source of the "difficulties" about interaction, and indeed, of "most of our philosophic ills." That source is "the prejudice that experience or knowing is a process in which the objects concerned do not participate and have no share." This error, it seems, has led philosophers to invent imaginary entities in order to solve spurious problems generated by the error itself. But "a careful inventory of our assets brings to light no such entities as those which have been placed to our credit. *We do not find body and object and consciousness, but only body and object. . . . The process of intelligence is something that goes on, not in our mind, but in things:* it is not photographic, but creative."[10] From such expressions one gathers that Professor Bode objects to the theory of interaction because it presupposes psychophysical dualism—because it implies the reality of two classes of entities profoundly different in their attributes and modes of operation. "Bodies" and "objects" may, he intimates, be said to "interact," but not "bodies" and "minds"; for there are no minds. No facts are to be found in experience which require a "subjectivistic" or "psychic interpretation."[11] Even abstract ideas do not "compel the adoption of a peculiarly 'spiritual' or 'psychic' existence in the form of unanalyzable meanings."[12]

Of the two types of objection to interactionism thus suggested by Professor Bode, the former will not be considered in this paper. I omit it partly in the interest of brevity, partly because I am in doubt whether Professor Bode himself seriously means to assert the view which his words at this point seem to imply, and partly because it appears questionable whether other pragmatists share that view. But the second of his anti-interactionist arguments is an application to the question in hand of a thesis frequently recurrent in the writings of Professor Dewey and others of the same school. Most pragmatists apparently share with the neorealist and the behaviorist a violent aversion to psycho-

[10] *C.I., pp.* 254–55; italics mine.

[11] *C.I.*, p. 270

[12] *C.I.*, p. 245.

physical dualism. "Pragmatism," Professor Dewey writes, "has learned that the true meaning of subjectivism is just *anti*-dualism. Hence philosophy can enter again into the realistic thought and conversation of common-sense and science, where dualisms are just dualities, distinctions having an instrumental and practical, but not ultimate, metaphysical worth; or rather, having metaphysical worth in a practical and experimental sense, not in that of indicating a radical existential cleavage in the nature of things." [13] For pragmatism, therefore, "things are no longer entities in a world set over against another world called 'mind' or 'consciousness,' with some sort of mysterious ontological tie between them." The pragmatist "tends to take sensations, ideas, concepts, etc., in a much more literal and physically realistic fashion than is current." [14]

This hostility to dualism is, it is true, directed primarily and most frequently against dualistic epistemology, the doctrine that (as Mr. Dewey's unfriendly summary puts it) "the organ or instrument of knowledge is not a natural object, but some ready-made state of mind or consciousness, something purely 'subjective,' a peculiar kind of existence which lives and moves and has its being in a realm different from things to be known." [15] "To say the least," observes Professor Dewey elsewhere, this conception "can be accepted by one who accepts the doctrine of biological continuity only after every other way of dealing with the facts

[13] *Journal of Philosophy, Psychology and Scientific Methods,* II, p. 326.

[14] *Loc. cit.*

[15] John Dewey, *Influence of Darwin, etc.,* p. 98.

has been exhausted."[16] But it is evident that when the pragmatist denies the reality of any "psychic," "subjective," or "mental" entities as factors in cognition, he also, both by implication and intent, repudiates the dualistic presuppositions of the theory of psychophysical interaction.

Thus, to recapitulate, we find the pragmatist asserting the determination of (some) events—i.e., of certain motions of matter—by a causal factor called "intelligence" or "reflection"; insisting upon the uniqueness of this mode of determination, its irreducibility to purely mechanical or physicochemical or physiological laws; and at the same time denying the existence of any "psychical" (i.e., non-physical) elements in experience or in "behavior," whether as causes or effects or mere concomitants. The peculiar combination of doctrines, then, which constitutes the typical pragmatistic view upon the problem with which the older controversies between parallelism and interactionism were concerned, must apparently be described as an anti-mechanistic materialism.[17] Intelligence—it clearly seems to follow from the

[16] *C.I.*, p. 35.

[17] I do not wish to be understood to assert that pragmatists in general, or even that any of the school, adhere to this position consistently; for they appear to me to adhere to no position consistently. I am, for example, after careful study of Professor Dewey's utterances on the subject, wholly unable to reconcile such passages as have above been cited, as to the "physically realistic" implications of pragmatism and its harmony with the "realistic thought and conversation of common-sense and science," with numerous other passages of his in which pragmatism is identified with "immediate empiricism," i.e., with the doctrine that only that which is immediately experienced can be known, and that things *are* (merely) "what they are experienced as." Such a doctrine, Professor Dewey declares, "doesn't have any non-empirical realities," such as "things-in-themselves," "atoms," etc.

conjunction of the passage already cited—is an affair of "bodies," not of "mind" or mental entities of any kind; but bodies, when they behave in the special fashion called "intelligent" or "reflective," are exhibiting a mode of action not exemplified elsewhere in nature; and by this action they cause the directions and velocities of motion of other masses to be different from what they would be if intelligence were (and where it is) inoperative. As Professor Bode puts it, we must recognize in what (with seeming incongruity) he calls "*conscious* behavior, a distinctive mode of operation," "the advent of a new category"; if we do not, "intelligience becomes an anomaly and mystery deepens into contradiction." [18]

Is this combination of doctrines, this attempt to vindicate the creative efficacy of intelligience while repudiating psychophysical dualism, a stable logical compound? Is it consistent either with pragmatistic principles or with the facts of that particular type of "situation" with which pragmatic analysis has been characteristically preoccupied?

In the preceding part of this article it has been pointed out that the most characteristic and most emphasized thesis

---

(*Influence of Darwin*, p. 230); yet such things, surely, play a great part in the "realistic thought and conversation of common-sense and science." The truth is—as I have, I think, shown in a paper in the volume of *Essays in Critical Realism*—that the pragmatism of Professor Dewey and others involves a hopelessly incongruous union of two fundamental principles, "radical empiricism" and the true pragmatic method, of which the former is idealistic and the latter realistic in its implications. In the present paper, I am assuming that pragmatists mean what they say in their realistic passages and am disregarding utterances which are in flat opposition to those passages.

[18] *Loc. cit.*

of pragmatism, in the more recent utterances of its advocates, is the doctrine of the potency of "intelligence" to bring about modifications in the physical world; that Professor Dewey, Professor Bode, and others are consequently in avowed and vigorous opposition to parallelism or epiphenomenalism in all its forms and disguises, and to the kindred assumption of the universal reducibility of bodily actions to mechanical laws; but that, at the same time, most pragmatists are altogether averse from any sort of psychophysical dualism. They seek to combine in a single doctrine the assertion of the efficacy of thought with the denial of the existence of any distinctively "psychical" or "subjective" elements in experience. We are now to inquire whether both these views can consistently be held by the same philosopher, without a falsification of the facts of those "concrete practical situations" which it is peculiarly the concern of the pragmatist to observe and describe truly.

It is to be noted at once that such a combination satisfies but poorly the pragmatist's antipathy to dualism as such, and hardly accords with his attachment to the principle of "biological continuity." A dualism of types of causal process, of laws of action, means just as deep a "cleavage in the nature of things" as a dualism of modes of existence; to a pragmatist, indeed, it should seem much the more significant cleavage of the two. If the appearance of "intelligence" upon the cosmic scene means, as Professor Bode says, the "advent of a new category"; if bodies, under the influence of intelligence, move in ways in which the same masses of matter would not move under the action of any forces known to physics or chemistry—then it follows that an irreducible discontinuity is to be found in the system of natural laws. I make this point merely because of its bearing upon the presumption which seems to be one of the principal grounds for the pragmatists' denial of the existence of anything "mental" or "subjective." We have already seen Professor Dewey urging the methodological presumption of "continuity" as a reason why the hypothesis that "consciousness is something outside the real object, is something different in kind," should, at the least, be not accepted until "after every other way of dealing with the facts has been exhausted"; [19] and in practice this presumption is treated by him as decisive. He repeatedly assails the dualistic epistemology on the ground that it "makes consciousness supernatural in the literal sense of the word" and implies that "the organ or instrument of knowledge is not a natural object"; what this apparently means—unless "supernatural" is used merely as an abusive epithet—is that "ideas" and "states of mind" are conceived by the dualist as a "peculiar kind of existence" essentially different from "things," i.e., from the physical things with which natural science is conversant. But since the pragmatist himself believes, not, indeed, in a peculiar kind of existence, but in a peculiar kind of causal agent or mode of action, his "creative intelligence" is, in the same sense of the adjective, quite as "supernatural" as the dualistic epistemologist's "representative ideas." It may, in fact, be said to be *more* "supernatural." For after all, mere "representation" is a function which, though external to the system dealt with by the physical sciences, does not disturb the system, or limit the range of applicability of the

[19] *C.I.*, p. 35.

laws of those sciences. But the control of "things" by a unique, nonmechanistic process of "intelligence"—nay, the creation of new content of reality, the introduction into the physical order of genuine novelties, by man's reflection and contrivance—this is not a mere external addition to, but an interjection of a foreign element into, the system of nature known to physical science. Indeed, Professor Bode, after setting forth in pragmatistic fashion the process of selective and purposive control of bodily behavior, refers to it as a "miracle."[20] Mr. Santayana's parallelistic dualism, as it seems to me, deviates less conspicuously from the presumption of "continuity," when it refuses "to attribute to thought a power, by virtue of its intent, to bring about what it calls for," while admitting the distinctive existence of thought as a physically ineffectual accompaniment of bodily processes.

These considerations, however, are merely preliminary; they serve to show only that the pragmatist is not steadfast in his loyalty to that *realwissenschaftlich* point of view in the name of which he appears to condemn psychophysical dualism. The presumption which he invokes as virtually decisive at one point, he quietly disregards at another. Perhaps it may turn out that it is a presumption contrary to fact in both cases; and, indeed, that it can not be rejected at the one point without being rejected at the other also.

From the question of antecedent methodological presumptions, then, we turn to the question of fact. We must directly scrutinize the process of "intelligence" or practical reflection, to note what elements are observably contained in it,

[20] *C.I.*, p. 240.

and what other facts must necessarily be presupposed, if it is to be credited, as it is credited by the pragmatist, with causal efficacy in the world of "things."

An answer to this question has been attempted by Professor Bode in the essay already cited; and it will serve our purpose to consider his answer first. He seeks to determine the differentia of what he calls (though apparently without any "subjectivistic" implications) "conscious behavior." That, at any rate in man, responses to stimuli occur which are not "purely mechanical reactions" he finds to be a plain matter of fact. These specifically "conscious" responses have three distinguishing peculiarities: (*a*) They are "processes of organization not determined by a mechanism previously provided"; they have "a peculiar flexibility, so as to meet the demands of a new situation. . . . The response to the situation is tentative or experimental in character." In this respect these reactions are essentially unlike reflex arcs. "The reflex arc is already set up and ready for use by the time the act appears upon the scene. In the case of conscious activity we find a very different state of affairs. The arc is not first constructed and then used, but is constructed as the act proceeds; and this progressive organization is in the end what is meant by conscious behavior."[21] (*b*) But this is not the whole story; for this "progressive organization" has, furthermore, a "selective or teleological character." The selection "is determined by reference to the task in hand, which is to restore a certain harmony of response. Accordingly the response is selected which gives promise of

[21] *C.I.*, p. 238.

forwarding the business of the moment."[22] (*c*) This selective control, furthermore, operates in a unique and highly significant way. "It consists in giving direction to behavior *with reference to results that are still in the future.*" Thus, in the case of an organism capable of conscious behavior, "a perceived object is a stimulus which controls or directs the organism *by results which have not yet occurred* . . . [e.g.] a 'sharp' razor, as perceived, does not actually cut just now, but it bodies forth the quality 'will cut,' i.e., the perceived attribute derives its character from what the object will, or may, do at a future time. . . . The uniqueness of such a stimulus lies in the fact that *a contingent result somehow becomes operative as a present fact; the future is transformed into the present, so as to become effective in the guidance of behavior.*"[23] Thus, finally, "*to be conscious is to have a future possible result of present behavior embodied as a present existence functioning as a stimulus to further behavior.*" It is this "conversion of future results or consequences into present stimuli" which constitutes the "miracle of consciousness."

This description is given by Professor Bode not merely as an account of "conscious" behavior, but also as an account of the nature of "intelligence." To "act intelligently" is to act "with reference to future results which are sufficiently embodied in present experience to secure appropriate reactions." But for certain qualifying and explanatory clauses which Professor Bode adds, we might very well

[22] *C.I.*, p. 240.
[23] *C.I.*, p. 242; italics mine.

accept this as an accurate and illuminating, if not complete, statement of the distinguishing peculiarities of intelligence in its practical aspect. But it has now to be noted that when Mr. Bode speaks of "acting with reference to future results," he apparently means what would ordinarily be called—and what, in fact, he himself calls—an *unconscious* reference to such results. He writes, for example: "A living body may respond to an actual cut by a knife on purely reflex principles, but to respond to a cut by anticipation, i.e., to behave with reference to a merely possible or future injury, is manifestly an exhibition of intelligence. *Not that there need be any conscious reference to the future as future in the act.*" [24]

What this means, as I judge from certain other passages, is that any response is, in Professor Bode's sense, "controlled by a reference to future results," provided only that (*a*) the response does in fact (however little the organism be aware of the fact) serve to adapt the organism to meet some future situation in a more effective way; and (*b*) that this adaptive character of the present response is the effect of previous experience in a situation similar to the future one. In any given situation in which an organism may find itself, and to which an immediate, reflex response is in any way impeded or inhibited, there are present in the organism a variety of "nascent motor impulses." If one of these impulses has already, in one or more previous experiences of the same organism, been carried out, its "adaptive value" has thereby been already tested, at least to some degree. In so far as this previous experience influences the present

[24] *C.I.*, p. 242; italics mine.

response, we may say that the "future possible result" of that response "is embodied as a present existence functioning as a stimulus to further behavior." For the future result will, after all, be the same in kind as the past result which is one of the actual determinants of the present response.[25]

When Professor Bode's analysis is construed in the light of these explanatory clauses, it becomes instructive chiefly by its omissions. It is a description of "intelligence" from which all that makes intelligence intelligent has been expressly excluded as nonessential. The terms used are as applicable to the behavior of a *paramecium* as to that of a man, to the activities of a trained flea as to those of an inventor, an engineer, an architect or a statesman. But, whatever be true of the *paramecia* or the fleas, we happen to know that, in the case of inventors and engineers, and even

[25] The passage in Bode's essay upon which I chiefly base this interpretation of his notion of "unconscious reference to the future," is the following: "The uniqueness of the conscious stimulus lies in the fact that the adaptive value of these nascent motor impulses becomes operative as the determining principle in the organization of the response. The response, for example, to 'sharp' or 'will cut' is reminiscent of an earlier reaction in which the organism engaged in certain defensive movements as the result of actual injury. That is, the response to 'sharp' is a nascent or incipient form of a response which at the time of its first occurrence was the expression of a maladaptation. . . . The character of the stimulus is determined by the adaptive value which the incipient activity would have if it were carried out." (*C.I.*, pp. 243–44.) I assume that the "reminiscence" in question need, for Professor Bode, to be more conscious than the future reference; and that, therefore, the "intelligent action" which he is describing would be sufficiently exemplified by any case of the formation of adaptive habits of response through the simplest process of trial and error, without either actual recall of past experiences or actual predelineation of future situations.

of statesmen, there is a "*conscious* reference to the future as future"; [26] and such conscious reference is a part of the essential differentia of that class of acts commonly regarded as "exhibitions of intelligence." An intelligent act, in short, is an act controlled by a plan; and a plan of action obviously relates, not merely in fact but by its explicit intent, to the not-yet-existent. It also, in so far as it is the fruit of reflection, involves an explicit reference to the no-longer-existent. "Imaginative recovery of the by-gone," Professor Dewey somewhere remarks, "is indispensable to successful invasion of the future." That, of course, overstates the case, as the felicities of instinct and of acquired adaptive habits may remind us. But it is manifestly true that imaginative recovery of the past is indispensable to *intelligent* invasion of the future. Thus the familiar and characteristic form of human "response to situations" which is known as planning consists essentially in two paradoxical-sounding processes—in the two-fold "present-ation" of the not-present. The "function of effective reflection" is performed only where there is both a partial reconstruction of the past and a partial pre-construction of the future. The principal constituents of the planning-experience are things which, though in a sense present in that experience, are—to use a happy phrase of

[26] I note in passing the odd circumstance that Professor Bode, even while offering a definition of "consciousness," refers to something else, also called "consciousness," which is excluded from that definition. In substance his formula reduces to the following: "Conscious behavior is behavior determined by a reference to future consequences, but not necessarily by a conscious reference." This, I suspect, is more than an accidental verbal slip; the inconsistent use of terms arises naturally from an error of fact in the analysis.

Professor Dewey's—"present-as-absent." For, as Professor Dewey justly adds, "we must not balk at a purely verbal difficulty. It suggests a verbal inconsistency to speak of a thing present-as-absent. But all ideal contents, all aims (that is, things aimed at), are present in just such fashion. Things can be presented as absent, just as they can be presented as hard or soft, black of white."[27] Thus Professor Bode would have truly described the process of intelligence if he had taken his first formulation of it quite literally, without the subsequent qualifications by which he renders it false to the observable fact. Reflection about a plan of action *is* in a certain sense, "a conversion of possible future results or consequences into present existences."

But if the meaning of this fact be considered, it should become evident that the pragmatists' attempt to avoid psychophysical dualism, while at the same time affirming the efficacy of "intelligence," has broken down. For in what sense is the future "converted into a present existence" at the moment of practical reflection? Not, obviously, in a physical sense; the "things aimed at" are not at that moment included among the contents of the physical system. If physical science were able to take a complete inventory of that system at the moment in question, it would find therein no "future existences" and no "results which have not yet occurred." There would be such and such a number of particles, acted upon by such and such forces, disposed in certain spatial groupings, and moving in various determinate

[27] *Influence of Darwin, etc.*, p. 103. I have discussed the epistemological bearing of this pregnant remark of Dewey's at some length in my contribution to *Essays in Critical Realism.*

directions. None of the particles, nor of the forces, nor of the movements (*pace,* with respect to the last, the theory of relativity) would bear either tomorrow's or yesterday's date. Doubtless, "yesterday this day's madness did *prepare*"*;* but it was not, either in existence, or in kind or "essence," that which it prepared. The category of "presence-as-absent" is foreign to the vocabulary of physical description. The material universe, at a given time, consists of things that *are* at that time, at particular places in space—not of things that have been or are possibly going to be, and are at no particular place in space. Literally "em-*bodied*" in present experience, "contingent future results" can not be said to be, without completely falsifying the concept of body, as held either by common-sense or by natural science.

On the other hand, it is, as we have already reminded ourselves, of the essence of a plan that it shall be made up largely of elements that do not now exist. Yet there is no paradox in this, nor need we talk mystically of it, as if the thing were a "miracle." For the sense in which the elements of a plan of action are present is different from the sense in which they are not present—are past or future; and this distinction of senses has been perfectly familiar and easy to the entire human race with the exception (apparently) of some very primitive peoples and certain recent groups of philosophers. "Present" the future results are, in so far as they are elements in the experience of the planner at the moment of planning, and are at that moment, as Professor Bode has said, functioning as stimuli to present behavior. "Present" the future results as obviously are not, in the sense that the anticipated or desired outcome is already a fact of that external order into which the planner intends to introduce it. A plan of physical action would not be a *plan* of action, if that which it contemplates existed, or were already going on, in the physical world; for a plan requires to be "realized." To realize, in the meaning in which the term has when used in this connection by common sense, is to *physicalize*—to act upon matter in such a way that the relative positions or configuration of things which was formerly but a dream, a hope, a purpose, takes its place among the solid, stubborn, noncontingent, public facts of the sensible world.

Thus it is only in consequence of an incomplete analysis of the nature of practical reflection and intelligent action that pragmatists have been able to avoid giving what Professor Bode calls a "subjectivistic or psychical interpretation" to those functions. They have failed to see that a plan of action *must* be a "psychic existence," in a perfectly definite and intelligible sense. There is, be it noted, no mystery about the meaning of the terms "mental," "psychic," "subjective." A thing is a "mental entity" if it is actually given at any moment in any context of experience, but can not be regarded as forming a part, at the same moment, of the complex of masses and forces, in a single, "public" space, which constitutes the world of physical science. But if plans of action are, or include, in this sense, mental elements, and are also—as the pragmatists assert—genuine causes or determinants of physical events, it follows that, rightly construed and consistently thought through, pragmatism means interactionism.[28]

[28] Neorealists will, no doubt, at this point take refuge in the grateful

A plan of action, however, as we are rightly reminded by pragmatists, is not, as some of the foregoing expressions might seem to imply, a static thing. We may, for purposes of analysis, take a temporal cross-section of the planning-experience, may view it as—what, at any given moment, it is—a complex of content made up of such and such elements. But as a whole it is essentially a process, a sequence of complexes constantly developing one into another. And the process is, as Professor Bode has observed, one of "progressive organization" having a "selective or teleological character." The plan itself and the measures for its realization are gradually built up, through the bringing together of such thought-material as is recognized as having relevancy "to the business in hand," and through the deliberate selection of some possible and nascent responses and the neglect or conscious repression of others. What are the "causes" which control—or which, at all events, seem to the subject to control—this process of selection and organization? In other words, what are the constant correlations of factors discoverable in the process, and what is the nature of the factors correlated? By virtue of what property or relation does one possible bit of content get attended to, taken account of, perhaps taken up into the organized plan itself, while other bits are ignored or eventually excluded? For an answer we have but to recall examples of the way in which "creative intelligence" actually operates.

An architect, for example, is called upon to design a group

---

obscurity of the conception of "neutral entities." As I have dealt elsewhere with that conception I shall not consider it here. It is not, at any rate—so far as I know—usually accepted by pragmatists.

of college buildings for a given site. Considering the uses to which the buildings are to be put, the character of the site, etc., he decides that the style of architecture to be adopted must not be "monumental," must be "flexible" and capable of an extensive variety and irregularity in size, elevations and ground-plans, and must permit the use of a certain local stone. With these criteria in mind he reviews the historic styles and, rejecting all of those now in fashion, decides upon the "rustic" Renaissance architecture of northern Italy. In such a typical process of planning can the determinants of the sequences be properly said to be exclusively either "physical" things or "physical" forces? Not if the adjective is used with definite meaning, and if, at the same time, we avoid confusing the attributes of one moment or situation with earlier or later ones. The "cause" of the behavior of a material system at a given moment is stated by physical science ultimately in terms of the masses, positions, velocities, electrical charges, of that system relatively to other existing masses or particles (and of its chemical composition, in so far as this is not yet reducible to the former terms), at the same moment or the immediately antecedent moment. In no such terms can planning be described. The controlling factors in the whole process by which the architect first defined his criteria, then by means of them selected his style, and finally worked out his detailed designs, were presentations of physically nonexistent things, of future possible results and of past experiences taken as throwing light upon future results. With these purely ideal, and at first highly general and abstract, models, every potential element of the final plan was compared;

and its adoption or nonadoption depended upon the nature of the logical relations between its properties and those of the imagined, the not-yet-realized, consummation. To tell the architect that the true reason why his process of selection and organization took the course it did is adequately stated by giving, for each of a series of moments, the distances and mechanical relations between the molecules composing his body and other coexistent masses of matter—to tell him this is to talk what to him, at least, must appear obvious nonsense. However little or however great the efficacy of a plan as a force in the physical world, it is the inner developing logic of his purpose, not the laws of mechanics, that inevitably seems to the planner to determine what the plan itself shall include and how its elements shall be combined with one other. In the recognition of the relation of means to the end to be realized, and in the complex processes of logical analysis and inference which this may involve, the reflective agent is carried along from one momentary phase of experience to another by what may analogically be called "forces"; but, in so far, at least, as the process is what it purports to be, the nature of these forces is falsified as soon as the attempt is made to formulate them as functions of the space-relations of molecules or electrons. It is true that, as psychoanalysis is showing us, the agent is frequently mistaken as to the real determinants of his choices and even of the results of his "reasoning." But not even psychoanalysts, I take it, would generalize this conclusion so far as to make all planning and all reasoning a mere expression of unconscious impulses, which explicit intents and the recognition of facts and logical relations never either modify or supplement. So sweeping a generalization would, of course, render all reasoned conclusions meaningless, including those of the psychoanalyst.

Professor Bode, at any rate—as we have already seen—expressly accepts the assumption of the distinctiveness of the determinants controlling the sequences which constitute "intelligence." He emphatically repudiates the notion that those sequences "are nothing more than an interesting indication of the way in which the neural machinery is operating" and that "the progress of an argument is in no way controlled or directed by the end in view, or by considerations of logical coherence, but by the impact of causation." But this again—when conjoined with the pragmatist's affirmation of the physical efficacy of intelligence—must be recognized to mean psychophysical interactionism; since "ends in view" are, before their realization, "mental" or ideal, i.e., nonphysical, things, and since "considerations of logical coherence" are not among the forces, or determinants of the relative motion of bodies, of which physics and chemistry take account in their formulas. The view to which Professor Bode commits himself, and which seems to be the typical pragmatic view, either excludes the idea of causation altogether from purposive action, or else it must finally "interpolate mental links into the causal chain."

Thus, whether we consider the "creative intelligence" of pragmatism analytically or dynamically, as a state or as a sequence controlled by certain distinguishable causes, the interactionist implications of the conception are evident. Fundamentally—to sum up—the doctrine of instrumentalism, in the present stage of its development, is a revolt against that strange nineteenth-century aberration, epiphenomenalism—a result, however, which can not maintain itself without an alliance with an honestly dualistic conception of the psychophysical relation. Pragmatism insists that, whatever philosophical propositions be true, one class of propositions must certainly be false—all those, namely, which either assert or imply that human intelligence has no part, or no distinctive part, in the control of physical events and bodily movements, in the modification of environment, or in the actual determination, from moment to moment, of any of the content of reality. That man is a real agent—and that the distinctive character of his agency consists in the part played therein by the imaginative recovery and analysis of a now physically nonexistent past and the imaginative prevision of a physically nonexistent future—these are the first articles of any consistently pragmatic creed. Such a creed is simply a return to sanity; for these two theses are the common and constant presuppositions of the entire business of life. Never, surely, did a sillier or more self-stultifying idea enter the human mind, than the idea that thinking as such—that is to say, remembering, planning, reasoning, forecasting—is a vast irrelevancy, having no part in the causation of man's behavior or in the shaping of his fortunes—a mysterious redundancy in a cosmos which would follow precisely the same course without it. Nobody at a moment of reflective action, it may be suspected, ever really believed this to be true; and even the composing and publishing of arguments for parallelism is a kind of reflective action.

VIII

PRAGMATISM AND THE NEW MATERIALISM *

One of the most striking phenomena in recent American philosophy and psychology has, manifestly, been an extensive recrudescence of materialism. To or toward this outcome have converged several theories diverse in name and, in part, in the considerations which have given rise to them. The tendency finds its most unequivocal expression in behaviorism, whenever behaviorism, as in the later writings of Professor J. B. Watson, abandons the modest status of a special subdivision of experimental biology, and sets itself up as—or as a substitute for—a general psychological theory. To say that in the processes commonly known as sensation, feeling, and thought nothing whatever occurs, or need be presupposed, except gross or microscopic movements of various portions of the musculature of an organism is obviously equivalent to the reduction of the entire content and implications of experience to motions of matter and transfers of physical energy. In some of the American forms of neorealism a scarcely less thorough-going materialism has been manifest, so far as the

* First published in *The Journal of Philosophy*, Vol. XIX, Jan. 5, 1922.

world of concrete existence is concerned; though the tendency here has been curiously conjoined with a revival of a species—a very unplatonic species—of "Platonic realism." In most of our neorealists, the latter seems an essentially otiose addition to their doctrine. Universals are asserted to "subsist" merely; and though subsistence is declared to be a status independent of consciousness, this independence renders it only the more alien to nature and irrelevant to experience. Since *mere* subsistents have neither date, nor place, nor causal efficacy, they are pertinent to the phenomenal order only in so far as they are embodied in particular existences; and by the neorealist their embodiment is apparently construed in the literal sense of the word. For him too the only entities existing in time and in the causal nexus are physical bodies, and—if the two be ultimately distinct—physical energy.

American pragmatism has often manifested a disposition to join forces with behaviorism and neorealism in their campaign against the belief in the reality of psychical entities; indeed, if certain utterances of its spokesmen be considered separately—apart from certain other utterances which to the uninitiated appear simply to contradict them—no contemporary philosophical school has given plainer expression to the materialistic doctrine. In a recent paper in this Journal [1] I cited several instances of this sort; one of them it is pertinent to repeat here:

> A careful inventory of our assets brings to light no such entities as those which have been placed to our credit. We do not find body and object and consciousness, but only

[1] *Journal of Philosophy,* XVII (1920), pp. 589–96 and 622–32.

body and object. . . . The process of intelligence is something that goes on, not in our mind, but in things. . . . Even abstract ideas do not compel the adoption of a peculiarly "spiritual" or "psychic" existence, in the form of unanalyzable meanings.[2]

In the paper mentioned I attempted to show, among other things, that this materialistic strain is incongruous with the most characteristic and essential thesis of pragmatism in its latest formulations. That thesis is to the effect that "intelligence" is efficacious and "creative." By "intelligence" the pragmatist appears to mean nothing mysterious or metaphysical; the word is for him merely a name for a familiar type of experience, that, for him merely of practical reflection, of forming plans of action for dealing with specific concrete situations. This process of reflection is, he maintains, in certain cases a determinant of motions of matter, i.e., of the movements of human bodies and of other masses with which they physically interact. But upon the materialistic hypothesis practical reflection itself is nothing but a motion of matter; if "bodies and (physical) objects" are the only factors involved in "intelligence," it should be possible to describe the phenomenon called "planning" wholly in physical terms—i.e., in terms of masses actually existing, of positions actually occupied, of molar or molecular movements actually occurring, *at the time when the planning is taking place.* The *laws* of that class of physical processes called "practical judgments" may, of course, be unique, incapable of reduction to the laws of physics or chemistry; and pragmatism declares that they are in fact thus unique and

[2] B. H. Bode, in *Creative Intelligence,* pp. 254–55, 245.

irreducible. But the things whose behavior these laws describe must—if the pragmatist is to avoid psychophysical dualism consist solely of real parts of the material world.

Now since "intelligence," in the pragmatist's sense, is an observable and analyzable phenomenon, the question whether any entities are involved in it which are *not* real parts of the material world is a question of empirical fact, to be settled by analysis of the specific type of experience under consideration. And in my previous paper I sought to show that this question must be answered in the affirmative. A plan of action, as I pointed out, obviously requires the presentation of both past and possible future states or contents of some part of the material world. But a past or possible future state of the material world is not, at the moment at which it is represented in the experience of the planner, a part of the real material world. The content of my memories or of my expectations, as such, would find no place in any inventory of then existing "bodies and objects" which would be drawn up even by a perfected physical science. It is of the very essence of the planning-experience that it is cognizant of and concerned with things, or configurations of things, which have yet to be physically realized, and are therefore not yet physically real. Thus in fixing his attention especially upon "intelligence" in its practical aspect, the pragmatist is brought face to face with that type of experience in which the empirical presence of nonphysical entities and processes is, perhaps, more plainly evident than in any other.

This fact, it may be remarked parenthetically, is the reason why I have thought it useful to select pragmatism as the immediate point of attack in a critical examination of the new materialism in general. The pragmatists have rendered a service to philosophers of all schools by directing attention to the significance of certain undeniably real aspects of the cognitive experience, which happen also to be the best possible touchstone for the determination of the issue between those who assert and those who deny the existence of psychical or immaterial entities. That issue has hitherto been discussed mainly in connection with the problem of perception; with that problem, in fact, the neorealists seem to have been somewhat obsessed. The believer in the presence of distinctively mental factors in the cognitive situation has not failed to meet the issue on this the favorite ground of his adversary. But in this part of the field the controversy, though not logically indecisive, has grown somewhat tedious and repetitious. There remains, meanwhile, a region of experience in which the dispute seems capable of being brought more speedily to a decisive conclusion; and it is with this region that the pragmatist is especially preoccupied. He is primarily interested, not in the question how we can know an external object, but in the question how one moment of experience can know and prepare for another moment. It is, in short, to what I have elsewhere named intertemporal cognitions that his analysis is devoted; it is by man's habit of looking before and after that he is chiefly impressed. Now to look before and after is to behold the physically nonexistent; it is to possess as data in experience objects or events which cannot be conceived to be *at that moment* existent in the material universe. Since, moreover, the pragmatist affirms the potency of intelligence, that is to say, of this function of foresight and recall, in the causation of (some) physical events, his philosophy, if consistently worked out, should lead him to an interactionist view upon the psycho-physical problem—in other words, to a dualistic view.

Such, in brief, was the argument previously set forth. To that argument Professor Bode has very courteously replied in an article in the *Journal of Philosophy*.[3] Certain phases, I will not say of pragmatism, but of the opinions and doctrinal affinities of pragmatists, are greatly illuminated by his paper, which is, moreover, manifestly inspired by a genuinely philosophic desire to co-operate in an endeavor to promote a common understanding. Nevertheless—such are the difficulties of philosophical discussion!—even this most generous and fair-minded of critics has apparently altogether overlooked the principal point of my argument; and the reasonings which he presents appear to me to be not only inconclusive, but almost wholly irrelevant to the particular issue upon which I had hoped to focus attention. Yet they are apparently believed by their author to controvert the conclusions I defended; and it seems needful, therefore, to examine carefully the chief considerations which Professor Bode contributes to the discussion.

1. A great part of his reply is devoted to an explanation of what the pragmatist means by "consciousness." He is not disposed wholly to reject this term; he too is ready to formulate, in his own way, a "differentia of the psychic" and a criterion "which makes it possible to draw a sharp line between conscious and mechanical behavior." This, of course, is of much interest in itself; but it has no pertinency to the

[3] *Journal of Philosophy*, XVIII (1921), pp. 10–17.

reasons for affirming the existence of "psychical" entities which were presented in my paper. To say that in the terminology of the instrumentalist "consciousness is identifiable with" such and such a "type of behavior," is equivalent to the two propositions (1) that by the word "consciousness" the instrumentalist means the defined type of behavior; (2) that such a type of behavior is empirically discoverable. The first, being a verbal proposition, requires no proof. The second is a proposition of fact and therefore subject to verification. But its truth might be conceded without the least logical detriment to the considerations which I had advanced. For I have not questioned the pragmatist's right to define the word "consciousness" as he likes; I have not denied that the "peculiar type of behavior" to which Professor Bode prefers to apply that name *is* a fact of experience; and I have not maintained that this type of behavior affords evidence that "mental entities," in my sense of the term, exist. What I have maintained is that there is *also* found in human experience a phenomenon differing in certain important respects from that which Professor Bode describes; and that this does afford evidence of the existence of mental entities. This other sort of experience, exemplified in planning and all forms of practical reflection, is what I had supposed the pragmatist to mean by "intelligence"; but I am less interested in ascertaining the pragmatic name for the thing than in pointing out that the thing is a fact. Throughout most of his paper, then, Professor Bode, instead of looking at the evidence offered for this conclusion, which he ostensibly rejects, appears to fix his gaze upon another subject altogether. Let me show this in detail by outlining more specifically the pragmatic account of "consciousness," as set forth by him. The pragmatist observes that some stimuli are of a "peculiar kind," i.e., have specific characteristics which others lack. For example, a noise in some cases has, in addition to the "various properties or qualities that are appropriate subject-matter for the physicist, a further trait or quality" of which the physicist takes no cognizance. This further trait is, it appears, an "elusive" one, difficult to express in words; but its nature is indicated by such expressions as "an indescribable 'what-is-it' quality," an "inherent incompleteness." When a noise possesses, besides its mere noisiness, this special and unique quality, it "causes the individual concerned to cock his ear, to turn his eyes, perhaps to step to the window in order to ascertain the meaning of the noise." Stimuli (a term which is for Bode apparently synonymous with any complexes of sensible qualities) are, then, said to be "conscious" if they have this peculiarity; and "consciousness" is a name for the "function of a quality in giving direction to behavior." The conscious stimulus, in other words, is differentiated by its tendency "to set on foot activities which are directed towards getting a better stimulus." The word "directed" here, however, must not be understood to imply any representation of the better stimulus *as* future; for a reaction possesses the "psychical" character "irrespective of any explicit reference to the future." There need be no actual anticipation of the "conceptual" sort. Any case of organic response which exhibits the phenomenon of trial-and-error would apparently exemplify "conscious" behavior, in the pragmatist's sense; in fact I can not see that there is any kind of actual response which would not correspond to the definition.

There are—it may be observed incidentally—some inconveniences in using the words "psychical," "mental," etc., in this manner. One of them is that "psychical" apparently does not exclude "physical." If I understand Bode's language, a real physical object would also be a "psychical existence" whenever it "sets on foot activities directed towards getting a better stimulus." It is also a somewhat confusing feature of this usage that the adjectives "conscious," "psychical," etc., seem applicable both to stimuli and to the bodily behavior which the stimuli evoke, though it is difficult to see how they can be attached to both substantives univocally.

This, however, is by the way. What I wish to point out is that my argument rested entirely upon an analysis of the particular kind of reaction in which there *is* an "explicit reference to the future"—in which actual foresight is an essential feature of the experience. By transferring the adjective "psychical" to a kind of reaction defined as lacking this feature, Professor Bode does not answer that argument; he simply ignores it. Is it a fact that explicit reference to the future sometimes occurs, that when we form a plan of action unrealized possibilities are present as unrealized possibilities to our thought? Or again, is it a fact that when we think of such unrealized concrete possibilities we have present in thought objects which can not be regarded as parts of the present content of the material world? Only by answering the first of these questions in the negative, or, if that were answered affirmatively, then by answering the second in the negative, could Bode join issue with the reasoning actually contained in the papers upon which he comments. A radical behaviorist, I suppose, would answer one or the other of these questions with an unequivocal negative. But it is not clear from Professor Bode's article that he shares the behaviorist's fine a priori contempt for the facts of experience.

2. There is, however, a further aspect of the pragmatist's conception of "conscious behavior" which is not fully brought out in the summary above given; and this we must now examine, since it is this aspect chiefly which makes it clear "why instrumentalism is so reluctant to bring in mental states or psychic existences." (The latter expression is presumably here used in the sense defined in my previous papers; for Professor Bode has just told us that in another sense, pragmatism itself recognizes psychic existences.)

The argument, if I have understood it, rests upon a distinctive thesis about the attributes of "objects." The pragmatist, it would seem, holds that what are usually called the effects of a stimulus upon an organism should properly be called "parts" of the stimulus, or attributes of the object (for Bode apparently uses the two terms interchangeably). In the case of a noise which causes a dog to cock his ear, the attribute of causing-ear-cocking, "by which the present stimulus makes provision for its own successor," is designated in pragmatist terminology the "incompleteness" of the present stimulus; and this "incompleteness is intrinsic to the stimulus, or inherent in it"; in other words, it is "as much a part of the noise as any of its other traits." Since the behavior resulting, or capable of resulting, from a given stimulus is thus read back into the stimulus itself, and since the stimulus in turn is identified with physical objects (and, in the case of perception, apparently with *the* physical object perceived), there results for the pragmatist a radical revision of the conception of physical objects. "Traditional theory" has been wont to regard such an object as "characterized by stark rigidity and close-clipped edges"; to the pragmatist, on the contrary, it seems to be a soft and plastic entity with boundaries so wide that almost anything might be found within them. The notion of the "inherent properties of an object" is thus so enlarged as to include either (Bode does not seem to me to be clear here) all organic responses which the object's presence ever evokes, or, at any rate, an inherent *tendency* to evoke whatever responses in fact occur when it is present. Physical objects are consequently things which can control behavior directly, by virtue of their own nature and attributes; and it therefore becomes unnecessary to introduce mental entities in the explanation of behavior, in man or other animals. "The emphasis shifts inevitably from mental states in the traditional sense to this peculiar type of control as exercised by *objects*."[4] It is precisely because pragmatism has become aware of "this distinctive character of the stimulus" that it "can not afford to give countenance to entities or existences the chief purpose of which," as it seems to Professor Bode, is to obscure this character—to "translate it into mechanical equivalents."

To judge of the pertinency of this reasoning it is needful to recall once more—however wearisome the repetition—the precise argument against which it is supposed to be directed. That argument, it will be remembered, (*a*) dealt exclusively

[4] *Op. cit.*, p. 15; italics in original.

with the evidence for the existence of nonphysical entities to be found *in a particular phase of human experience,* viz., in intelligent planning, involving an explicit representation of things past and future: (*b*) used the expressions "psychical" or "non-physical entity" *in a specific and clearly defined sense,* viz., as meaning "an entity not assignable to real space and to the complex of matter and forces recognized by the physical sciences, at the moment at which the entity is actually present in experience." The reasoning offered as the principal reply to this argument (*a*) still wholly ignores the specific type of experience to which the argument related. It offers, not an analysis of anticipation and memory, but an analysis of sensory stimulation. I ask the pragmatist about "intelligence," and am given a description of responses for which no intelligence is requisite. I ask what precisely it is that happens when an architect plans a building, or when an engineer endeavors to analyze the defects in the design which explain the collapse of the St. Lawrence bridge several years ago; Professor Bode replies by telling me what it is that happens when a dog cocks his ear. As described, moreover, "conscious behavior" is not distinguishable from the kind of phenomenon which occurs when a phototropic plant is touched by a ray of light. In the case of the plant also the initial stimulus "makes provision for its own successor" and "sets on foot activities directed towards getting a better stimulus." (*b*) With respect to the question, irrelevant to my argument, with which Bode's reply is actually concerned, his conclusion is reached by a series of partly explicit and partly tacit alterations in the meanings of terms. He first includes the adaptive motor-responses to a sensation among the "traits" of the sense-datum itself; he next tacitly identifies the sense-datum ("the noise as heard") with the "stimulus" (which in the ordinary use of terms means, in the case of audition, the air wave set up by the vibration of an elastic body); he then identifies the stimulus with the "object"—presumably the object from which it proceeds, e.g., an automobile-horn. By this process of freely substituting one meaning for another, it is assuredly not difficult to prove that the dog's cocking his ear is merely an instance of "the control of behavior by objects." But the entire argument is of an essentially verbal character; and the first two steps in it—the identification of responses with sense-data, and of sense-data with external stimuli—beg the only question to which the argument can be said to be directed. For that question is whether sensory content *is* totally identical with either the stimulus or the physical state of the sensory nerves; and whether the stimulation passes over into a motor response without the generation or interposition, anywhere in the process, of any factor which is not "physical" in the ordinary sense, previously defined. That is a question of fact which is hardly to be settled by the short and easy method of *defining* physical objects *ab initio* as having an inherent *virtus excitativa* sufficient of itself to account for "intelligent" behavior.

What might at first be taken for a further distinct argument against psychophysical dualism and interactionism is suggested by Professor Bode's repeated remark that those doctrines imply a "mechanistic" conception of behavior. "Unless we abandon the category of interactionism we are back on the level of mechanistic naturalism, from which the position of instrumentalism is intended to provide a means of escape." But it is obvious that the adjective "mechanistic" must here be used in some peculiar sense; for nothing is more alien to "mechanistic naturalism," as that designation is usually understood, than the doctrine that nonphysical entities or processes can affect the movements of bodies. When, then, we seek to determine precisely what Bode means by "mechanistic," we find that the word apparently denotes any view which regards as incorrect or insufficient the account of the "distinctive nature of conscious behavior" given by the pragmatist. "Mechanical behavior," in short, is expressly antithetic to "conscious behavior," in the pragmatist's sense; and "conscious behavior" in his sense means, as we have seen, behavior controlled by physical objects directly, by virtue of their "inherent incompleteness"—this last expression, in turn, meaning a capacity to initiate in an organism (without the intervention of any other factors) a series of adaptive responses. In brief, the charge that psychological interactionism is "mechanistic" means, when translated, that that doctrine affirms the presence and efficacy of factors other than physical objects in at least some modes of human behavior. The charge, in short, is that interactionism is—interactionism. There is here, therefore, no argument which seems to demand separate discussion.

3. After having, through nearly all of his article, vigorously assailed the belief in mental or psychical entities (in my sense of the terms), Professor Bode in his penultimate paragraph suddenly and surprisingly utters a profession of faith in the creed which he had seemed to be attacking. "We need not," he writes, "take serious exception to Lovejoy's

contention that concepts are 'mental entities,' in the sense that they may be 'actually given . . . but can not be regarded as forming a part, at the same moment, of the complex of masses and forces, in a single public space, which constitutes the world of physical science.' That concepts exist in some form and that there is a discernible difference between them and physical objects is an indubitable fact." These "concepts," moreover, are functional. "They function in much the same way as physical objects;" they "control behavior." Here, it will be observed, it is explicitly in the sense which I had given to "mental" that Professor Bode grants the reality of mental entities. He adds, it is true, that "the important issue is not whether concepts exist, but whether the classification of them as 'mental' is to be made to accord with the foregoing (i.e., the pragmatic) theory of conscious behavior." This might be taken to mean that, after all, he regards "concepts" as "mental" solely in the pragmatic sense, not in the sense given in the definition which he quotes from my paper. But to construe his meaning thus would be to imply that he denies in one sentence what he had affirmed two sentences before; and no such interpretation, happily, is necessary. For a "concept"—i.e., an "idea"—e.g.—a representation of a building yet to be erected, may be "mental" *both* in the sense expressed by my definition and in a sense which includes at least the distinctive positive differentia of the "psychical" in the pragmatic definition. A nonphysical factor in experience may—and if it be efficacious, must—*function* like any other stimulus. The idea of the house to be built will necessarily have what Bode calls an "unfinished quality;" it too will be "directed towards the end of completing the present incompleteness." But its possession of this character does not alter the fact that, unlike other possible varieties of "psychical" stimuli—in the pragmatic meaning of the term—it consists in a representation of a future object, and is therefore "psychical" in another sense, a sense which excludes it from the class of physical things existing, i.e., of things belonging to the objective spatial system.

Professor Bode, then, though he has elsewhere represented the psychical as merely a special variety of the physical, now seems to tell us plainly (*a*) that there are two distinct classes of factors in our experience, "physical objects" and "mental entities;" (*b*) that both are efficacious in the causation of physical changes. These two propositions taken together seem to constitute the plainest possible affirmation of psychophysical dualism and interactionism—as, I take it, those terms are commonly understood. Yet the same passage concludes: "There is no ground for Lovejoy's contention that, if concepts are admitted to their legitimate place, it follows that, rightly construed and consistently thought through, pragmatism means interactionism." Here I must confess myself baffled. How this conclusion is to be reconciled with the admissions which immediately precede it, I am unable to conjecture. I therefore can not feel that Professor Bode has succeeded in making his position, or that of pragmatists in general, unmistakably clear. After careful study of his paper, I remain in some doubt whether he holds that pragmatism implies materialism or not.

It still seems to me desirable, however, that the matter should be made clear, and that pragmatists (not to speak of others) should actually give some consideration to the reasons offered in support of the view that the pragmatic doctrine of the efficacy of intelligence properly implies psychophysical dualism and interactionism. And in the hope that Professor Bode himself, or others of the same way of thinking, may again deal with the subject, I venture, by way of conclusion and résumé, to set down a few questions to which I think it would be illuminating to have clear answers. (1) Does the pragmatist hold that only physical things exist, i.e., that they alone are disclosed by, or present as factors in, experience ("physical" meaning "occupying a position in objective space and existing as a part of the sum of masses and forces dealt with by physical science")? (2) Is it not a fact that in the formation of intelligent plans of action there are involved both "imaginative recovery of the bygone" and imaginative anticipation of objects and situations not yet physically realized? (3) If so, can every bit of the content presented in the two types of experience just mentioned be regarded as forming a real part of the physical world, as constituted at the moment of such experience? (4) If so, *where* in that world, and in what form or manner, does the "bygone" that is "imaginatively recovered," or the future that is not yet realized, exist? (5) If it does exist physically at the moment of the experience of planning precisely what is meant by calling it "bygone" or "future"? To the last four of these questions I can not but think that all partisans of the new materialism might profitably address themselves.

IX

THE ANOMALY OF KNOWLEDGE *

I

There are two or three familiar ways of distinguishing the province of philosophy from that of the other sciences which, though not untrue, conceal an important part of the truth. The most generally prevalent notion of the matter, I suppose, is that philosophers constitute a variety of the human species characterized by a peculiar craving for comprehensive generalizations, for *vues d'ensemble*—that they are men who cannot rest content with fragments, with partially unified knowledge, but demand a synoptic vision of the nature and meaning of things as a whole. According to another account, the philosopher is primarily distinguished, not by the greater breadth of generalization of the knowledge that he seeks, but by its logical priority. The questions which it is most characteristic of him to ask are not the last but the first questions. He scrutinizes long and critically the tools which the special sciences unhesitatingly use and raises more exigent doubts than either science or common sense are wont to face. The trait distinc-

* First published in the University of California *Publications in Philosophy,* IV (1923), pp. 3–43.

tive of his intellectual temperament is—to change the figure —conceived to be an obsessing curiosity and concern about the *foundations* of his structure of belief, and consequently a more far-reaching and resolute skepticism than is natural to the generality of our easy-going kind or is customary with those who build the towering superstructures of science. Or again, the philosopher is sometimes said to have, not, indeed, for his only province, but for his most characteristic and perhaps his only permanently inalienable province, the realm of values, especially of moral and aesthetic values. While the natural sciences represent man's attempt to correct, to systematize, and to extend his judgment of fact, his knowledge of things as they are—or, in the case of the applied sciences, to discover the best means to desired ends—philosophy alone, we are told, is mindful that men also, constantly and irrepressibly, make judgments of worth; that these too require correction, systematization, and extension; that the criticism of ends is not less a part of the life of a rational animal than the intelligent choice of means; and that the question of ultimate human interest is the question how the good stands related in this world of ours to the real, how far values have a basis and a backing beyond the transient likings and dislikings of our feeble race.

One or another, and in not a few cases all three, of these accounts truly enough describe propensities and preoccupations of those whom it has been customary to call philosophers. Yet I think the effect of the emphasis upon these aspects of the philosopher's business, and especially upon the first two, has not been wholly fortunate. That business is made to appear very widely different in kind, and in temper, and in its pretensions, from the work of the scientific investigator; and the philosopher has often, I suspect, had to his scientific *confreres* the look of a rather queer fellow, either dangerously disposed to hasty generalization; or else full of barren doubts and hesitancies about things that all other men take for granted, and have so taken for ages with the happiest results; or else so infected with moralistic preoccupations, so eager to find the edifying in the real, that his inquiries into any question about reality are open to the gravest suspicions of emotional bias. However unjust such conceptions of most philosophers and most philosophy may be, they have, I think, some currency; and while I should not wish to see the philosopher abandon these three interests, or abdicate his claim to these provinces of thought, I think it may help to make him more intelligible to other animals of his species, and especially to workers in the natural sciences, to point out another aspect of his business which is hardly made evident by the accounts of the field and purpose of philosophical inquiry that I have mentioned. There is, I suggest, a special class of empirical matters-of-fact which—with one possible and ambiguous exception—none of the other sciences investigates or is, for reasons which will presently appear, in a position to investigate. And this class of empirical matters-of-fact constitutes the starting point and primary subject-matter of the sort of philosophy with which I am here concerned. The philosopher, as I conceive of him, is first of all a man whose interest and desire to understand have been aroused by a certain biological phenomenon, and who therefore becomes a specialist in the study of that type of phenomenon. Doubtless he should be more than that; but he ought never, I think, to be less; and in any case, that is what many modern philosophers essentially are.

The class of biological phenomena to which I refer is that consisting of making judgments about things, having doubts about them, having knowledge about them. Whatever more knowing may be, it is on the face of it, and in the first instance, a phenomenon sometimes occurring in the life of the organism man, a function of which the featherless biped is capable; and it is as such, and without other preconceptions than those of the man of science, that the philosopher does well to approach it. Its empirical occurrence is at least as certain as the occurrence of any other phenomenon; for being certain of anything either is or purports to be an instance of this phenomenon. Its occurrence is, indeed, more certain than that of any other phenomenon; for being *un*certain is also a variety of the same species of biological happening. In other words, knowing is a natural event that is taken for granted by biology and all the other sciences. But it is not *investigated* by biology, or by any of the natural sciences, with the dubious exception of psychology. The psychologist might but usually does not investigate it with thoroughness. Clearly, then, there is here a class of facts which it ought to be somebody's business methodically to describe, to analyze, to correlate with other facts. That business has historically fallen, and still falls, to the lot of the persons conventionally described as philosophers; and discussions relating to these matters form pretty certainly, I think, the most voluminous and characteristic part of contemporary philosophical literature.

The primary relation, then, of the philosopher to other men, including biologists or other specialists, is much the same as the relation of the biologist to his infusoria or other organisms, of the geologist to the processes of rock formation, of the astronomer to the celestial bodies and their motions. The biologist observes the infusoria and endeavors to reach conclusions concerning the nature of their activities and what is implied by them; the philosopher may be said to observe the biologist—or any other creature that is supposed to know anything—to ascertain precisely what it is that *he* is doing *when* he is reaching conclusions, and what is implied therein–not in the specific conclusions, but in the fact that he reaches them, and that, if there be any science at all, some of them constitute what we call knowledge.

There has, it is true, taken place in recent philosophy a curious revulsion against the customary name of this special inquiry into knowledge, and to some degree, also, a revulsion against the inquiry itself. Epistemology has become a word taboo among certain circles of—shall I say?—epistemologists. A former lecturer on the Mills Foundation writes as follows:

> The astronomer, the biologist, the chemist, the historian, the student of literature . . . are all engaged in increasing our knowledge of what our perceptions are and how they are related to one another. Their studies are not prefaced by an examination of how we perceive. They take their material as so much given stuff, and then proceed to tell us what, when so taken, they perceive it to be. If they are invited to examine first the mechanism of perception, they regard the invitation as impertinent and irrelevant. They

> have found such an examination unnecessary, and so believe that they can rightfully reject it. . . . The results of modern intellectual inquiry [have been built up] directly from considering the processes of perception, and also the results of those processes, without seeking any epistemological warrant for our procedure.[1]

Professor Woodbridge therefore deprecates epistemological inquiry into perception, and presumably into other modes of knowledge. Many scientific investigators, I suspect, have experienced a similar feeling of irritation at the curious preoccupation of philosophers with epistemology—their tendency to loiter in the vestibule of science, to spend their time in looking over the instruments of knowledge, instead of using them.

I refer to this state of mind in order to make it clear that the study of knowing of which I am speaking is not exactly the sort of thing that is referred to in the passage of Professor Woodbridge's which I have quoted; nor are the reasons for engaging in it the reasons which he rejects as invalid. I am not contending here that epistemology is a necessary propaedeutic to natural science, or that an experimentalist ought to await a license from the philosopher before entering upon his own business. Epistemology, as I conceive it, is not a preliminary and it is not a normative science; it is merely one descriptive or analytic science among others. But its results, when reached, will require correlation with those of the other sciences, will supplement and qualify their conclusions, will, perhaps, restrict gen-

[1] F. J. E. Woodbridge, "Perception and Epistemology," *Essays in Honor of William James* (1908), p. 142.

eralizations to which we might be led if we considered solely the data of those other sciences. Such a study of knowledge needs no more special or peculiar justification than any other study. Since knowing is an actual phenomenon presented in our experience, there is the same sort of reason for finding out what we can about it as there is for finding out about other things. The prosecution of epistemological inquiries is sufficiently justified by the undeniable fact that their subject matter exists—unless, indeed, it should be maintained that man, and man engaged in the function most characteristic of his species, is an animal less deserving of study than the *paramecium* or the dancing mouse.

The inquiry I speak of, then, should begin—where it will end is another question—with a plain descriptive account of what knowing is, what goes on when it occurs. Only it must be an account of *knowing*, and not of something which happens to be associated with it. And here certain obstacles to the serious study of this phenomenon have arisen through entirely natural and comprehensible causes. In the first place, since knowing is, in a sense, the thing we know best of all —since it is what all men are doing, or supposing themselves to do, during most of their waking life—it is difficult to arouse in most men, and, I sometimes think, especially difficult to arouse in men of science, sufficient intellectual detachment from this phenomenon to permit them to feel a philosophic wonder concerning it, or even to observe with particularity just what it is. Many collateral questions are, indeed, often raised with respect to it; but for the prime question: Precisely what am I doing when I know—or what should I be doing if I were correct in supposing myself in any given instance to know?—for this prime question it is often hard to get consideration. This is, I think, further due to two developments in the history of science which have tended to substitute for this question other questions which look like it but are not in reality the same. The first of these —a natural consequence of the legitimate custom of the physical scientist to forget the knowing he is engaged in and to fix his attention upon the object—is the substitution of a description of the physiological conditions of knowledge for a description of knowledge. I am not assuming at this point that a physical account of man's cognitive function cannot be given; I am merely pointing out that you certainly have not described a case of knowing when you have merely described the movement of a number of molecules, or still more minute units of matter, in the animal's brain and nervous system, with accompanying changes in their electrical charges. These movements may be conditions without which knowing cannot happen in the human organism; but to study them is to study the correlates of the phenomenon of knowing, not to observe and analyze the phenomenon itself. It is at least what it is experienced as being, though it may be more; and it is assuredly not experienced as being a movement of molecules under your cuticle or within your cranium. This is an awkward sort of remark to have to make; for some of my readers are sure to regard it as a truism too obvious to need mention, and others are likely, in these days, to regard it as an unintelligible philosophical prejudice. To the former I make my apologies; to the latter I address the suggestion that one of the pregnant causes of muddle in contemporary thought, especially in the case of some of those given to taking the name of "science" in vain, is precisely a tendency to treat things as being what they observably are not, by substituting a description of their causes or concomitants for a description of the things themselves—especially when the concomitants are readily amenable to the methods of investigation and the principles of "explanation" of the physical sciences, and the things themselves are not.

The other tendency in nineteenth-century scientific thought unfavorable to an appreciation of the nature of and necessity for a direct examination of the organic phenomenon of knowing has been observable in evolutionary, and especially Darwinian, biology and in the vogue of what is called "functionalism" in psychology. It is a tendency in a sense the reverse of the preceding—namely, to substitute the question what knowing *does* for the question what knowing *is* or consists in; to offer a description of the thing's effects and uses in lieu of a description of the thing itself. General surveys of organic evolution are accustomed to mention the gradual development of intelligence in the higher animals, culminating in the scientific and technological activities of man, and to point out the new adaptations and new ranges of physical action which this made possible. Such a study of the role of mind in evolution is assuredly of the highest interest and importance; but, once more, to tell how knowledge assists man, and possibly in its rudimentary forms some animals below him in the scale, in the struggle for existence is not to tell what knowing is—any more than giving the clinical picture of a patient suffering from an infection is equivalent to isolating and describing the microorganism responsible for his condition. No physiologist or pathologist would for a moment fall into the latter confusion; yet a good deal of what is written about the function of intellect as a late-evolved acquisition of organisms is, I think, somewhat affected by an analogous confusion. And one part of that rich melange of incongruous ideas commonly known as pragmatism apparently consists in setting up this confusion as a methodological principle. You are never to inquire what anything is, but only what it does, what its consequences are; pure descriptive analyses of temporal cross sections of reality are to be avoided, and the character of any datum of experience at a given moment is always to be stated in terms of some other experience in which it is to eventuate. The paradoxical consequences of such a program, if consistently carried out, are obvious; but of course it never is consistently carried out. It is used in practice only as a means of evading those particular problems of descriptive analysis, of telling just what is *there now*, in which some adherents of this school are not interested, or for avoiding consideration of those facts, such as the fact of knowledge itself, which seem incongruous with opinions to which these philosophers incline.

We are, then, to try to describe a case of knowing as such, to make explicit what it is that is happening while a given instance of this phenomenon in the life of the human organism is going on; and we are to avoid substituting for this question any of the collateral questions which I have been mentioning. By "knowledge" here is not meant perception of data immediately and sensibly present at the moment of experience to be considered, but "knowledge about" things not in that manner present; and to make the question more specific, we may take the instance of knowledge about a no-longer-existing object or a bygone event—whether it be a remembrance of a past experience of the knower, or an inferential reconstruction of a past situation, such as the historian and the geologist are supposed in some measure to achieve. We are not, however, be it understood, concerned with the process and grounds of the inference but only with its outcome. It at once becomes evident, when you examine such a case of knowing, that it is a happening of a highly anomalous sort, when considered from the point of view of the physical sciences, including biology; that it is a type of event which no other science assumes to occur in any of the objects of its study. A knowing of a past object or event manifestly consists in a species of presence, within the experience of some organism at a given moment, of an object which is not at the same moment present in nature—i.e., in the system which the so-called "natural" sciences investigate —though it *is* present in the system of which those sciences themselves, considered as phenomena, consist. Knowledge, in other words, is a kind of evocation of the absent, and, in the particular case in question, of the physically nonexistent. Suppose, for example, you collect a thousand persons of different ages, all of them educated in different places, into one room, and that you first get them all to attend to some present physical object perceptible to their senses. Even in this case it is not strictly true that their percepts of a given state of the object are simultaneous with the existence of that state; but ignoring this slight difference, we may say that the thousand observers are experiencing—whether directly or indirectly—objects and processes now going on in nature, in the space in which their bodies and organs of perception also are. But now let the thousand persons be called upon to remember each his first schoolhouse and the scenes and incidents of his first day in school. Thereupon there suddenly appears in the experience—that is, in the actual life as organisms—of these persons, a host of objects of memory—elements and aspects, probably for the most part visual aspects, of a thousand differing groups of animate and inanimate bodies and of their movements. But the world of the physical sciences is not at the same time suddenly augmented by this rich, chaotic, fleeting mass of new material. For no physical observation discloses to the investigator, watching the thousand silent human organisms, the presence of these memory-objects; and even if this were not true, the entities which such observation revealed would find no place in the system of physical science. These quasi-bodies, or substitutes for bodies, which have no mass, which are not bearers of energy, which jump about in space—at least in *some* space—in the most erratic and discontinuous manner, do not and should not *as such* figure in the analyses of the chemist or the equations of the physicist—even of the physicist since Einstein. True, the scientific investigator will presumably find some difference between the neural processes of the thousand persons in the case when they are directly perceiving an (approximately) coexistent object or event, and the case when they are remembering past objects or events. But what the thousand themselves are experiencing is not the neural processes; and the difference for them between the two cases is not stated, certainly is not exhaustively stated, in terms of the differences between the two neural processes. What they now have present in their environments are more or less confused and blurry visual aspects of schoolhouses, teachers, schoolmates. Of their actual environments, of the surroundings with which their organic life is now really occupied, these things are even more certainly a part than are the unperceived though temporally coexistent changes in nerve fibers and cerebral cortex.

The same is true, of course, of all objects, other than immediate sense-data, about which any science claims knowledge, when we consider these objects, not in themselves and as of their own date, but as items in the present experience of the man of science. Dinosaurs are happily extinct upon our globe, and therefore, so far as we know, they are not a part of the environment of present subhuman animals. But they are certainly in some sense a part of the environment of present geologists—in the two specific senses, namely, that the geologists have these creatures actually, though not sensibly, within their present fields of consciousness, are "referring to them," and that the geologists' reactions to the sense-impressions which they are at a given time receiving are modified by the presence of these other items in their content of experience. The effect, it is true, is curiosly unilateral; the dinosaur, by being known, now makes a difference to the geologist, but the geologist by knowing makes none, or none of the same kind, to the dinosaur; and the *kind* of difference which the dinosaur makes to the geologist is fortunately very unlike that which he would probably have made, if the two had physically, and not merely cognitively, coexisted. But the significant and anomalous fact remains that, when exercising the function of retrospective knowing, the organism has to do—and, since knowledge of the past is the guide of practice, has to do in a highly practical way—with things which are not physical realities at the time when the organism is a physical reality and while the knowing is going on. When a knowing animal first appeared in the course of evolution, many prior events and vanished objects, though in one sense remaining as past and irrecoverable as ever, were in another sense rescued from the maw of the all-devourer. In short, then, when you make a valid retrospective judgment, some bit of the past, as we say, comes "before you"; and it is *now* that it is before you; and nevertheless it is before you *as* past.

The same characteristic of the knowing experience is, of course, often put in other terms, which merely express a complementary aspect of the same fact. I have been speaking of the phenomenon of knowing with reference chiefly to the peculiar status of the objects known, as entities not at the moment of knowing to be found in physical nature, yet, somehow, quite unmistakably factors at that moment in a physical organism's total environment. Stated on the other hand as a function of the organism, knowing consists in a power which the organism has to reach beyond, to transcend, both the place and the date of its own existence as an observable object in nature. It is able to range up and down through time, annulling in some measure the transiency of things; to penetrate also into the world of the unborn and thereby to make it possible for the cognitive animal to be affected by events which have not yet happened and to adapt itself to things that have not yet entered into nature—though, happily no doubt, it possesses a far more limited vision in that temporal region than we commonly believe it to have in the region of the past. Whatever the specific content of knowing, in whatever direction of time or space it is, in any given instance, turned, it proves to be generically an organic process characterized by a reference to, an evocation and apprehension of, a spatial and temporal Beyond, to which the physical sciences offer us no counterpart among the phenomena which they describe. This, I repeat, is not presented as a theory or an inference, but as a mere description, and a description of the obvious—but not of the unimportant. If there is any such thing as knowing, then that is what it is; whenever anyone asserts that he has a knowledge of anything more than the blank, momentary, uncorrelated content of his present sensations (which we do not usually term knowledge), he is asserting as a fact the occurrence of the type of organic phenomenon which I have been describing. To recognize this simply *as* a fact, an empirical datum, and as a fact which constitutes a prima facie anomaly among the phenomena of nature is, as it seems to me, the beginning of wisdom in philosophy; to endeavor to connect the fact intelligibly with other facts, to elucidate and, if possible, to alleviate the anomaly is a large part of the philosopher's task. "Just why and how," writes W. P. Montague, "a system of mere cerebral molecules should have this self-transcending reference is in my opinion the key-problem of philosophy." Though I do not find Montague's very original and ingenious solution of the problem satisfactory, I am entirely at one with him in this emphasis upon the primacy and decisiveness of the problem itself.[2]

[2] Montague observes that in causality there is a similar relation of present and past. A prior event may be in some sense said to be

It will, however, already have been perceived that the apparent anomaly of knowledge of which I have been speaking is really twofold—that there is a lesser and a greater anomaly. These should now be formally distinguished. (1) The lesser anomaly is the one which arises when you view the phenomenon of knowing from the standpoint of physical science; and it consists in the fact that there exists an organism, itself physical, which at some moments of its life has as items in its experience, as factors in its environment, things that are not, at those moments, any part of the sum of masses and motions and forces which for the natural sciences then constitute the physical world. That fact is so queer and troublesome to a good many contemporaries who have been trained in the categories and presuppositions of natural science, that they feel the strongest possible repugnance to admitting it—and in some cases may be seen denying on purely a priori grounds that it is a fact. To the consideration of these bold and simple methods for getting rid of the lesser anomaly we shall return presently. (2) The greater anomaly consists in that peculiarity of knowing which philosophers call "meaning" or "transcendent reference"; that is, in the fact that when we know we appear somehow to have within the field of our experience at a given moment objects which we must at the same time conceive as existing

present in its effects; and thus in any organic response the organism is really concerned with past (and with future) entities or events. Finding, then, a certain analogy between knowing and a relation which pervades all nature, Montague boldly identifies cognition and causation. Unfortunately the analogy breaks down at the critical point. A cause is *not,* as such, recalled or "represented" in its effects in the *same* sense in which a past experience is recalled in memory. We do not, for example, always remember the errors from which we suffer.

entirely outside of that field—for example, as having their being at a time other than the time of the knowing of them. The anomaly here, at first sight, and so long as the philosopher is able to offer no conceptual device for alleviating it, seems to look much like a logical paradox. It is not merely that, in knowing, some organisms deal with entities which are not *physically* coexistent with the organisms themselves, or with their present exercise of the knowing function; the greater anomaly is that these entities—at least in the case of retrospective and anticipatory knowledge—must apparently be said not to coexist *at all* with the organism, or with the particular exercise of the cognitive function through which they are known. Yet how can I in any way have to do today with that which does not exist today, which is not a reality contemporaneous with myself? How can a being whose activities are all in a fleeting present, and the entire sum of whose knowings falls temporally within a brief span of years, really behold that which was ages before it or shall be decades, possibly centuries, after it? When a distant and unperceived object or a past event is known, it seems that it must be present to the knower; but it also seems plain that it is truly known as what it is—namely, as distant or as past—only if it is spatially or temporally absent. It must be content of present experience; and yet what is known *about* it is that it is *not* content of present experience. In knowledge, in short, as Dewey has put it—in a phrase which I perhaps quote too often—something must be "present-as-absent." But that, obviously, is a rather peculiar way of being present which calls for elucidation.

Common sense has, of course, long had its own way of

dealing with these anomalies—a way followed also, until recent times, by many philosophers and most psychologists, but now increasingly out of fashion among both classes. The apparent oddity that a thing absent should, when known, become present (while still remaining absent), and that a thing bygone should in some manner and some degree become coexistent with a living organism, disappears—according to this long established *interpretation* of the fact of knowledge—when that which is present is regarded as a partial and immaterial *simulacrum* of a past or otherwise absent object, this shadowy replica being called an "image" or "idea." The present-ation, or making present, of the absent, in which knowing consists, is declared to be simply a representation—not in the etymological sense of a literal "making present over again," but in the sense of "effective substitution." The object is represented by an understudy or deputy or surrogate, not having all the powers or attributes of its principal, but sufficient, it is assumed, for all cognitive purposes. But this simple and familiar way of construing the phenomenon of knowing, as a mere occurrence of what are called "mental images," manifestly does nothing to eliminate the lesser anomaly; and it has been held by a number of philosophers of different schools that it is incapable of elucidating or alleviating the greater. If "ideas" are conceived of as a sort of psychical stuff indispensable to the organic function of knowing, then the assertion of their existence does but increase the anomalous appearance of that function from the point of view of natural science. That assertion would compel biology to one or another troublesome conclusion. One alternative would be to hold that at a certain stage of evolution an animal appears which produces a species of intangible, imponderable, immaterial secretion, extended, yet not localizable in any space of which the biologist or even the relativistic physicist takes cognizance; and that this secretion has the extraordinary property of reproducing, with some loss of vividness, past phases of the organism's life, and even bits out of the physical world as it was before the organism's birth. The other alternative, to which biology would apparently be constrained, if it admitted ideas as a feature of the life of human organisms but rejected the conception just mentioned, would be the attribution to *all* organisms of the power to throw off these imponderable secretions. And the question would arise in either case, but in the latter perhaps more insistently, whether this function could, after all, be supposed to be wholly otiose in the determination of animal behavior or even vegetal response—whether it is reasonable to assume so vast a redundancy in nature as that hypothesis would imply. The hypothesis of ideas, then, would in any event fit into the habitual preconceptions of the biologist, and into the general theory of biological evolution, only with difficulty and at the probable cost of some revision of those preconceptions. Dewey somewhere remarks that such a hypothesis "can be accepted by one who accepts the doctrine of biological continuity only after every other way of dealing with the facts has been exhausted."

And to many, as I have said, the theory of representative ideas seems at worst to aggravate, and at best to be unavailing to lighten, the greater anomaly. Some of those who take this view of the common-sense explanation of knowing do not deny the reality of ideas or images; but they point out that these are insufficient to render the present apprehension of absent objects intelligible. For what we mean by "knowing" evidently is not at all equivalent to what we mean by simply "having ideas." Human creatures obviously (if they have ideas at all) have many such which do not even purport to constitute knowings; and all that do purport to do so seem to involve something more than the simple presence of certain ideas in a given field of consciousness. If the geologist professes to know anything about the fauna of the Jurassic period, he is not merely reporting the emergence in his thought of various "mental pictures" of queer beasts. A poet may be content to tell us of his images as they rise, but not the man of science. A scientific statement is not intended to be taken merely as a contribution of the scientist who propounds it to introspective psychology. To know, in short, even supposing that it requires the occurrence of "ideas," requires also a judgment in which these ideas are recognized as disclosing, or corresponding to, something not identical with themselves in its time and place of existence and in many of its attributes.[3] The present simulacrum alone cannot, for cognitive purposes, take the place of the absent object or the past event. Even its factual correspondence with a past event is not enough; the correspondence must be *apprehended*, the idea must be *referred to* the object, before there can be the reality or even the appearance

[3] Some Berkeleian idealists may demur at this remark. Suffice it to say that any of my readers who do not suffer from total amnesia or do not suppose themselves to have been born simultaneosly with the beginning of this sentence are realists enough to be committed to a recapitulation of *some* cases of the kind of knowledge here referred to.

of knowledge. And this means that the absent object also, when knowing occurs, must be within the conscious field of the cognitive organism; that it, as as well as the idea of it, must, as the common phrase goes, be "before the mind." You cannot, it would seem obvious, "refer" an idea to something else of which you say it is a representation without at the same time having the something else present to your thought. And thus it is contended that the hypothesis of ideas, whether well-founded or not, does not serve to remove or even diminish the apparent paradox of the presentness of the absent in the cognitive experience. The ideas do not, it is urged, bring you any nearer to the object; on the contrary, they interpose themselves between the knower and the object and make it more difficult than before to conceive how the knowing function attains its objective.

I now pass on to present some illustrations of the part played by these two anomalies of knowledge in recent and contemporary thought, some specific examples of the diverse reactions of philosophers upon them.

II

No one, I think, ever felt the greater anomaly more strongly nor expressed it more effectively than our own Californian philosopher, Josiah Royce; it seems, if one may judge from the argument of his first book (*The Religious Aspect of Philosophy*) to have been the difficulty through reflection upon which his own metaphysics was generated. His reasoning on the point is, I am sure, familiar to many here, but as I cannot assume that it is so to all, it is worthwhile to recall it. A case of knowledge, Royce observes, is generally defined as a judgment that agrees with its object, and error as a judgment which fails to agree with its object. In either case it is assumed that the judgment—the knowing or would-be knowing—*has* an object wherewith it can agree or not agree. This assumption Royce accepts. But he points out that you get into difficulties as soon as you raise the question: What is meant by *the* object of a judgment? If a judgment is to have an object of its own,

> there must be something about the judgment that shows what one of the external objects beyond itself this judgment does pick out as its own. A judgment has as its object only what it intends to have as object. . . . But the essence of an intention is the knowledge of what one intends. . . . So then judgments err only by disagreeing with their intended objects, and they can intend an object only in so far as this object is known to the thought that makes the judgment.

In other words, the absent object, if it is to be discriminated from all other absent objects and now recognized as the object-now-referred-to—if it is to be "spotted" or identified at the moment of knowing it—must be compresent with the thought of it, must be given in consciousness along with the idea whose recognized as well as actual agreement with it would constitute knowledge. But on the other hand, it seems impossible that the object-referred-to should be thus compresent. For if it were, error would be impossible. I cannot err with respect to what is actually and totally given within my present consciousness. Thus it appears necessary to say that when anyone knows, or even errs about, any definite object or situation, he must have before him, as a thing now literally given in consciousness, the actual object of his judgment, in order that he may recognize it as that which his judgment is about and at the same time contrast it with his conceivably erroneous idea of it; and it appears equally necessary to say that the actual object *cannot* be literally given in consciousness, since if it were, his idea of it could not conceivably be erroneous—and (as we may add) its true temporal externality to the knowing and to the idea could not be asserted.

Such is the seeming paradox of knowing which Royce felt was the primary task of philosophy to remove. But his conclusion was that it can never be removed so long as we conceive of knowing only as a temporal event in the life of a human organism. By no finite knower is the required conjunction, in a single moment of consciousness, of idea and object-intended achieved. Only by assuming that there is a more comprehensive consciousness within which that of every finite knower is contained, and for which the idea and its object and the relation which unites them are all simultaneously compresent, can we escape from the paradox. And this larger consciousness must, of course, be an eternal, a nonsuccessive, consciousness. In Royce's own words:

> To explain the possibility of error about matters of fact seemed hard, because of the natural postulate that time is a pure succession of separate moments, so that the future [or past] is now as future [or as past] nonexistent. Let us then drop this natural postulate, and declare time once for all present in all its moments to an universal all-

> inclusive thought. And to sum up, let us overcome all our difficulties by declaring that all the many Beyonds, which single significant judgments seem vaguely and separately to postulate, are present as fully realized intended objects to the unity of an all-inclusive, absolutely clear, universal and conscious thought, of which all judgments, true or false, are but fragments. . . . Then all our puzzles will disappear at a stroke.

But for whom do they disappear, one must ask. Doubtless they disappear, or have never existed, for the supposed time-transcending and universal Knower, since he by hypothesis has all things compresent to him. But does this make them compresent to me? And if not, does it in the least solve the puzzle how *I*, temporal creature that I am, can ever know anything, or even be in error about anything in particular? The cases of knowing we are concerned with are knowings which occur at this date or at that, as incidents in the life of this or that human organism. It will not serve to say that all these organisms are, by the hypothesis, fragments of the Absolute, that it is the eternal and all-inclusive Mind that thinks through their poor transitory thoughts. Even if this were true, it would still be in their fragmentariness and transitoriness that men must know, if *they* are to know at all; and we are assuming that they, and not merely the Absolute, sometimes do know. The problem therefore remains entirely unaffected by the monistic idealist's proposal that—in a homely phrase—we should have all our knowing "done out." So far as the present complication is concerned, the Absolute is not even a god out of the machine; he is a god who remains forever upon the Olympus of his eternity, helpless to straighten out any of the tangles which arise upon the actual temporal stage of human knowledge.

Whatever, then, be the difficulty of dealing with the greater anomaly within the limits of human experience, it is within those limits, if at all, that the escape from the seeming paradox must be reached; and we may, I think, set it down as a principle on which a large majority of contemporary philosophers would be found agreed, that the peculiarities of knowing are not rendered more intelligible by supposing that organic function to be carried on always with the supernatural assistance of an omniscient and eternal Mind.

III

Contemporary Anglo-American philosophy is chiefly distinguished, as it seems to me, by the number and energy and ingenuity of the efforts made to escape from both the anomalies of knowledge, and by a convergence of the efforts made on the one side and on the other toward a repudiation of the old hypothesis of representative ideas. In other words, motives arising through reflection sometimes upon one, sometimes upon the other, sometimes upon both, of these difficulties, incline several otherwise discordant schools in philosophy and psychology to hold that the notion of ideas, as present "mental," i.e., nonphysical, content through which knowledge of things absent in time and space is mediated, must once for all be given up. Of many it is now undeniably true that, as Dunlap has declared, the "world of representational 'ideas' or 'states of consciousness,' dim shadows through which we may look at the objects casting them, or on which alone we may fasten our gaze, attracts no longer faith or interest."

When based solely upon an aversion for the first or lesser anomaly of knowledge, these attacks upon the belief in ideas often take a very simple form. There can, we are sometimes told, be no such things as ideas or mental content or mental states, no nonphysical element in cognition or other modes of what is called consciousness, for the sole and sufficient reason that such things *are* anomalies from the point of view of the natural sciences. This view is perhaps most often expressed by psychologists of a certain type, with respect to the procedure of their own science. These lay it down as a fundamental rule, primarily for their fellow-specialists, but by implication for all who would make any pretensions to scientific respectability, that no "mental" or "psychical" factors shall be admitted within the purlieus of science. "As long as psychology deals with conscious or mental states of any sort," writes one representative of this fashion [4]—so long as psychology does this, "it cannot attain to the dignity of a science, as Kant long ago asserted." (Kant, I may interpolate, has been credited at one time or another with the paternity of many doctrines; at none of his reputed speculative descendants would he have gazed with more amazement and less sense of family likeness, I suspect, than at this latest claimant.) To quote again from the same writer: "Clearly there can be no science which has as its subject-matter intangible and invisible subjectivistic states. . . . If we assume that what is studied in psychology is the development of

[4] J. R. Kantor, in *Psychological Review* (1920).

the complex reaction-patterns and the means whereby they are put into complete or incipient function by various types of stimuli, we need never invoke any mysterious [you observe this word seems here synonymous with 'non-physical'] —any mysterious or inscrutable entities." To the mere logician, all this necessarily has the appearance of the ancient trick of question-begging definition, done on the grand scale. You first define a "science" in such a way that no study of "consciousness" or "mental states" or activities or content—even if by any chance they should happen to exist —would conform to the definition; you then define psychology as a science. You further tacitly assume that nothing that is *not* the potential object of a science (as defined) can exist—or at all events be known to exist—and so, by means of these convenient verbal premises, most of the problems of psychology, not to say of epistemology and metaphysics, are settled for you at the outset by a single stroke. You are no longer under any troublesome necessity of examining the facts in each case with an open mind, in order to make certain whether, in some obscure corner of human experience, there may not peradventure be found lurking some "mental thing."

It is, for example, suggested by psychologists who are still under the influence of what the writer quoted calls the "mentalistic tradition" that the experience commonly called perception is (as Stout puts it) "essentially cognitive," and that it "involves a reference to an object present to the senses." The psychologist who uses the a priori premises indicated does not need to analyze perception, as he himself experiences it, in order to assure himself that such a view as

Stout's is mistaken. It is enough for him to note that if that view were admitted it would bring back into psychology those troublesome alien enemies whom he is resolved to exclude from it. If *he* is to give a description of perception it must be one which "consistently complies with the rigorous canons of natural science," [5] and since those canons expressly forbid him to deal with "conscious or mental states of any sort whatsoever," he knows, before addressing himself to the phenomenon to be described, precisely what kind of elements should, and what should not, be found therein. His account of the facts, in short, must be made to fit a dogmatically predetermined formula. "Only upon the *assumption* that the perceptual reaction is a natural psycho-physiological response," observes the writer last quoted,[6] "*may we hope to escape* the arbitrary and confusing concept of a mental content, *which is an unavoidable consequence of the presupposition that perception is a knowledge process*"—i.e., that it is "the consciousness of an object present to sense." An investigator who, dealing with a concrete factual question, "assumes" what may be necessary to enable him to avoid a consequence which he "hopes to escape"—is not unlikely to have his hope realized.

This sort of thing—which I mention because there appears to be a good deal of it going on in present-day American psychology—manifestly violates, in the name of science, the most elementary principles of scientific method. "Thou shalt not settle questions lying in the region of empirical fact by

[5] Kantor, *op. cit.*, p. 192; the following quotations are from the same article.

[6] Kantor, *op. cit.*, italics mine.

a priori arguments drawn from definitions"—this first commandment of science, at least, one might have supposed to be sufficiently promulgated; but the writer quoted argues as if he had never heard of it. Yet there is one thing admirable in the passage cited; it is the candor of the admission that if perception—or by implication, any other function of the organism—is regarded as "cognitive," as a "knowledge process," then "the confusing concept of a mental content" must be accepted "as a necessary consequence." In other words, what we have here is a heroic endeavor to escape, primarily from the lesser, but in fact from both the anomalies of knowledge by denying the reality of knowledge altogether. And this is the essence of the view of the school of psychologists known as behaviorists—at least of that straiter sect of them who alone, as it seems to me, have a valid title to the name. The fact is not always so clearly recognized or so plainly expressed as by Kantor; yet, implicitly or explicitly, behaviorism amounts to the proposition that cognitive phenomena are not legitimate subjects of scientific inquiry—a view which inevitably develops, and has as a matter of historical fact developed, into the thesis that those phenomena do not really occur—that there are no functions or "reactions" of an organism which cannot be described in terms of (theoretically if not always actually) observable motions of the portions of matter composing the organism's body. The best-known representative of behaviorism, seeking some particular motion of matter which can be regarded as the specific "behavioristic" fact corresponding to what has commonly been called "knowing," finds it in the movements of those muscular mechanisms, chiefly in the region of the larynx, which are concerned in speech. When you have described these you have, he believes, told the whole story about thought and knowledge. As for "ideas" or "images," those terms are mere nonsense-words, standing for no fact of experience at all.

But manifestly this is a description of knowing with all the knowledge left out. It bears not the least resemblance to what anybody—including the behaviorist—means by knowing, and claims for himself when he professes to know. It states wholly in terms of alterations of position of physical particles within an organic body a function which, as we have already seen, has for its essence the effective presentation in an organism's experience of things outside its body and sometimes external to its date of existence and to its entire physical environment as constituted at the moment of the exercise of that function.

Behaviorism, nevertheless, is a phenomenon of much interest to the historian of philosophy and of science, because it brings into perfect sharpness of definition the contrast between two modes of approach to the more general problems of science, and the consequences of one of these, when universalized. It has been the usual custom of the specialist in any of the physical sciences, as I have observed, to forget himself and keep his eye upon the object. The testimony of his senses respecting the qualities and behavior of observable external things and theories, conceptual constructions, suggested and in the end tested by such observations, have constituted the content of his science. And since he has not found it necessary to assume the occurrence of the cognitive phenomenon in any of the objects of his study, he has been able to ignore the fact that he himself is all the while exhibiting that phenomenon. The historically interesting and crucial thing that has been recently happening in psychology is the attempt to apply this procedure in thorough-going fashion to man himself. It was natural enough that the attempt should be made; it is, perhaps, useful that it has been made. If, as some have hoped, a comprehensive unification of knowledge on the basis suggested by the results of the more "fundamental" natural sciences is ever to be achieved, that unification must include all the functions and processes that make up the life of the organism man. And, as a step toward that ultimate unification, it was inevitable that the experiment should be tried of bringing all human phenomena at least within the categories of ordinary biology—that is, of a biology which begins by disregarding the very fact of knowing which it exemplifies. It is the behaviorist who has performed this logical experiment for us; and the result—which might, I should have supposed, have easily been foreseen—is both conclusive and amusing. What it is I have recently pointed out elsewhere; but I may perhaps be permitted to recall the point briefly here. The behaviorist is faced by an embarrassing dilemma. He must either exclude himself and his activities as a man of science from his generalization as to that in which all animal and human activity consists; or he must include himself and his activities therein. If he excludes himself, he is admitting the occurrence in at least one organism, himself, of precisely the kind of knowing which was described at the beginning of this paper; he is claiming an acquaintance with things that are not present muscular or other movements inside his own body—for example, with his own past movements, with the muscular processes of other organisms, with stimuli external to all organic bodies, and the like. He is, in short, admitting that there figure in his organic life entities transcendent of both the time and place of *his* existence as a physical entity. If, on the other hand, he includes himself in his generalization (as in consistency he should) he is thereby disclaiming any pretension to knowledge, and admitting that the utmost that he as an organism can at any time accomplish is to move his laryngeal or other muscles, or other portions of his anatomy, in certain so-called "reaction-patterns." That is doubtless an interesting exhibition; yet it hardly seems equivalent to the creation or advancement of a science.

Such are the ironic revenges which logic takes upon those men of science who begin by refusing, because of dogmatic methodological preconceptions, to look even one fact in the face—at least when that fact is the nearest at hand of all, and the one in which the conduct of scientific inquiry and the attainment of scientific conclusions themselves consist. But if the behaviorist's logical experiment is thus a complete though instructive failure, it would seem to follow that what may be called a generalized biology, and a generalized conception of the process of evolution, can be possible only upon condition that the cognitive function be fitted into its place as a biological fact, with whatever supplementation or revision of the rest of the scheme that may make necessary.

IV

I have time to touch upon only one other contemporary attempt to deal with the two anomalies of knowledge; and I select the most important example of an especially influential and interesting tendency of current opinion on these matters. The tendency is more largely represented among British realists of the present time than in America, though it is not without American spokesmen. My colleague, Professor Knight Dunlap, a distinguished graduate of this University, holds a kindred view, so far as the issues here under consideration are concerned. But the specific example to which I shall limit myself is the doctrine developed by Samuel Alexander in a long series of papers, chiefly in the *Proceedings* of the London Aristotelian Society, and recently systematically set forth in his *Space, Time and Deity,* one of the most considerable, ingenious, and carefully elaborated contributions to philosophy which the present century has produced.

The lesser anomaly is a good deal attenuated but not altogether abolished in Alexander's theory. Whenever knowing occurs, a "mental event"—an event which *in a certain sense is* not physical—admittedly occurs; without this, Alexander holds, there can be no such thing as knowing. This event consists in an activity apparently peculiar to some organisms, and in its higher forms to man—called generically "mind" or "consciousness" or "awareness." It is always directed upon objects; the name of it, indeed, is not complete unless followed by the preposition "of." And these objects in no case owe their existence or their qualities to it. With this unique activity Alexander thinks we have an immediate or "inner" acquaintance which he calls "enjoyment"—a term, however, which is not to be understood as implying that all awareness is accompanied by agreeable feeling. We "enjoy" our own consciousness, then, and—by what Alexander seems, at least at times, to regard as a radically different type of activity—we "contemplate" objects; more precisely, consciousness itself *is* a contemplation of objects.[7] But the residuum of the distinctively "psychical" thus left in Alexander's universe seems, at first sight, to be decidedly scanty. For, first, consciousness itself is declared to be "identical" with certain physiological phenomena. Since we discover, "partly by experience, partly by reflection, that a process with the distinctive quality of mind or consciousness is in the same place and time with the neural processes," we are "forced to go beyond the mere correlation of the mental with these processes, and identify them. . . . That which is experienced from the inside or enjoyed as a conscious process is, as experienced from the outside, or contemplated, a neural one." But it is not clear that this "identity" is not compatible with a very large measure of difference—though I confess that Alexander's exposition of his views on the point seems to me extraordinarily elusive. At times he goes so far in the direction of pure materialism as to suggest that "mental process may be expressible completely in physiological terms,"[8] though, of course, in *distinctive* physiological terms, which would not correctly describe a "non-mental" physical process. It appears, in some passages, to be suggested that what "chiefly" differentiates those neural

[7] The attempt to show that there is a different activity, and a distinct relation to the entity apprehended, and not merely a different *kind* of entity, in "contemplation" and "enjoyment" appears to me wholly unsuccessful; but as Alexander attaches great importance to the distinction, it is best to use his terms in explaining his position.

[8] Samuel Alexander, *Space, Time and Deity* (1920), II, p. 7.

processes which can also be named "psychical" is their "locality in the nervous system" or their high degree of physiological complexity and organization. Elsewhere the language of the identification theory is abandoned, and we are told merely that the neural process "carries thought"—which last, therefore, can hardly *be* the neural process. And Alexander expressly argues against the view of some American neorealists that consciousness can be adequately represented merely by conceiving of "an environing world of things provoking specific neural responses." Such a doctrine appears to him "to fail to account for a vital feature of the cognitive situation, namely, that in being aware of a fire, the fire is before *me*, it is I who see it." There is, in other words, not merely the fire and the neural response, however complex, but also "an act of consciousness" whereby the response "is something which *experiences itself*." This "experiencing of itself" would appear to be something quite distinct from what is usually understood by a neural process, viz., a particular type of molecular motion or an electromagnetic transaction between electrons. Unfortunately Alexander fails to face this issue definitely, and his position consequently remains hard to define; he does not tell us plainly whether "consciousness," or a "mental act," is a motion of molecules (of a complex sort and in a special portion of the brain), or whether it constitutes an event of which no description of even the most complicated molecular movements could give us any true notion. The impression one gets, however, is, I think, that the author of *Space, Time and Deity*, if he should deal expressly with this question, would answer that "mental processes" are *not* merely movements of particles—that the "enjoyment" of a given neural process (viz., of the change of position of a group of particles moving at a given velocity) is not literally the same occurrence as either *that* change of position, or some other change of position of some other particles, taking place at the same time. If this interpretation is correct, there is an irreducibly nonphysical element in the *process* of knowing, as conceived by Alexander, though that element is only one side of a two-sided fact: a cognitive act is, as "contemplated," truly a physical phenomenon in the nervous system, though as "enjoyed" it is not a physical phenomenon, nor in any respect similar to one. As regards the *objects* of knowing there is, happily, no such obscurity in this author's presentation of his doctrine. The objects of awareness, he tells us, are exclusively "non-mental or physical realities," "some part of the whole world of Space-Time." The act of knowing merely, so to say, illuminates what is there entirely independently of it; that which is "before the mind" is not composed, either in whole or part, of nonphysical "ideas," but of a selection out of the actual content of the physical world, apprehended without mediation or representation.

Whatever be the percise measure of the nonphysical element in this philosopher's world, it seems, at any rate, sufficient to exclude that "biological continuity" which I have quoted Dewey as desiderating. The evolutionary process is here conceived as literally creative. There are sudden transformation scenes in it; new types of reality "emerge," to use a favorite word of Alexander's; and "consciousness" is, at all events on this planet, the latest of these saltatory innovations, though we have no reason to suppose that it will be the last—indeed we are offered a "speculative assurance" (on what real grounds it is difficult to see) that it cannot be the last. So far, then, as the first anomaly consisted in the implication of such biological discontinuity by the phenomenon of knowing, it still stands. The *content* of experience and the world of objects contemplated have, indeed, been purged of everything mental or subjective; but knowing itself, at least as it is "enjoyed," apparently remains (in spite of its so-called "identification" with neural processes) a sheer external addition to that world, having no attributes, beyond presence in the same time and space, in common with its processes.

But what precisely does Alexander mean when he asserts that—for example, in the specific case of memory—consciousness is conversant exclusively with "physical realities"? What and when is the physical reality upon which memory is directed? Is it the actual past object or event? And if so, does the assertion that the object apprehended is always "physical" mean that the past object is *now* a part of the physical world? Alexander's language at times might lead one so to construe him. He observes, for example, with reference to his own view, that it doubtless "seems in the last degree paradoxical to ascribe to the image of a landscape regained in the memory—and still more to one which one has never seen—an existence, in this case physical, independent of the mind. . . . Images appear to be patently psychical, to be mere ideas and in no sense realities." Now the principal reason why memory-images have appeared to most philosophers and psychologists of previous generations to be psychical is simply that there does not seem to be room for them, at the moment of their being experienced, in a *present* physical scheme of things; and the air of paradox which to such persons might seem to invest Alexander's conception might be due to the supposition that he declares this imaginal content to *have* a place in the present physical world. But it turns out that the adjective "physical" is used by Alexander in a temporally unbounded sense. It does not imply presence in any particular physical system synchronous with the act of knowing. The remembered object, he writes, "is physical insofar as [it] behaves according to the laws of physics." A remembered friend "does not speak now, but he is remembered as speaking, or, to vary the example, the memory object is the physical man cutting physical trees yesterday." In short, the object of my retrospective knowledge is *not* declared to be any part of my present physical environment; it is asserted to be "physical" only in the past tense. In so far as Alexander affirms the physicality of the remembered object merely in this innocuous sense, he will hardly be charged with paradox.

There is, it is true, a real and, as I think, fatal paradox in his doctrine; but it is precisely the reverse of the one suggested. It consists, not in putting the known past event or object into the present physical order, but in leaving it in all its pastness and providing no present substitute for it—in giving to the act of cognition nothing whatever that is synchronous with itself to deal with. Here, however, we pass again from the lesser to the greater anomaly of knowledge; and we must now consider some observations of Alexander's which have the look of being intended as his solution of the latter difficulty.

He often writes, namely, as if he had framed a way of conceiving of the cognitive situation which eliminates the anomaly of transcendent reference altogether. "The relation of the conscious subject to an object which transcends it," he declares, is not "unique"; it is, on the contrary, merely "an instance of the simplest and most universal of all relations," that of "compresence within one space and time." There is no mystery about the compresence of two physical things, and just as little about the compresence of a "mental process" with "some existent of lower order." But it presently appears that "compresence" here does not mean simultaneity; it means merely the existence of two things at *any* two times and in *any* two places within the entire range of an assumed single Time-Space system. This meeting is compresent with the first meeting of the Philosophical Union which I ever attended, thirty years ago; George Washington is compresent with Mr. Harding, and the fiftieth President of the United States is compresent with both. In this large and liberal sense, undeniably, compresence can be asserted equally and univocally of all objects or events, whether mental or physical. It happens, however, that in knowledge of the past or future, there empirically occurs a compresence of quite a different sort. The relation between George Washington and my "consciousness," when I am thinking of him, is scarcely the same as the relation which subsists when I am thinking, not of him, but of something else; yet in both cases my "consciousness" and the Father of his Country are equally compresent, in Alexander's sense. Nor—leaving the temporal difference aside—is my consciousness of the things in front of me, which I see, the same relation as my mere compresence with the things behind my back, which I do not see. Alexander thus finds himself constrained to recognize that "there is nothing in the relation of two material finites comparable with the situation" exemplified by genuinely cognitive consciousness, and, in particular, by the remembrance of a past experience, and only imperfect analogies with it among noncognitive organic phenomena.[9] This being the case, his remarks about "compresence" seem to have no relevancy to the actual anomaly of transcendent reference.

[9] Alexander, *op. cit.*, II, pp. 83–84. On this point also, however, Alexander's language seems to me obscure and wavering. He manifestly desires to minimize the difficulty by "using 'knowing' in an extended sense for the relation between *any finite* and those of lower empirical order," i.e., for all cases of compresence where there is a difference of grade between the entities compresent. Thus, "just as objects [e.g., sensible qualities] are to our mind partial revelations of the thing from which the object is selected," so to an amoeba inanimate things "are revealed in their material characters," and to one inanimate thing are "revealed" the primary qualities of another. This at first sounds like panpsychism. But we are at the same time told that the paramecium reacts to stimuli "without, it would seem, the vaguest consciousness of any object." In short, in its "extended sense" the word "knowing" lacks precisely the signification which is of its essence when we speak of *our* "knowing"; we are, indeed repeatedly warned to "remember that the 'mind' of a [merely] living thing is not conscious mind, and has not the empirical character of consciousness at all." In short, as Alexander grants, the "extended use" of the term is merely a metaphor; and the things to which it is figuratively applied are avowedly without the specific characteristic which the word connotes when it is applied literally. Thus, to lend support to the proposition that "all that knowing" (i.e., admittedly "conscious" knowing, or awareness) "implies is the compresence of a mind and an object at a lower level," "knowing" is given a new meaning from which awareness is expressly excluded.

His real procedure with respect to that anomaly is, if I have understood his meaning, to accept—though not always unambiguously—one of the two horns of the dilemma in which it consists. The believers in ideas, as we have seen, have held that belief largely because it seemed to them evident that, when they thought of the past, they must necessarily have—and also, as an experienced fact, did have—in their consciousness some *present* content which could not be considered identical with the past object simply because of the difference of date between them. It has, in short, usually been assumed that when, to use Alexander's word, I "contemplate" something, that which is directly contemplated must exist simultaneously with the contemplation. Alexander, however—and this is his real paradox, to which I referred a moment ago—appears (in common with several other contemporaries) to reject this assumption and to maintain that a present act of knowing may be directed immediately upon past or future objects. He writes, for example, in what seems to me his most definite passage on the subject: "The truth is that remembering and expecting do occur at the present moment, but we are not entitled therefore to declare their objects simultaneous with the present." The word "object," to be sure, is even here not wholly free from equivocality. There is a sense in which anyone who supposes us to have any knowledge of past or future at all might subscribe to the sentence just cited. But I do not suppose the statement to be intended in this truistic sense. I take it to mean—and this seems the only meaning congruous with the doctrine as a whole—that when you remember, as I now invite you to do, the appearance of the Tower of Jewels at the Panama-Pacific Exposition in 1915, there occurs an act or state of being conscious which is entirely distinct from anything that you are conscious *of*, and is an existent of the present date; but that on the side of experienced content—of that which you have before your thought—there is nothing whatever which can be said to exist at the present date, but only things existent in your past experience, and, in the chronology of the physical world, belonging to the year 1915 as reckoned in the local time-system of this planet.[10]

And just here, as it seems to me, we come upon the crucial issue concerning the anomalies of knowledge, and upon one of the crucial issues in contemporary philosophy. If this conception of an act of consciousness with no simultaneous content of consciousness is tenable, the greater anomaly ceases from troubling, and a long step is taken in the argument against the existence of representative ideas. Knowing, so conceived, would reach the object in all cases directly, and no intermediaries would be necessary. But is such a conception tenable? I am unable to think so. It seems to me to conflict both with the observable facts and with the logical necessities of the case. I cannot recall having myself ever enjoyed a state of cognitive consciousness in which there was nothing simultaneously before the mind. When I think of past or future events I always find myself confronted with present images. To remember, as common speech testifies, is to recall—to give present (though not physical) existence

[10] Here too, however, it is difficult to be quite sure what Alexander means; and the view mentioned should perhaps be described rather as a possible than as a certain interpretation of his position.

to some of the characters of a bygone item in experience. Nor can I so much as conceive how the sort of long-range yet unmediated knowing—a kind of cognitive *actio in distans*—which Alexander's theory implies, could take place. That an activity of apprehending, which of itself, it must be remembered, is entirely distinct from anything that may *be* apprehended, should occur at a given date and have nothing at that date, nor within that moment of experience, *to* apprehend—that the process of knowing should operate, as it were, *in vacuo*—is a notion to me totally unintelligible. If it is asserted that the only existent given in memory, when we think of a Philosophical Union meeting of thirty years ago, is the original meeting, that this remains fixedly in the year 1892, and that there now occurs no manner of revival or presentation of it, even of the most fragmentary sort—then the second half of this assertion appears to me expressly to deny what the first half assumes, namely, that we *are* now remembering that bygone meeting. I recognize that Alexander and others who are of his way of thinking have been driven into this paradox through the pressure of the greater anomaly of knowledge, that they have sought in this conception a way of escape from a genuine difficulty. But in no such absolute temporal sundering of the process and the content of thought or knowledge can, I think, any real escape be found.

With respect to the greater anomaly, then, we seem driven upon the horn of the dilemma alternative to the one apparently chosen by Alexander; in other words, we must conceive of all the content or material of an act of knowing as temporally present along with the act. To use one of Alexander's terms in a sense perhaps not quite his, what I *contemplate*—what is "*immediately* before the mind"—when I bethink myself of yesterday's events is not something existent yesterday, but something existent today.[11] But is not this horn of the dilemma, it will be asked, as impossible as the other? For what, in the case supposed, *I know about*—if there be any knowledge involved in the matter at all—is not today, but yesterday. And how is such a knowing of things past conceivable, if the only content of present consciousness is present content? Is not the alternative proposed tantamount to a denial of the possibility of knowledge? If we were compelled to answer this question in the affirmative, our conclusion would necessarily be that the problem is insoluble—that neither of the conceivable alternatives is tenable, and that the very idea of knowledge is thus involved, for reflective thought, in an irremediable antinomy. The past or otherwise absent object of knowledge, we should be obliged to say, cannot in fact be absent, or external to the content of present consciousness; for in that case it would not now be known. But on the other hand, it *must* seemingly be absent—for it is of past or otherwise not-present objects that we are supposed to have knowledge. But in truth, I believe, we are not forced to accept so strange and disturbing a conclusion. The two sides of the seeming antinomy are not of equal logical force; one of the alternatives is meaningless, the other,

[11] This does not mean that, when not engaged in philosophical or psychological reflection upon the point, I necessarily think of yesterday's events as existing as today's content of consciousness. The observation that the content is in fact present, not past, arises only when the question here dealt with is raised, and is not explicit in ordinary memory experience.

though it undeniably offers some difficulties to our ordinary habits of thought, is nevertheless capable of intelligible formulation, and is, in fact, simply an accurate description of the common natural event called knowing. To speak of a present awareness of things blankly absent, of known past events that, in being known, undergo no recall or translation into the present tense, is, as we have seen, a mere self-contradiction; it is to say that one has now before one's mind something which is at the same time declared not to be now before one's mind—since it is declared to have *now* no sort of existence at all. The content or make-up (I do not speak of the causes) of a concededly present experience cannot without absurdity be described in terms of past events. But if, on the other hand, we begin our account of knowledge by recognizing the invariable and indispensable presence therein of content existentially synchronous with the act or event of knowing, we can then, I believe, find within such content all that is necessary to make knowledge of the not-present comprehensible. For the content given in memory, in other retrospection, or in anticipation is not a simple, flat, one-dimensional thing. Temporal perspectives are contained within the limits even of a single "specious present"; elements which are presented simultaneously are nevertheless also presented *as* not simultaneous, either with one another or with the present in which they are experienced. The present images without which, as I have already maintained, it is impossible to "recall" the events of yesterday, have two dates—their date of existence in consciousness, which is today, and what may be called their date of reference, which is yesterday. But the pastness of their date of reference is itself a present quality of the memory-images. It is something which I directly experience as one of the attributes of the now given content; and I do so without performing the miraculous feat either of actually turning backward time in its flight, or of being aware of an object without having any present content of my awareness. In other words, we apprehend the various elements of our present content as fitting into a framework of *conceptualized* temporal relations—which in fact appear in consciousness largely in the form, or by the aid, of spatial imagery, as of a calendar or a timetable. And this temporal framework in which our images appear has a curious twofold relation to our present consciousness. As a datum for psychological observation, as an existent now given in consciousness, the framework is *included in* the present moment's content; but at the same time, as a conceived scheme of relations, it logically includes the present moment and its content as a single unit in the larger system represented. The solution—as it appears to me—of the anomaly of the presentness of the absent in cognition lies precisely in this dual and (to use a term of Royce's) "self representative" character of thought. A given moment of thought may consist in a representation of a whole world of objects in relations of many kinds—temporal, spatial, logical—in which it is itself, *as represented,* a mere fragment. Thus it is that a given thought, e.g., a memory, can, and does, cognitively or representatively transcend itself, without any existential self-transcendence. The memory-image which I am at this moment evoking exists as a transient bit of reality now, and at no other time; but that which *does* thus exist now is a representation of a more comprehensive whole in which the now is an element consciously distinguished from the not-now. Because our thought has this obvious peculiarity, we can see how it is not only possible but necessary that an act of rational cognition should be conversant with a Beyond, while yet as a natural event it is limited in its existence to the here-and-now; we can see how it is conceivable that a bit of present content should "mean" the past and future without *being* past or future, and how the experience or awareness of such a meaning is not any sort of removal into the past or the future.

And we can now also see precisely what is meant when it is said that the content of a cognitive experience—of memory, for example—is "present-as-absent." That content (the memory-image) is present in the literal sense; it is an existent contemporaneous with the event of knowing. But it is presented "as absent" in the sense that, in the conceptual scheme of temporal relations which is also now presented, the memory content is assigned a position external and prior to that occupied in the same scheme by the present moment. And there is no contradiction in this; for the presentness and the pastness are not predicated of the same content in the same sense. The content has a date and it also includes or represents dates; and the date which it has is not necessarily the same as the dates represented. It is true that such an account of the matter implies that all knowing of things remote in time or place is indirect and substitutional. The conceptual pastness of my memory-image is not an experience of pastness; and the bygone event remembered does not itself now enter my experience. If it did it would not be what we mean by a remembered event, namely, one which has ceased before the remembering of it occurs. Pastness is never—and from its own nature cannot be—experienced at all; [12] it figures in experience only through a present peculiarity distinguishing certain present data from others. We have a meaningful idea of it, but no "acquaintance with" it; and the idea means it partly because it is one of those ideas which present themselves in consciousness saying: "I stand for something not myself; the thing that I am is not the thing that I mean." The same is, of course, true of the idea of the future; but the two are differentiated, they have distinctive *present values,* through their utterly dissimilar relations to our volitional and affective life.

There are, however, some minds which appear to have an unconquerable repugnance to such a conception of knowing as indirect. Nothing less than literal and complete possession of the object known will satisfy them. They wish to transact their cognitive business only with principals, never with deputies, however extensive the powers of attorney these may exhibit. If it is a question of dinosaurs, they would presumably insist upon meeting the original reptiles in the actual Jurassic period, before admitting that those monsters are "known" at all. Such a craving for immediacy in cognition, however, is simply a rebellion against the limitations of

[12] This is said without prejudice to the view, held by some psychologists, that in a single "specious present" we directly experience a small lapsing bit of the past. For a past which is admittedly external to a given present (e.g., a remembered past) is obviously past in a very different sense from one which is supposed to be contained within a so-called present experience, and is thus somehow both present and past. It is only with pastness in the former and more rigorous sense that I am here concerned.

our human powers—limitations arising chiefly from the fact that man, the knower, is himself a temporal creature, whose existence is meted out to him in successive drops persisting each but for a moment. Because his life is of such a sort, he can never enter into actual present possession even of his own past—nor of his own future, so long as futurity is intelligibly predicable of it. His knowledge, therefore, of aught that is not present, or not his own experience, is inevitably vicarious; the objects which he often would most wish to make fully his own—his lost youth, an expected good fortune, his fellows' thoughts and feelings—keep their distance, preserve inviolate the distinctions and reciprocal exclusions which make up the order of the world. Knowledge thus, in Santayana's admirable phrase, is a salutation, not an embrace. Instead of denying these unescapable limitations of our knowing, we do well, while recognizing them, to fix our attention upon the other half of the story. Indirect though knowledge is, it is yet a presentation, within the limits of the passing moment and the individual consciousness of things apprehended as transcending those limits. Within the microcosm of my present thought is reflected, as in a mirror, a macrocosm of other objects and other thoughts—and they are known to *be* other simply because their images bear the marks of "otherness" upon them. And this means nothing mysterious or "metaphysical"; it merely names a fact of the commonest everyday experience, namely, that data which are immediately and indubitably present—which offer the conclusive evidence of present existence which consists in actual givenness in this moment of conscious life—yet carry with them familiar, though not infallible, *indicia* of pastness or of futurity or of presence in the conscious life of others.[13]

Such, then, I suggest, is the solution of the chief paradox of knowledge. But such a solution is obviously impossible except upon the assumption which I have throughout been making in expounding it—the assumption of the existence of representative ideas. In other words, the only available way of escape from the greater anomaly seems to require us cheerfully to accept the lesser. The content synchronous with a given act of knowing by means of which alone temporally or otherwise absent objects can be brought "before the mind" clearly cannot be assigned to that public, coherent, measurable, ponderable world of moving masses or particles with which the physical sciences have to do. And if we mean by the adjectives "mental" or "psychical" simply "existing but not as a part of the simultaneously existing physical world," then, aside from other considerations which have been intimated, the occurrence of mental entities in nature has been sufficiently demonstrated by the result of our analysis of the phenomenon of knowing.

I am well aware that the positive thesis concerning the greater anomaly which I have presented stands in need of a more elaborate formulation than it has here received, and that some difficulties may still naturally suggest themselves. So large a theme can hardly be adequately dealt with in a single hour's lecture; and I must here be content but to have

[13] The question how tests of validity in our knowledge of not-present objects can be applied in accordance with the general view here indicated lies beyond the scope of this lecture.

sketched a way of thinking about this strange activity of ours which seems to me at least worthy of consideration, in view of the apparent failure of the other attempts to rid our knowing of the paradoxical look which it wears when we take the trouble to reflect upon it. For the rest, this discourse will have perhaps served its purpose if it has done something, first, to make a little more vivid to some of my readers, the queerness of knowing, its distinctiveness among natural processes; second, to trace some conflicting tendencies in contemporary philosophy to a common source, and, what is more, to a common and genuine difficulty in interpreting an indubitable and familiar fact of experience, and thus to render these conflicts a little more intelligible, to make it more understandable why philosophers are so; and lastly, to suggest some reasons for suspecting that funeral orations may have been prononunced prematurely over the hypothesis of representative ideas. For I will conclude by repeating the confession that, in spite of the ingenious reasonings of many contemporaries, I am still much inclined to believe that I have ideas, and that without them I and other men would know even less than we do—would, to be precise, know nothing at all.

INDEX

A

B

C

D

E

F

G

H

I

J

K

L

M

N

O

P

R

S

T

U

V

W